REPRESENTATION OF PLACES

The Publisher gratefully acknowledges the contribution provided by the Art Book Endowment Fund of the Associates of the University of California Press, which is supported by a major gift from the Ahmanson Foundation.

Representation of Places
Reality and Realism in City Design

PETER BOSSELMANN

University of California Press
Berkeley   Los Angeles   London

An earlier version of Chapter 4, entitled "Times Square," was published in *Places* 4, no. 1 (1987). An earlier version of Chapter 6, "Urban Form and Climate," was published in the *Journal of the American Planning Association* 20 (1995).

University of California Press
Berkeley and Los Angeles, California

University of California Press, Ltd.
London, England

Library of Congress Cataloging-in-Publication Data
Bosselmann, Peter.
Representation of places : reality and realism in city design /
Peter Bosselmann.
p. cm.
Includes bibliographical references and index.
ISBN 0-520-20658-4 (cloth : alk. paper)
1. City planning. 2. Communication in architectural design.
1. Title.
NA9031.B69 1997
711'.4 – dc21   97-81

Printed in the United States of America

9 8 7 6 5 4 3 2 1

The paper used in this publication meets the minimum requirements of
American National Standard for Information Sciences—Permanence of Paper
for Printed Library Materials, ANSI z39.48–1984.

For Dorit, Thea, Sophia, and Margerete

CONTENTS

ACKNOWLEDGMENTS

Many friends helped me with the preparation of the manuscript. Puja Kumar drew the historical maps. Cheryl Parker dedicated Tuesday morning every week for an entire year to tracing thirty-nine drawings of a walk through Venice. Thomas Kronemeyer not only prepared the footprint maps and completed the historical maps but also modeled, by computer, the Minerva Temple in Assisi. His dedication went far beyond what I could reasonably expect from a busy graduate student. Jennifer Avery prepared the perspective of multiple station points in Chapter 1, a challenge to her, and to anybody else, for that matter. She correctly refers to Brunelleschi's view from Santa Maria del Fiore as "her image." Jennifer also rendered the computer images for the San Francisco chapter and supervised the production of all other computer-generated images. Jeff Clark provided essential help with image rendering in the final phase of the production. Ray Isaacs—one of the first doctoral students I have met who is interested in writing on pedestrian movement and the sense of time—created image sequences of the San Francisco computer model. Leila Pozo, who came from Milan to work at the Berkeley Environmental Simulation Laboratory, began the work on the San Francisco computer model that Ray and others completed.

Mirelle Rodier inked drawings for the Times Square chapter and prepared facade drawings for the density study in Chapter 8 from designs produced by Lotte Johansen, who came from Copenhagen to the simulation laboratory. Lotte's work influenced all aspects of the density research.

Stephano Fantuz, from Udine, came two years in succession to learn about visual simulation. I am very grateful to him for arranging with officials in charge of the Florence cathedral to open the main portal of Santa Maria del Fiore. He took the 90-degree images of Brunelleschi's view with a special camera. To see the heavy doors swing open and reveal the famous view from inside is unforgettable.

Jim Bergdoll did library research for me on Leonardo da Vinci and Brunelleschi.

Jack Kent, Professor Emeritus and founder of the Department of City and Regional Planning at the University of California at Berkeley, read and commented on an early draft of this book. Jay Claiborne, Raymond Lifchez, and Nezar Alsayyad gave valuable advice after reading successive versions. My friend Allan Jacobs, working in an office adjacent to mine on his book *Great Streets*, coached me and all my helpers on mapmaking and the preparation of eye-level views. In fact, the map comparisons in Chapter 3 were triggered by his work on streets. Allan repeatedly went over chapters of my book and gave me his insights on how to present the information. I hope we can spend many more years teaching and doing research together. Kenneth Craik from the Psychology Department at UC Berkeley was responsible for the validation study described in Chapter 3. He was one of the co-founders of the Environmental Simulation Laboratory and has continued to be involved in its work. Donald Appleyard started the laboratory in 1968 after teaching and working with Kevin Lynch at the Massachusetts Institute of Technology. Donald did not see his laboratory applied to the projects described, but his influence on this book is significant.

David Van Arnam and Kaye Bock were responsible for the work of word processing. Neither of them complained about my handwriting, although it offered them plenty of opportunities. Stephanie Fay's careful editing at UC Press strengthened the book.

Kevin Gilson, who had been involved with the Environmental Simulation Laboratory in one form or another since 1979, was responsible for its day-to-day operation and worked on all the projects presented in this book. He also developed the tables for determining correct viewing distances in Chapter 7. I am very grateful to him and learned to depend on his insights. William Kanemoto, who took over from Kevin in 1994, contributed a sequence of images from one of the current lab projects.

Tony Hiss, who was writing for the *New Yorker* when the Times Square project was developed, volunteered his help and turned my matter-of-fact descriptions of the simulations into a finished film script. Jason Robards volunteered to narrate the film. Darleen McCloud, Nicholas Quinelle, Hugh Hardy, and Kent Barwick helped direct the New York project described in the fourth chapter. The Toronto project (Chapter 6) was awarded as a contract to the Environmental Simulation Laboratory, but the city of Toronto insisted that I select Canadian partners. Klaus and Marjut Dunker and Robert Wright from the University of Toronto offered to help. The work in San Francisco (Chapter 5), chronologically the first of the three case studies, became possible with the help of two former students, Terrance O'Hare and Juan Flores, who stayed on at the laboratory after finishing their studies. My Berkeley colleague Edward Arens was essential in carrying out the work for Toronto and San Francisco.

Funding for the preparation of the manuscript came from the UC Berkeley Committee on Research, from the Beatrix Ferrand Fund at the UC Berkeley Department of Landscape Architecture, and from the Environmental Simulation Laboratory at the Institute of Urban and Regional Development, UC Berkeley.

As dean of the UC Berkeley College of Environmental Design, Richard Bender has watched protectively over the growth of the laboratory and helped to expand the idea of it to New York City, where a laboratory was underwritten by the Kaplan Fund, the Vincent Astor Foundation, and the Revson Foundation. Later Dean Bender generously offered his advice and assistance to Shigero Ito and Osamu Koide, who established a similar facility at Roppongi, in the heart of Tokyo.

Professor Koide invited me to Japan to join the Advanced Science and Technology Research Center at Tokyo University during the time I was working on the manuscript. My Japanese friends Shigeru Sato, Naomishi Kurata, and Toshio Oyama gave me many opportunities to present the themes of this book to professional audiences.

I thank all my friends and my family. Dorit read the manuscript, and her comments included the final changes I have made.

INTRODUCTION

This is a book about the visual representation of city form. It asks how the experience of cities can be represented and explores the influence of representation on city design. The architects, engineers, and city planners trained in the design of cities acquire the skills necessary to represent what exists and what might become reality. But because the richness and complexity of the real world cannot be completely represented, they must, out of necessity, select from reality an abstraction of actual conditions. For them the process of representation is a complex form of reasoning. What they choose to represent influences their view of reality and very significantly defines the outcome of designs and plans, and thus the future form of cities.[1]

This book asks how the creation of images affects what gets built. How good are images as surrogates of reality? Can images be made that represent a match between design as a product of the mind and a future reality?

Much has been written about the form of cities. People in various disciplines have explained why cities have taken on their forms and how they might develop in the future. Although much has also been written about ideal communities—how people should live in cities—the literature includes comparatively little on the conception of city design. Professional planners and designers generally know the power and limitations of representation, but they may take for granted how representation influences design thinking. An examination of the relationship between design, the design media, and reality is timely now, as the computerized production of images is changing the way designers do their work. It may also change their thinking about design.

Design images portray change, which members of the public view with their own concerns in mind; the representation of places to be built triggers emotions as well as calculated thought. People ask who is likely to be affected by design, who will gain from it, and who might lose. Although the people who live in cities experience urban places firsthand, design professionals explain these places conceptually. Charts show statistics, diagrams show flow or movement, and maps indicate structure and layout. Most professional representations are like theory in that they reduce reality into easily and clearly communicable facts or measurements. But the facts remain abstract. Professionals understand conceptual representations—or claim to—but few people outside the professions can read the information, let alone understand what it would be like to walk through the streets or neighborhoods described in such representations.

Professionals rarely represent the way people move through urban places, looking down streets or standing in a square alone or with others—actual conditions that people can imagine. Representing the experience of urban places means showing conditions as they are perceived by the human senses, chiefly vision. Animation for special-effect cinema, sketches, photo montage, watercolor paintings, or computer-generated eye-level views—all these are better understood than conceptual representations, and for that reason some professionals have searched for ways to combine the conceptual method with the vibrant and empathic experiential method. Much is to be gained from such a union in representation. The combination might help to overcome the split between sense and thought that Rudolf Arnheim has termed a deficiency disease in modern man.

Professionals increasingly rely on computer technology to store geographic and other detailed spatial information. They can use it to display both conceptual and perceptual images. Although in practice few designers and planners have integrated the two modes of representation, such an integration is technically possible. It would make project information more accessible and proposals more readily comprehensible to the public. But the new technology can also be employed to communicate design more persuasively, and this possibility raises important questions: about the documentary quality of images, that is, the values and biases that representations encourage or discourage, and about the credibility of the professionals who produce them.

The ideas illustrated in this book have sprung from experiments conducted in the Environmental Simulation Laboratory at the University of California at Berkeley,[2] dedicated to improving visual communication in urban design.[3] Although the question this book tries to answer—about the influence of representation on the design of cities— might rarely be asked, the problems implicit in it have been with us for a long time. Part One presents a history of professional representation in the West, where during the Renaissance Italian architects perfected conceptual and experiential representation in a form similar to that used by architects and urban designers today. The chapters of Part One discuss urban places in Europe that have come into being through conceptual design during the centuries since the invention of accurate town maps in 1502. The analysis is based on comparative map studies and secondary sources.

Part Two presents case studies carried out over a ten-year period in which design and planning proposals illustrated concept and experience combined. The application of more understandable media has not improved all the environments studied; that I can already admit at this point. The chapters of Part Two illustrate how the visual capabilities of the Environmental Simulation Laboratory at Berkeley were applied to projects in New York City, San Francisco, and Toronto.

Part Three looks at the new imaging technology that allows professionals to explain their designs more clearly than before. The chapters in this section of the book discuss where technology is likely to take professional representations and where professionals might like to take technology to bridge the split between concept and experience. Good representations improve our ability to imagine and to conceive designs. But those preparing such representations also exercise control over information. Because of the adversarial context of city design and planning, professionals must appraise the aesthetic and ethical implications of their tools.[4]

A book about images, even specialized professional images, has to draw from the various arts and sciences of our culture; therein lies the pleasure of studying the topic. The sources for this work include the writings of architects, planners, and historians in the visual arts as well as physicists, computer scientists, and perceptual psychologists.

I ask for patience from experts in these fields. The words "representation" and "places," frequently used in the text, have different meanings in the various disciplines. For some, the relationship between visual perception and representational images is necessary and intimate; for others, it is unnecessary, artificial, and misleading.[5] Architects, engineers, and planners belong to the first group. Their representations capture elements of reality for manipulation (that is, design) and for presentation to others as a substitute for reality.

When designers speak of representation, they do not mean only images that show an observer what the representer has seen. More frequently, designers represent things they have never seen but have only imagined or invented.[6]

Equally in need of clarification, the word "places" refers to conditions we can imagine: inside or outside, in front or behind, beside something or someone, viewing out from, or being sheltered. To choose among such conditions is part of being human.[7] People define places according to their own position in space, their relation to physical space, and to fellow humans within space. But places can discourage and encourage, exclude and include. I use the word "places" broadly in all its dimensions—physical, social, psychological, economic, and political.

Those who write about the making of places rarely concern themselves with representation, nor do those who write about representation mention places. Thus this book. It is written primarily for urban designers, architects, and landscape architects, who depend on concrete representations for their own understanding of what they do and for the evaluation of their work by others. Concrete representation—that is what this book is about.

PART ONE

A History of Representation in City Design

CHAPTER ONE

Concept and Experience: Two Views of the World

Pictures do not mimic what we see. In fact, no optical system exists to mimic the tasks performed by our eyes, although now, more than 150 years after the invention of photography, we assume that photography truthfully records the world around us. But photography is based on a convenient geometric fiction called "central projection." Picture taking, film, television recording, and eye-level drawings rendered by hand or computer all rely on the concept of central projection, or linear perspective, a technique that offers a somewhat limited representation of reality.

These limitations have been with us since Filippo Brunelleschi (1377–1466) carried out an experiment associated with the discovery of linear perspective,[1] a method for representing a place in a manner that approximates reality. This artisan-engineer gave Florence the magnificent dome (1420–1436) of the cathedral, the first such engineering accomplishment in the Western world since Roman antiquity. He was also a painter. Much has been written about his experiment with a painting—what Rudolf Arnheim calls Brunelleschi's peep show. A decade prior to the construction of the dome, Brunelleschi had painted from the portal of

the Cathedral of Santa Maria del Fiore the view of the Baptistery San Giovanni di Firenze. Apparently he executed the painting in perfect linear perspective. It is known that he painted the picture on a wooden panel, although there is much speculation in art-historical literature about both the method Brunelleschi used to produce it and the date he finished it.[2] The painting is lost, and the method used was not recorded until after his death.

According to his biographer Antonio Manetti, Brunelleschi's demonstration went as follows:

> He [Brunelleschi] had made a hole in the panel on which there was his painting.... The hole was as small as a lentil on the painting side of the panel, and on the back it opened pyramidically, like a woman's straw hat, to the size of a ducat or a little more. He wished the eye to be placed at the back, where it was large, with one hand bringing it close to the eye and with the other holding a mirror opposite, so that there the painting came to be reflected back...which in being seen, it seemed as if the real thing was seen. I have had the painting in my hand and have seen it many times in these days, so I can give testimony.[3]

Indeed, Brunelleschi's contemporaries must have been stunned when he took viewers to the exact spot where he had painted the Baptistery. Brunelleschi had set up his painted panel on an easel, five feet inside the cathedral's main portal.[4] He had drilled a hole in the center of his picture to control the position of the viewer's eye. Brunelleschi asked his viewer to look from the back of his painting through the hole into a mirror that he held approximately a foot from the painted side of the panel. The observer saw the reflection of the painting in the mirror. When the mirror was lowered, the observer could confirm the painting's accuracy by comparing the painted scene with the reality framed by the dark doorway of the cathedral. When the mirror was raised, the observer would again see the reflection of the painting. A person standing where Brunelleschi stood when he painted the image could see the Baptistery in the center of the scene, the Misericordia on the left, and the Canto alla Paglia on the right.

Brunelleschi sought to increase the realism of the picture: "For as much of the sky as he had to show, that is where the walls in the picture vanished into the air, he put burnished silver, so that the air and the natural skies might be reflected in it; and thus also the clouds which are seen in that silver are moved by the wind, when it blows."[5]

More than a decade after the experiment, Leon Battista Alberti credited Brunelleschi as the inventor of linear perspective and called it *constructione legitima*.[6] Now, nearly six centuries later, art historians believe Brunelleschi's experiment "ultimately was to change the modes, if not the course of Western history."[7] Brunelleschi demonstrated a technique for representing the world as we see it.

We can only speculate that the late-fourteenth-century invention of flat mirror glass, produced on the Venetian island of Murano, gave him the idea of a two-dimensional representation of the multidimensional world around him.

Since Brunelleschi, instructions in perspective generally start like those in Alberti's *Della Pittura*: "First of all, on the surface on which I am going to paint, I draw a rectangle of whatever size I want, which I regard as an open window through which the subject to be painted is to be seen."[8] In Brunelleschi's experiment, the frame of the cathedral door (today, as in Brunelleschi's day, 3.80 meters wide) was his "window." The distance between the doorway and the exact place where the picture was painted was approximately 1.75 meters. The two-to-one ratio of door width to distance means that a person standing where Brunelleschi stood to paint and looking out toward the piazza could take in a 90-degree view between the uprights of the door.[9]

Such explicit instructions guide an effort to re-create what Brunelleschi's painting must have shown and what could be seen through the hole in it. The re-creation of Brunelleschi's experiment clarifies the shortcomings of linear perspective.

What is most noticeable when the cathedral's heavy doors swing open (they open only on special occasions) is the immediate presence of the Baptistery, with the morning sun illuminating the splendid gold panels of the Portal del Paradiso. When the eyes grow accustomed to the scene, they begin to take in the details of the Baptistery (the arches, the inlaid marble) and the people in front of the Portal del Paradiso who, noticing the open cathedral doors, step inside, as if that were the normal way to enter the cathedral. All this the spectator sees while looking at the facade of the Baptistery. The square to the right and left is visible, but only with a turn of the head. Similarly, the sky above the Baptistery can be seen only by tilting back the head.

Portal del Paradiso, 17-degree horizontal angle, 80 mm focal length.

View from the Portal of Santa Maria del Fiore, taken with a 90-degree
angle of view, 21mm focal length (60 mm camera format).

A modern camera equipped with an adjustable zoom lens can reframe the view to take in everything Brunelleschi would have seen through the frame of the cathedral door. To take in the entire 90-degree field of view, the zoom lens would have to be adjusted to a 21 mm focal length.[10] In the viewfinder (at 21 mm), however, the Baptistery appears farther away than it actually is, and the piazza more spacious. If the zoom lens is adjusted until the dimensions of the Baptistery in the viewfinder are identical to those of the Baptistery as the eye sees it, that is, to a 65 mm focal length, the field of view in the viewfinder becomes much narrower—approximately 30 degrees, or one-third of the view seen through the cathedral door frame. Although the Baptistery appears at the same distance and size, one cannot take all of it in through the viewfinder.

Brunelleschi must have given distance perception serious consideration. If he wanted to verify the painting's accurate recording of the view, he must have concerned himself with the match between the objects in that view and their reflection in the mirror held up to the painting. Only if the mirror was held at the correct distance could there have been such a match. That distance would have depended on the size of the painting and the angle of the view. The view through the hole to the mirror image of the painting showed no more than what can be seen in a 30-degree cone of vision; that is, it included only slightly more than the portal of the Baptistery. The painting in all likelihood showed more; and if the hole in its back side was large enough, it might have been possible to move the eye, thus seeing the buildings and the sky Manetti so vividly described.

The experiment with an adjustable focal length demonstrates one of the shortcomings of a linear perspective as a two-dimensional recording of the three-dimensional world around us. The problem lies in its imposed conditions. To close one eye and hold the head still at a single predetermined point in space is not the normal way of looking at the world. Under such conditions, matters that relate to the distance and dimensions of objects cannot be judged with certainty.

Portal del Paradiso, 27-degree horizontal angle, 65 mm focal length.

Portal del Paradiso, 60-degree horizontal angle, 35 mm focal length.

It would be possible to overcome some of the problems inherent in linear perspective by keeping the zoom lens fixed at 65 mm and using the camera to scan the scene. The resulting series of pictures would start at the Misericordia on the left, move toward the Baptistery and the Canto alla Paglia, and end where Via de Martelli meets the piazza on the right. This photographic survey would require a matrix of pictures and would scan the scene in four horizontal rows.

Photographic prints of these negatives at a size of 4 x 6 inches mounted on a large board show the full 90-degree field of view. If the photoboard is held at eye level, approximately 12 inches away, it shows the actual distance relationship the eye sees in the scene. The scene on the board can then be scanned more naturally with both eyes, which would not be limited to the narrow predetermined field of view seen in the viewfinder but could wander across the scene as they would if one were to stand in the actual place, looking at a slightly different perspective with each split-second move of the eyes. Painters of large canvases commonly practiced such multiple-station-point perspective. In a large urban scene like a view down Venice's Grand Canal, a Canaletto might give a detail its own focal

Portal del Paradiso, composite view created from twenty images taken with a 27-degree horizontal angle, 65 mm focal length.

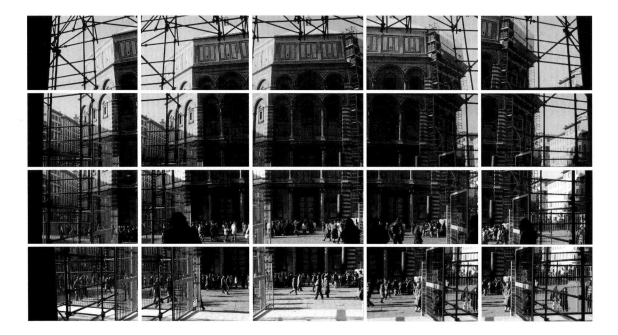

point and vanishing lines, slightly different from those of the main scene. Such a painting has a stronger spatial effect on the viewer than even a very large photographic print. As the eyes of the viewer wander across the canvas, the picture places the viewer in the scene. The viewer appears to be part of the picture because with every move of the eyes, a correct perspective is seen.[11] The line drawing created from photographs taken through the portal of Santa Maria del Fiore captures the multiple station points of a 65 mm lens; it also captures time, showing how people opposite, in front of the Portal del Paradiso, move on. The reader, holding the drawing close to the eyes, can now judge the distance to the Baptistery and the dimensions of the structure more easily. The eye perceives a multitude of reference points, and therefore the viewer appears to be part of the scene.

Anyone interested in the dimensions of the square in front of the cathedral and the proportions of the buildings surrounding it, however, would be well advised to step out of the cathedral portal and stroll around the square. Much of the experience of

such a stroll is taken in with the eyes. But all the senses work together in the experience of the square. The sense of touch registers the condition of the paving between the cathedral and the Baptistery. Body orientation conveys a sense of the proximity of walls, even those outside the field of view. Hearing is involved. Sound is reflected back by the buildings that frame the square. After taking such a stroll, one can look at the Baptistery from different angles and judge its dimensions more accurately than before, because these now relate to the dimensions of the body. ■

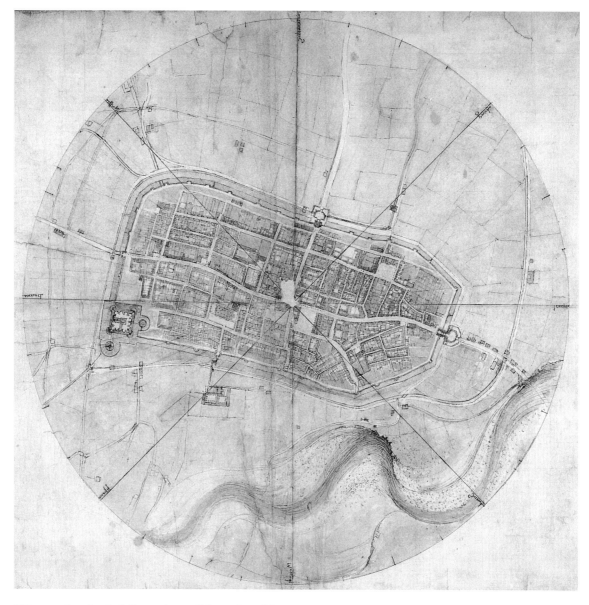

Whereas the physical dimensions of the real world
can be judged by direct experience, any future
reality has to be modeled. It is not coincidental that
the art of modeling was perfected at the time that
linear perspective came into use. During the
Renaissance it was common to build large and
precise models of building designs. James Ackerman writes that Giuliano da Sangallo built a model
of St. Peter's in Rome that was big enough for a
person to stand inside.¹²

Brunelleschi's view tries to capture the world as
the eye sees it. Almost ninety years after his experi-

Map of Imola by Leonardo da Vinci, 1502, Royal Library at Windsor,
Codex Atlanticus, no. 12284. © Her Majesty Queen Elizabeth II.

ment, on the eve of the Renaissance, a second method of representing the world was perfected. Originally called ichnographia, or plan view, it is an abstraction of reality in which a place is viewed from above.

Certainly the plan view does not depict a city in the way it is experienced. This method of representation was first used, as it is used today, to show accurately the dimensions of streets and city blocks as well as the general layout of a city, with its relationship to surrounding places.

In the first known example of a plan view resembling modern city maps, Leonardo da Vinci drew the small town of Imola, located on Italy's Emilia Romana halfway between Bologna and Faenza.[13] Leonardo's map differs from plan diagrams like the early-ninth-century parchment of St. Gall. Although the historian Howard Saalman has traced the composition of cloisters, church, and chapter hall on the St. Gall map to the great colonnaded square of the Forum of Trajan in Rome, framed by a basilica and temples,[14] the map itself represents neither historical reality nor a plan for building. It was an organizational scene that served as a guide in the layout of numerous abbeys from the ninth century on.

Leonardo da Vinci's Imola map showed actual conditions. In 1502 Cesare Borgia commissioned Leonardo to design repairs for the city's fortifications, ruined during a siege in 1499. As Architecto e Ingegnero Generale, Leonardo drew an image of this town that drastically departed from representations common at the time. Late medieval plans represented cities iconically. They showed a single perspective, with selected buildings chosen to symbolize the city, drawn in elevation. These buildings were distinguished in size according to their chiefly religious virtue, not their actual dimensions.

For Leonardo, such a representation was of little use. New ballistic methods required attention to a fortification's plan dimensions and the accurate measurement of angles. For determining exact bearings, Leonardo used a transit, known since antiquity, and a magnetic compass,[15] an invention

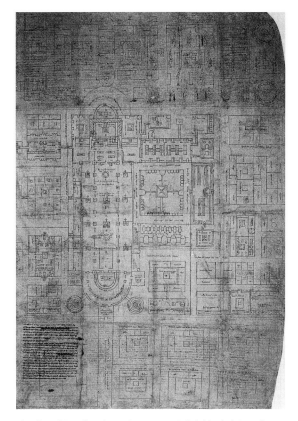

The Plan of St. Gall, early ninth century. © Stiftsbibliothek, St. Gall, Switzerland.

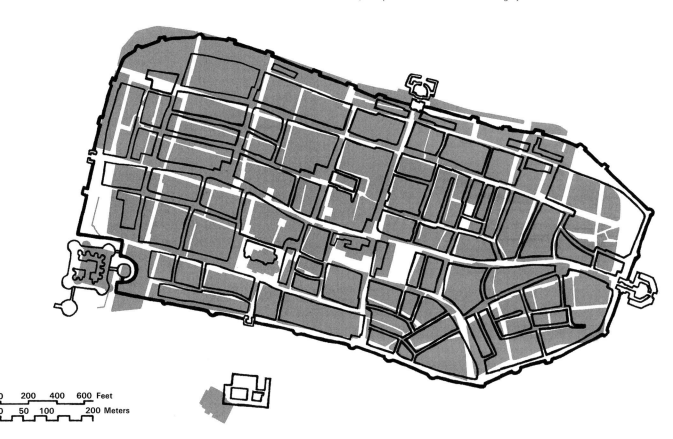

Imola in comparison, 1502 and 1984. The 1984 plan view (shaded area) is imposed on the 1502 line drawing by Leonardo.

0   200   400   600 Feet
0   50   100   200 Meters

from China that had come to the Western world through the Arabian Sea. Leonardo also used a modified odometer, a device known since Roman times, to measure distance.[16]

With these three instruments, Leonardo surveyed Imola and constructed an ichnographic city plan.[17] He was inspired by Leon Battista Alberti's *Descripto Urbis Romae,* a brief description of a survey of Rome, written between 1443 and 1455. Although no example of Alberti's survey work has survived, his methodology is clear in another of his writings, the *Ludi matematici.* Apparently Alberti did not use a compass but wrote that any point in a city can be fixed by establishing its polar coordinates. Using Alberti's technique, Leonardo drew a polar grid, with the town square at the center of the map, locating all plan measurements of the town on the grid.

The Imola map is the earliest surviving artifact of the Renaissance revolution in cartographic techniques. Every element of the town in the ground plan is represented as if it could be seen from an infinite number of viewpoints, each perpendicular to the earth's surface. Every point on the map is rendered equidistant from the observer. Modern high-altitude photogrammetry of the town largely concurs with Leonardo's map, confirming Leonardo's astonishing achievement. Since no written document of Leonardo's technique has survived, we rely on a letter Raphael wrote while in service to Pope Leo X, proposing to map Rome according to Leonardo's specifications.[18] Raphael died in 1520, before he could finish his work. ∎

New ways of looking at reality, however, can provoke surprising reactions from those unaccustomed to them. One sixteenth-century source reports that Leonardo was ridiculed when he presented an unsolicited map of ancient Rome to the courtiers of Pope Leo X:

> In telling you something about the kind of consideration that courtiers have for men of ingenuity and draftsmanship, I recall a wonderful cartoon which is impressed in my memory. A *gentile intelletto* had portrayed Rome as it was in antiquity, not as it is now; he presented his work to the courtiers believing that they would express their enthusiasm for it, as it is customary of people who have no other way of prising themselves than that of giving credit to the ingenuity of others. And while he was explaining to them how he had subdivided the city into seven parts, that is in as many parts as there are hills, they started to let the wax of their candles pour down on the drawing. He was so intent on his explanation that he did not notice that, and he went on saying that this is the Pantheon, which Marcus Agrippa dedicated to all the Gods, and this is the Templum Pacis, and here are the Baths of Diocletian, here the Antoniane, and again: through this passage, above such great columns, one could go from the main Forum to the Campidoglio. In the meantime the wax of the candles continued to pour down, and he continued to go on by saying: here in the Vatican was the foundation of the Domus Aurea of Nero, here is the bridge of Horace, here Hadrian's sepulchre, which is now the Castle of S. Agnolo, and from which one could watch the bellum navale. And when he arrived to point out the Colosseum, the courtiers raised their candles pretending to praise the Ancients. Our good man continued his explanation, pointing out the places of the performances of the gladiators and of the fights of the wild beasts, and giving measurements of aqueducts, of painted grottoes,

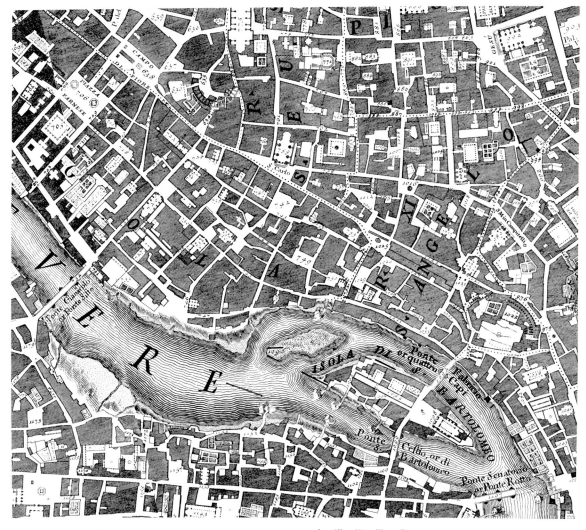

Detail, map of Rome, 1736–1748. Giambattista Nolli, *The Pianta grande di Roma of Giambattista Nolli in Facsimile*, Highmount, N.Y.: J. H. Aronson, 1984. Note the Theater of Pompeii in the upper middle of the map between the numbers 635 and 633.

of the Metae, of obelisks, of the Column of Trajan, of the arches of Titus, of Septimius, of Constantine, and of all the others. Then he explained how many colossi and marble statues there were in Rome, and how many statues of bronze and gold; really, as I can tell you, he was explaining every detail in a marvellous way. And the courtiers, who as architects of human suffering could understand the Ionic, the Corinthian, and the Composite Orders in the same way as they could understand Chaldean, Hebrew, Greek, and Latin, set fire to one of the sides of the cartoon with their candles, breaking into such laughter that one could only feel utter disgust at their behavior.[19]

More than two centuries after Leonardo completed his Imola map, Giambattista Nolli undertook his famous survey of Rome. The map that resulted from his work is a high point of mapmaking. Nolli began as early as 1736 and finished in 1748. He started work on the survey of Rome after being given an extraordinary pass by the Vicar of Rome, Cardinal Gandagni, that reads: "Since His Holiness

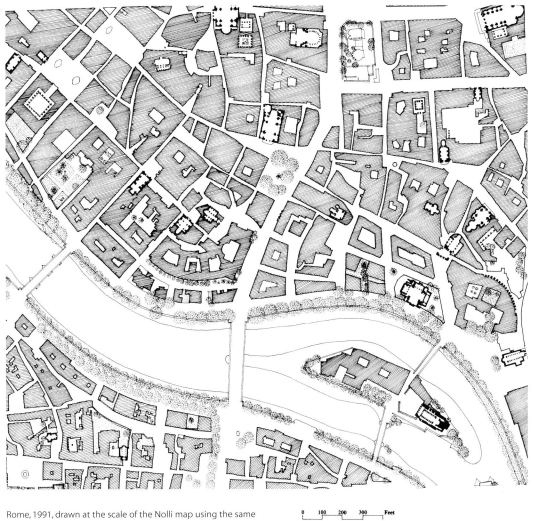

Rome, 1991, drawn at the scale of the Nolli map using the same graphic conventions.

```
0    100   200   300   Feet
0         50        100   Meters
```

has given permission for the publication of a new, exact Map of the City of Rome, and since the geometra surveyor assigned to this task, Giambattista Nolli by name, must have access and entry to all the Basilicas, churches and convents, even those of Cloistered Nuns, in order to take the necessary measurements, His Holiness orders that the above-named geometra be permitted to enter with 4 or 5 Companions."[20]

The first use of Nolli's map appears to have been political. In 1744 a print of it was used to redefine the borders of the city's fourteen administrative districts.[21] In his surprisingly accurate map, Nolli employs a simple and effective convention of using voids to represent publicly accessible space and solid black to represent the coverage of buildings on a given block. His map holds up well in comparison with the detailed modern maps made for the 1991 Atlas of Rome,[22] though Nolli made some interesting mistakes. For example, the representation of the Roman ruin of the Theater of Pompeii is largely Nolli's invention. (The theater is situated in the upper middle portion of the Nolli map.) The location is correct, and the large arch can still

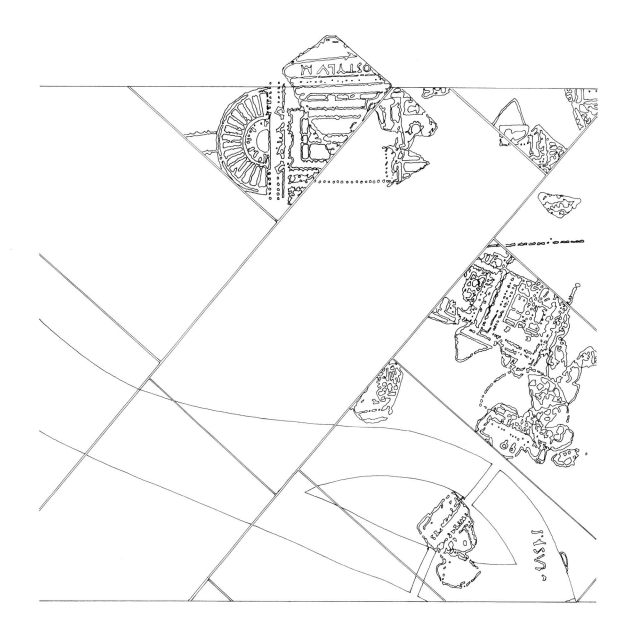

Detail of a map of Rome produced at the time of the Emperor
Septimus Severus, 203–211 A.D. Only fragments of the map have
survived. Traced and reproduced at the same scale as the Nolli map.
Note the location of the Theater of Pompeii and its orientation in the
upper portion of the map.

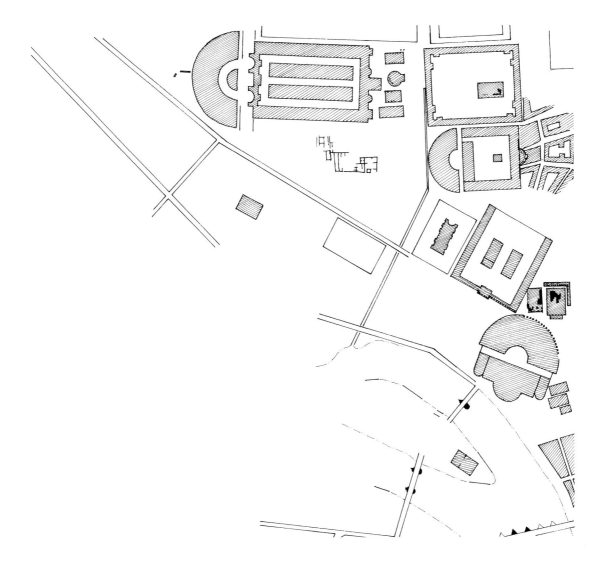

Location of ruins according to an archaeological survey. Source:
Carta de Centro Storico di Roma, 1988 (1:1000). Three survey maps
were used to reproduce the detail shown here: Largo Argentina,
Isola Tiberina, and Campo des Flori.

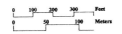

be seen in the fabric of Rome today, but the theater opens to the east, not the north.

Over the centuries, the Nolli map has sustained its appeal. The map reads like a written language, describing the dimensions of streets and piazzas, interiors of churches, public buildings, courts, and gardens. Nolli's graphic convention produces an abstraction of physical reality and, like all abstractions, conveys selective information.

Both methods of representation, Leonardo da Vinci's and Brunelleschi's, have been developed over the past six centuries. Brunelleschi's *constructione legitima* made possible the invention of photography, which led to motion pictures, which led to television and now digital image recording. Leonardo's cartography developed into modern mapmaking, with photogrammetry used to record selected points through triangulation.

These two methods, fundamentally the only means available for depicting the world, represent two ways of looking at and understanding that world. In the development of a human individual and of our civilization, Brunelleschi's painting represents the earlier view—an understanding of the world based on the evidence of the senses. We believe those things to exist and to be true which we can take in through our senses. Leonardo's map symbolizes our need to go beyond direct experience, to explain the structure of things, the theory behind the phenomena we can see. Both methods of representation made possible design and planning work as we know it today, remote from the actual place of construction.

It is not entirely fair to associate the two men with opposing methods of representation. We admire Leonardo's sensuous paintings and sculptures as much as his meticulous engineering studies and scientific records. Likewise, the concept governing Brunelleschi's dome above Santa Maria del Fiore still inspires engineering students. Creative achievement draws from both concept and experience.

The chapters that follow suggest that the two methods of representation—map and perspective—introduced a division in professional thinking about places between the clarity of abstractions (the view from above) and the befuddling richness and confusion of the ground-level view. These two mind-sets rarely achieve balance; but when they do, the effect is that of a bull's-eye hit.

CHAPTER TWO

The Search for a Visual Language in Design

How to describe a city? Even for an old inhabitant it is impossible: one can present only a simplified plan, taking a house here, a park there, as symbols of the whole.

Graham Greene

Giambattista Nolli's map of Rome and the earlier map of Imola by Leonardo da Vinci are beautiful examples of spatial representations drawn in graphic terms now commonly used in Western society but unusual for their time. Few people could relate the information on the maps to what they knew existed in the real world. And even today many people are not entirely comfortable with the graphic convention of maps or plan views.

Of course, maps of cities simplify reality; they are intended not to contain all available information but—like a scientific theory—to contain the least possible information, arranged as unambiguously as possible, to permit a skilled map reader to extract an adequate image of reality. Nolli's map was not a commercial success. Only 340 copies sold of the 1,874 printed. Romans of the time, like one particular art dealer of the day, "would have preferred a map that showed the palaces, churches, obelisks, columns and other relevant things, rather than spending money for a work whose principal merit is only that it shows the exact measurement of all the places of the city."[1] The public had little need for the highly abstract map; for orientation and as a record of memory, people preferred bird's-eye views, or maps that reminded them of buildings by showing the facades of important structures.

Certainly Leonardo's Imola map, intended as a tool to assess and plan fortifications, was not made for public consumption. Leonardo prepared it in his capacity as a salaried consultant on military architecture to the "splendid and magnificent" Cesare Borgia—who, according to Machiavelli, the Venetian representative to the duke's court, conquered a new fortress once a month and "arrived in one place before it is known he has left another."[2] In conducting his campaigns, either by subterfuge or an open show of force, the duke needed to know the city's entrances and exits and the routes within it, and these are exactly what the map shows. Its abstraction is a real advantage, not only in maintaining the secrecy of information intended for military use but also in obliging the reader to recognize that interpretation is an integral part of representing reality.

Few of Leonardo's contemporaries understood the Imola map. The new convention of representing cities was rarely used. In fact, none of the four surviving sixteenth-century maps preserved in a collection of maps of Rome from antiquity to modern times follows Leonardo's convention.[3] The seventeenth-century portion of the collection includes eighteen maps, only two of which are presented in ichnographic form. And even among the eighteenth-century maps, only six of thirteen (including two by Nolli) follow Leonardo's plan view. But the thirty-nine maps produced during the nineteenth century all follow his ichnographic convention, and only three show Rome in the older picture-map tradition. Not until the second half of the eighteenth century had the new convention taken hold among professionals concerned with the form of cities.

No one except God could see a city from above; a plan drawn on flat material does not correspond to human experience in the way a "prospect" does. The idea of seeing a city in the mind's eye from above was born of the Enlightenment and its fascination with rational thinking and with abstractions or generalizations.

Through the power of abstraction, urban planning became possible. A map of a town could be made, taken to an office (sometimes in another city), spread on a table or hung on a wall, and looked at. A professional looking at such a map could imagine a city as a system. Even if it seems to a pedestrian to have no clear order, layers of order are readily visible in a city drawn in plan and viewed from a few feet away. Cities generally have centers, boundaries, and edges. Streets connect places; major streets run from squares to gates and bridges. Frequently there is a hierarchy of squares, as there is a hierarchy of quarters and the activities associated with them. If urban structure becomes obvious on a map, intervention in it might be equally obvious. With a ruler, one could mark a straight avenue through the ancient congestion of alleys. Indeed, throughout history, physical changes to the form of cities have been justified as a cure for every ailment of urban society. Reasons for placing the ruler on the map have been articulated inside and outside the profession of city planning, but the placement of the line is the act of a planner because the planner understands best the meaning of this graphic convention.

Although a designer like Leonardo may have searched for new conventions in the graphic representation of cities for practical military reasons, designers also experiment for reasons of professional prestige. Those who mastered Leonardo's graphic convention achieved greater standing vis-à-vis those in power. A proposed design no longer had to be visualized on the site. Instead, the designers could come to court and spread out a plan. In doing so, they gained access to power and became the equals of the courtiers, who depended on them to interpret what was to become reality.

At the same time, as designers' access to power increased, the new graphic convention opened up the possibility of working on large-scale projects, which previously would have been possible only with piecemeal design. But power and the potential to work on large-scale projects came at a price: gradually, conceptual representation removed the designer from the reality of the site—not only from the physical, or ecological, reality, but also from political, economic, and socio-psychological reality.

The examples that follow have been selected from an extensive history of city design. I have selected one city design per century to show the gradual introduction of conceptual representations, from the invention of Leonardo's map of Imola in 1502 to the end of the nineteenth century, when a reaction to the conceptual representation of cities set in. The places and the professionals searching for ways to perfect conceptual representations are well known and require only brief introductions.

LONDON, 1666

Steen Eiler Rasmussen, in his book on London, explains how the conceptual planning method might have been applied to that city.[3] In 1666 the Great Fire destroyed the entire center of London. It broke out late in the evening of September 1, burned fast, and stopped on September 6, only to break out again. Historians say it smoldered for months. On September 10 the king received Christopher Wren, who came with a plan to rebuild the city. Immediately after the fire, according to his son, Wren prepared a survey of the city. But when his design is compared with Wenceslas Hollar's "Exact Surveigh of the City of London," commissioned in December 1666, three months after the fire, and published in 1667, the comparison reveals that Wren's survey was probably traced from an earlier inaccurate map brought up-to-date by a hurried walk through the smoldering ruins,[5] an improvisation similar to what a modern-day professional might do. The designer quickly records an image mentally and on paper in order to work with it. Compare Wren's map with the hatched area on Hollar's survey, and note how carefully Wren depicted the edge of the fire-damaged areas.

Wren was only thirty-four years old but had distinguished himself as a mathematician and held a professorship in astronomy at Oxford. Architecture was new to him; he had taken it up only four years before the fire. His interest in the construction of buildings and towns had led him to Paris, where he spent the year 1665—the year of the plague, a good year to be away from London. The geometric clarity of the map Wren presented to Charles II reminded the king, who had lived in Paris himself for many years, that London could be rebuilt according to the latest French planning methods.

Two monuments stand out in Wren's proposal: St. Paul's and the Stock Exchange. The Guild Hall remained in its original place. All three structures are linked by straight roads where none had been. From the Stock Exchange, a road leads directly to London Bridge, again where no such connection

had existed before. Wren connected St. Paul's with the Tower of London in a straight line; the road that had linked them before had curved in several places. Other intersections shaped as stars or squares had only graphic significance. New buildings would have to give them meaning over time. For example, Wren moved the parish churches from their existing locations to intersections and alongside important roads. Wren also rotated St. Paul's Cathedral to make the building respond to the axes of the new streets. Wren's drawing is nothing more than a conceptual diagram; major modification would have been required to make it a design. The drawing's details do not correspond to the actual ruins, the Thames River, or the Tower of London.

A letter signed by Will Morris, the king's secretary, went out to the Lord Mayor of London the day of Wren's visit, asking the Lord Mayor "to inhibit and straightly forbid all persons, whatsoever that they presume not to build any dwelling houses until further order," because "his Majesty had before him certain models and drafts for re-edifying the city with more decency and convenience than formerly."[6]

Wren's design responded to the prevailing view that epidemics like the plague were caused by bad air, which became stagnant in narrow, congested streets with open sewers. The same narrow streets were correctly blamed for spreading the fire, which had jumped from one roof to the next. The alleys had been too narrow to serve as firebreaks between houses made primarily of wood. Moreover, buildings had been too high for the roofs to be reached by ladders.

Wren's recommendations for rebuilding London went beyond physical improvements for health and safety. His plan was influenced by a growing literature on ideal cities, with clear geometric patterns, applied first to the construction of fortified new settlements in Northern Italy and later to the planning of settlements in the New World and the resettling of religious refugees in the Protestant or Reformed countries in north central Europe.[7]

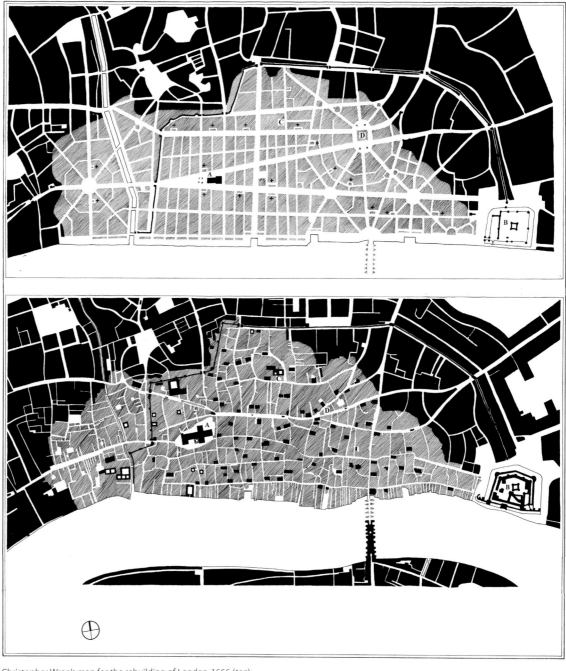

Christopher Wren's map for the rebuilding of London, 1666 (*top*);
and Wenceslas Hollar's survey of London, 1667; redrawn to the same
scale. Hatched areas indicate the extent of destruction after the 1666
fire: (a) St. Paul's, (b) Tower of London, (c) Guild Hall, (d) Royal
Exchange.

In the wake of the Thirty Years' War, the lords, bishops, and kings of central Europe rivaled each other in renovating the fortifications around their cities. At the same time, contradictorily, they engaged military engineers to design new subdivisions outside the remodeled fortifications. The geometric order of the new towns outside the walls stands out clearly on city maps of the period.[8]

Charles II saw that the Great Fire gave him the opportunity to introduce the same new geometry in London. During the days that followed Wren's visit, the king received proposals from John Evelyn, Captain Valentine Knight, and Robert Hooke. Evelyn produced three versions of his design, all grid patterns with diagonals. One of them bears a curious resemblance to the later L'Enfant plan for Washington. Hooke, like Wren a mathematician, prepared a gridiron plan.[9] None of the plans was executed. Each was considered for only a few days in late September 1666. The rejection of the September plans signifies the power of the City of London—a city that, in contrast to capitals of the Continent, desired to be self-governing, independent of the Crown.

Although all buildings had burned to the ground, citizens could stand on their property and point to where their houses had been and where the neighbors' property met theirs. If Wren's plan was to be carried out, the city's land would have to be assembled and somehow subdivided again in proportions based on ownership before the fire, with land for roads and public buildings subtracted. Such an enterprise would have required government expropriation of the land and a large bank to handle finances. With his government impoverished from the plague, the king needed no reminder of the impossibility of rebuilding London according to geometric schemes "drawn up by clever men in a few days' time."[10]

The reminder came from representatives of the city—the Lord Mayor, startled by the letter he received from the Crown the day after Wren's map was shown to the king, convinced the monarch how impractical it would be to carry out an ideal plan. Rather, attention should go to rebuilding: no wooden buildings; comparatively low buildings on narrow streets where light and air were scarce; taller buildings along wider streets. Fleet Street, Cheapskate, Cornell, and some other streets should be made much wider. The precise width was to be published later after consultation with the Lord Mayor and aldermen. Lanes and alleys were proscribed unless absolutely necessary. To give access to water in the event of future fires, a broad embankment along the river was created, free of buildings along the riverbank. In the rebuilding of London, practical reasoning prevailed. Decisions about the city's future form were made locally, with an eye to the problems at hand, and not by the monarch who lived outside the city.

Parliament voted on new controls for rebuilding London on February 8, 1667. The legislation had been prepared in a remarkably short time by a committee that included Wren and Hooke. One of their first tasks had been to commission a new, accurate survey of London and the 1667 map, to plan the widening of streets in detail. The commissioning of an accurate survey followed by the drawing of an exact map became the prerequisite of town planning. Without the map image, it would have been impossible to evaluate projects prior to constructing roads and city blocks.

Almost two hundred years later in Paris, Baron Haussmann wrote in his memoirs: "Before concerning myself with the piercing of the new public ways, whose networks constitute the most singular part of the transformation of our great city, should I not in effect, speak of the initial study for this long and laborious work, and of the instruments which have served me to undertake this project in its entirety and its details, to determine, on the spot, the line of each avenue, boulevard, or street, to be opened up, and to oversee the faithful execution of the whole."[11]

In Paris Haussmann's surveyors climbed high scaffolds or great wooden masts that Haussmann described in his journals as "higher than the houses, from where they could measure according to the method of triangulation by the means of the most perfect precision instruments. Angles were formed by the sides of each of the triangles determined on the spot by the extension of the central shafts of these temporary constructions."[12] To a surveyor holding on to the top, the sight lines from mast to mast "gave a real existence to the plan."

Haussmann wrote his journal entries before balloons equipped with cameras produced aerial images of cities. In the absence of such technology, the masts were an effective tool, permitting survey-ors to "draw" an imaginary design above the roofs of the city. It is not known whether Haussmann himself climbed into the skies to compare his plan against reality.

One cannot help wondering if a person— whether the prefect himself or any "geometer"— standing atop one of the masts might have imag-ined the run of a proposed street and the connec-tion such a street would make between known places. Might that same person not also have imag-ined the fate of the people who lived under the densely cluttered roofs in that same line of sight? By the end of Haussmann's tenure, the number of displaced Parisians squatting outside the city walls north and northeast of Paris had increased to 140,000.[13]

Although for Haussmann the new straight streets meant "disemboweling the old Paris"— the quarters of riots and barricades—because they "did not lend themselves to the habitual tactic of local insurrection," history repeated itself. The displaced citizens marched back into the city to take the Hôtel de Ville on March 18, 1871. For the fourth time since 1789, revolutionaries claimed the city, this time for the short-lived Commune of Paris.

BARCELONA, 1776

In 1776, at a point midway between Wren's plan for rebuilding London and Haussmann's remodeling of Paris, the military engineer Juan Martin Carmeno started work on a new street through the middle of Barcelona. Carmeno had become known in Catalonia for the planning of Barceloneta, a suburb for workers near the port of Barcelona.

The Ramblas ("riverbed" in Arabic) had been the site of a small creek, the Cagallel, that ran as an open sewer along the western edge of the Gothic quarter. In the thirteenth century a city wall had been constructed along the curving creek. The wall, made obsolete when a new wall was built further west, was taken down in 1779. Carmeno, guided by a survey, laid out a novel type of street, an urban bypass, a divided roadway with a wide median, connecting the port with a town gate, approxi-mately where the Plaza de Cataluña (Plaça de Cata-lunya on the map) is today. From there, highways branched out north, west, and east. The new right-of-way was marked by two straight parallel lines, 100 feet apart, a broad strip of road in a city where streets are rarely more than 30 feet wide. The east-ern edge of the right-of-way was drawn with some reference to the alignment of the old wall, but without its curvature.

On a map drawn in 1807, thirty years into the existence of the new street, some property owners have taken advantage of the new right-of-way in building structures up to the new frontage line. Carmeno's plan called for the razing of properties near the port, drawn by the author of the 1807 map in the same graphic convention (a dotted line) as the former placement of the city wall. Other, more substantial residences on the western side of the Ramblas were left standing, although they pro-jected into the new street.

For the design of the straight street, and as a legal instrument for adjustments to individual properties, a precise map was necessary. An earlier map, drawn in 1697, which followed the graphic convention of representing structures by their facades instead of by roof or ground plans, would

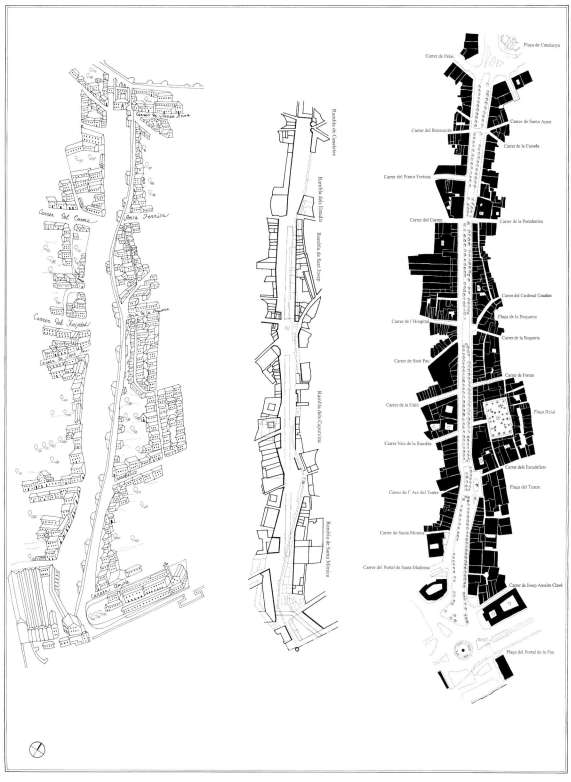

Ramblas, Barcelona, as it appears on maps in history (*from left*):
1697, prior to construction; 1807, thirty years into the existence of
the street; and 1987, in its current form.

Above: Ramblas, Barcelona.

Opposite: Joan Miró, 1925, *Lady Strolling on the Ramblas in Barcelona,*
New Orleans Museum of Art; bequest of Victor K. Kiam.

confuse anyone wanting to establish dimensions.
More misleading would have been the incorrect
angles of buildings and streets. Even a surveyor who
had learned to use a magnetic compass might not
have understood that frequent, precise readings
were necessary to determine accurate bearing angles
of buildings and streets. But an accurate map made
possible detailed planning away from the site; the
plan, moreover, could be presented to the military
governor for approval.

Barcelona in 1776 was an occupied city. The
straight line of the road that made the movement
of goods more efficient also carried a distinct mes-
sage of power: "You cannot fire a cannon around
a corner, or send cavalry charging through winding
alleys. The Barrio Gotico was the natural home of
the urban guerrilla—the Ramblas implied the
supremacy of the army."[14] But whatever its mes-
sage, the Ramblas was a vast improvement over the
old riverside walk, "thronged with people, choked
with dust in the summer, and mud in the winter."[15]

Carmeno's Ramblas is one of those rare planning
projects that achieves a balance between concept
and experience. The abstract line was modified by
the elements already in place. Because of this
balance, urban designers still borrow Carmeno's
concept. This street, a designer might exclaim of a
proposal far from Barcelona, will look like the
Ramblas. And the proposed street might have a
paved median strip for pedestrians. But it might
not be located near a high-density medieval quarter
where even to this day people stroll. The proposed
street may lack any number of design elements that
characterize the Ramblas, such as the slightly
changing width of pavement, a reminder of the
former riverbed. Generally, the median measures
from 42 feet, 14 inches, to 46 feet, 18 inches,
widening only at the beginning and end. The plane
trees are generally 18 feet apart, sometimes 36 feet.[16]
The straight plantation grows well in the well-
composted alignment of the former sewer.

And the proposed street might not share a number of other important elements of the Ramblas,
such as vendors selling birdseed, flowers, and

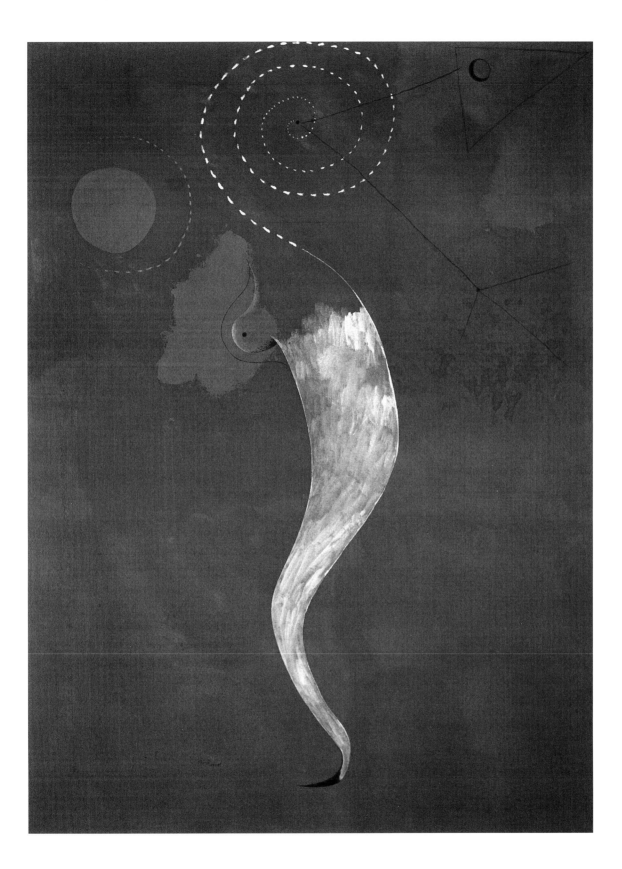

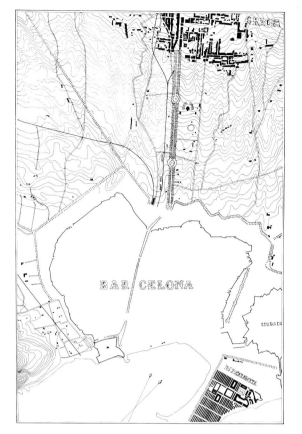

Ildefonso Cerda, Barcelona and environs, 1855, detail redrawn.

magazines—the only goods that can be sold there—and waiters rushing through the traffic lane to deliver drinks to customers in the median strip (and, when I first saw the street, a Civil War veteran keeping the chairs in line and renting them out for a peseta to people who wanted to rest and watch the crowd stream by).

Another memorable experience is to see the Ramblas framed by the buildings lining a narrow cross street. On a spring day, in such a narrow frame of view, the light reflecting in the leaves of the trees tints the air green. Such sights are part of the Ramblas experience. Joan Miró, in a 1925 painting, conveys another facet of this experience: the curvature of this relatively straight street.

BARCELONA, 1859

By the middle of the nineteenth century Barcelona had been freed of the much-hated outer walls built under Bourbon occupation. In 1855 Ildefonso Cerda, a civil engineer, had been commissioned to prepare an accurate topographic survey of Barcelona and its surroundings. Whereas the city's population in the eighteenth century was 64,000, by the 1850s it had grown to over 150,000. As a result, the density of Barcelona, at 315 inhabitants per acre (855 per ha), was one of the highest in Europe. (In Paris, density averaged 166 people per acre [400 per ha], and only in the third and fourth arrondissements did density approach that of Barcelona.)[17] The average life expectancy for a man ranged from 38.3 years among the wealthier classes to 19.7 years among the poorer laboring classes. The city was frequently ravaged by cholera epidemics. In the view of the public, Barcelona simply had to expand to accommodate the large influx of rural inhabitants seeking employment in the city.

Cerda, who had completed his studies in 1849 in Madrid, belonged to the generation of European planners born after the French Revolution who had grown up amid the great economic and social changes of the Industrial Revolution. He welcomed the commission to prepare an accurate topographic survey as a necessary prerequisite for the much

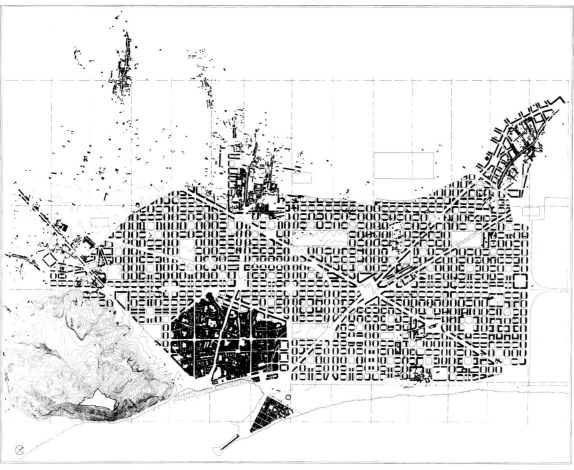

0 1000 2000 3000 4000 5000 6000 Feet
0 200 400 600 1000 1400 1600 Meters

Ildefonso Cerda, Ensanche de Barcelona, 1859, redrawn.

talked-about expansion. He presented the new map in November 1855.[18]

The map was a milestone in cartography. Cerda worked at a scale of 1:1250, intending to reduce the map to 1:1500. "He applied his habitual rigor to the scrupulous drawing of contour lines."[19] To avoid errors, he had all information independently checked by three teams of professionals. The 1856 Public Works Record pronounced Cerda's work "the clearest and most perfect topographic plan we have ever seen, in which the terrain is represented by level sections, one meter apart, whose figure is not even minimally arbitrary."[20]

Four years later Cerda's topographic map became the base drawing for those entering the 1859 competition for an urban extension plan, the Ensanche.

Cerda submitted his own entry but was not initially awarded the prize. The commission to plan the extension was eventually given to him after the central government in Madrid reversed the local decision to award the contract to the architect Antonio Rovira i Tias. Apart from having prepared the geographic survey, Cerda had another advantage. Three years prior to the competition he had published a different kind of survey: a statistical summary of Barcelona's working-class demographics and social conditions.[21] Cerda articulated his ideas for the expansion of Barcelona in his *General Theory of Urbanization and the Application of Its Principles and Doctrines to the Reform and Expansion of Barcelona*, published in 1867, eight years after the Ensanche competition.[22]

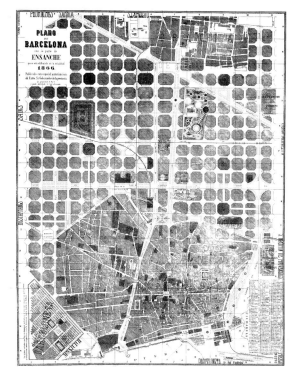

Ensanche de Barcelona, 1866. Source: Barcelona Public Works Department.

Even before construction of the Ensanche had officially started, on October 4, 1860, Cerda's plan was criticized by the local architectural community for its monotony, its lack of human variety.[23] In his book, Cerda reflected on this criticism and clarified his thinking regarding the intent shown in the competition plan. His plan, the now famous pattern of blocks with chamfered corners framing Barcelona to the north, west, and northeast, enclosed the old city. As an abstract pattern, it has visual appeal. Its 550 blocks cover 9 square kilometers, without reference to the gentle slope of the land toward the sea. In its modularity, the plan could have been expended wherever topography permitted such regularity.

What we do not see on the plan, or experience today walking through the Ensanche, is a city shaped by social concerns. Cerda's book is clear: the smallest unit of Cerda's structure is the city block, 113.3 meters (330 feet) square, with the famous 45-degree cut at the corners, resulting in four street facades, each 86 meters long, and four shorter facades facing squares at intersections. Typical streets are 19.80 meters (60 feet) wide, and the squares at intersections have 48-meter (150-foot) sides. Only one-third, approximately 5,000 square meters, of each block was to be used for buildings, constructed in rows two floors high above a basement. The rows would occupy two sides of each block; the other two would be open to gardens. A glance at Cerda's competition map confirms his intention. The pattern he drew corresponds to this description. If built as planned, Cerda's extension would have resembled a garden city. He intended that 25 blocks, five by five, should form a neighborhood, with its own school and church; 100 blocks, ten by ten, should form a district, with an entire block in each district set aside for a market and a park.

In the northern section of Barcelona, six districts are visible in Cerda's plan. In the section of the Ensanche just above the center of the old city, on both sides of the Paseo de Gracia, where construction started in 1860, the pattern of neighborhoods and districts is less clear.

Paseo de Gracia, Barcelona.

As a concrete image of city development, Cerda's proposal exercised only limited control over three-dimensional elements. An official map published in 1866 shows no trace of Cerda's two-sided block development with row housing. Instead, the height limit was set at 57 feet, or five floors; in 1891 the limit was increased to 65 feet, allowing for rows of seven-story buildings around the perimeter of each block.[24] The density increased from Cerda's original proposal of 150,000 square feet of floor space per block to 710,000.

In the eyes of the critics, the higher density led to disease and social problems. "The Middle Ages never escaped the common man." According to an 1888 medical survey made by a Doctor Faria, typhoid, scrofula, anemia, and tuberculosis were common in what should have been the "handsomest and healthiest of cities." Toilets drained into open pits, contaminating the air and water.

That same year another critic of the Ensanche wrote: "With two story rowhouses and a basement enclosed by gardens set out in pleasant and smiling perspective, built on only two sides of each block, meant for one family at a time, today they have become veritable slums, in which the Barcelona families are imprisoned. The forces of speculation unleashed without control."[25] Cerda's plan was untenable because it implied political conditions capable of controlling the speculation encouraged by the regular land division.[26]

Cerda's proposal did not exercise much control over private property; however, with regard to the publicly owned spaces, his plan had longevity. The layout of streets, blocks, and broad avenues was carefully studied with regard to all their dimensions.

Cerda proposed that one hundred trees should be planted in each block. Regularly spaced plane trees still line many streets of the Ensanche. Walking on the 30-foot-wide sidewalks under these trees, which are planted every 24 feet, is a very pleasant experience. The pattern of short blocks shaded by trees, alternating with squares open to the sky, introduces a rhythm to the walk. The rhythm is interrupted when the pedestrian must cross wide streets or diagonal streets, but since these also appear at regular intervals, the rhythm is reestablished.

Contrary to Cerda's early critics, such a walk is rarely boring or monotonous. Some portions of the walk present real treats, like a stroll on Antonio Gaudi's tiled sidewalk along the Paseo de Gracia or in the middle of the right-of-way on the Ramblas de Catalonia, one block west. These urban spaces afford pedestrians a sense of mastery, leaving them surprisingly unaffected by the onslaught of car traffic. ■

By the end of the nineteenth century, planners had grown accustomed to Leonardo da Vinci's convention of the conceptual city map and had used it to rationalize the geometry of urban form. The rubric of rational planning, which assumed the existence of political control, included a concern that public and private places in cities be healthful for residents, safe from fires, and efficient to move around in for inhabitants as well as the military. The elements of rational planning, moreover, could be quantified and evaluated: straight was better than curved and wide better than narrow for all matters of health, comfort, safety, and efficiency.

In Barcelona, the process of mapping a rational plan invited idiosyncrasies: with his straightedge, Cerda created the "Calle Diagonal" as well as the Square of the Glory of Catalonia where two diagonal streets cross the Gran Via. Despite the important-sounding name, the place shaped by the crossing of major roads had no geographic, symbolic, or other meaning prior to its creation,[27] and for that matter the square has not become a center of Barcelona corresponding to its geographic location in the grid and its accessibility. That situation may change, however, for finally, at the end of the twentieth century, a performing arts complex is emerging there.

The process of designing a town in plan does not in itself inform decisions regarding those dimensions and proportions that make the experience of urban form worthwhile. At the end of the nineteenth century, in response to rapid urbanization, the authors of books on city form stressed artistic principles, and in doing so started a search for representations that expressed the experience of urban geometry. For the English-reading audience, Raymond Unwin addressed the art of city design, using material from the German planner Joseph Stübben.[28] Both were preceded by Cerda's contemporary, the Austrian Camillo Sitte.

Sitte wrote his *Städtebau*, a book about artistic considerations in urban design, when the vast complex of public monuments and private apartment buildings in Vienna known as the Ringstrasse was nearing completion.[29] Sitte's ideas of urban life and form were opposed to those of his professional rivals, who had captured the imagination of the liberal government of Vienna with conceptual images of urban form shaped according to rational thinking. Camillo Sitte was a promoter of the Arts and Crafts movement. He had studied at the Vienna Polytechnic and founded the state professional school for arts and crafts in 1875 in Salzburg and later a second school in Vienna.

Carl Schorske has written that Sitte "won his place in the Pantheon of communitarian theorists where he was revered by other reformers, such as Lewis Mumford and Jane Jacobs."[30] Sitte's contribution is important to our discussion of representation and the influence of representational method on the design of cities. His graphic methods combined concept and experience. He produced comparative map studies of well-dimensioned urban places and eye-level drawings mainly of cities in Austria, Italy, Germany, France, and Belgium. He used graphic representations to exemplify physical enclosure and spatial definition.

If dimensions are important in the art of city design, then measured drawings are an essential record of places worth remembering. Sitte failed to indicate the scale of his drawings, and thus they convey only the relative spatial relationship of enclosure to openness. But Sitte's insistence on a three-dimensional survey of city form was new. He implied that the design of cities should be the work of professionals trained to imagine urban form three-dimensionally. Because of Sitte's writings, a change took place: military engineers responsible for the design of fortified cities had turned over to engineers the task of laying out boulevards when city walls came down; after Sitte published his *Städtebau*, however, the physical shape of cities became the responsibility of architects.

The most innovative element of Sitte's work was his insistence that urban places respond to the inhabitants' psychic state, an idea that can only be understood as an offspring of the turn-of-the-century fascination with the work of Sigmund Freud and a growing interest in the workings of the human mind.[31]

Vienna, in the mid-nineteenth century, had burst its seams. The old city, Roman at the core, with medieval extensions, was still surrounded by the massive defense works that had withstood the onslaught of the Turks. But already more of Vienna was outside the fortifications and beyond the extensive glacis than within. The new liberal government made plans to raze the old fortifications. In 1848 the city and its institutions, including the court of the emperor, appeared in danger not from invaders, but from revolutionaries.

Sitte intended to weave the streets and city blocks of the old inner core with the more regular pattern of the suburbs into a continuous fabric. Seemingly by accident, urban spaces would have resulted "in nature," shaped by a complicated geometry of street grids. In front of great buildings like the new Reichstag, the Austro-Hungarian Parliament, for example, Sitte proposed to build supplementary structures to frame and contain squares as islands of human community. Instead, in the official plan the *Prachtbauten* (splendid structures) dominated these squares. The vast urban spaces that resulted were too large for the traditional uses of urban space—for trade, assembly, celebration, and demonstration. Moreover, they were not connected to the streets that led toward them. They were voids.

A square, in Sitte's view, was not merely a piece of unbuilt land, but a space enclosed by walls, like an outdoor room, serving as a theater of common life. "No one thought of that," he complained.[32] In his view, the members of the City Expansion Committee had lost their senses. "The rage for open space," he proclaimed, would produce a new urban neurosis of *Platzscheue*, or agoraphobia, the fear of crossing, and of being dwarfed by, space and being

Vienna, 1844, redrawn.

impotent in the face of the vehicles to which it has been consigned.[33]

In his book Sitte had presented measurements and images of well-proportioned town squares to open the public's eyes to urban qualities too important to sacrifice. The psychological well-being of citizens, he argued, is as important as improvements in mobility and hygiene. Had Sitte's work been understood as an attempt to design for the psychic state of urban people, his critics might have seen its progressive aspects. But Sitte did not know how to express his concern in a form that could appeal to those interested in the new field of psychology. As a result, his method looked to his contemporaries like historicizing; and for that matter,

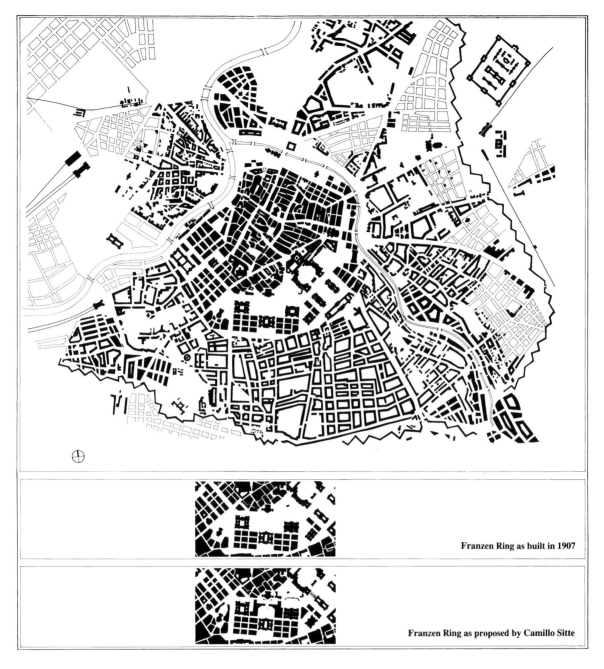

Franzen Ring as built in 1907

Franzen Ring as proposed by Camillo Sitte

Vienna, 1891 (*top*), with detail of Sitte's proposal redrawn.

0   500   1000   1500   2000   2500   3000   Feet
0   100   200   300   400   500   600   700   800   900   1000   Meters

designers of cities today face similar struggles. The irony in their work is that they frequently look backward in history in order to go forward. Sitte's critics, seeing images of largely medieval or baroque squares and winding roads, interpreted his work as that of someone who lived in the past, wanting to go backward.

Thirty-five years after Sitte first published his *Städtebau* (the first edition, in 1889, sold out within a month of publication), this reaction was given voice: "The winding road is the pack donkey's way. The straight road is man's way," wrote Le Corbusier in his 1924 book *Urbanisme* (published in English as *The City of Tomorrow and Its Planning*). The persuasive order of the machine age influenced the form of cities in the twentieth century. In his first chapter Le Corbusier contrasts Sitte's artistic principles—polemically caricatured as the pack donkey's way—with the new order, man's way. The "new urbanism" calls for rationalism, function, efficiency.

> The winding way is the result of happy-go-lucky heedlessness, of looseness, lack of concentration and animality. The straight road is a reaction, an action, a positive deed, the result of self-mastery. It is sane and noble.
>
> The city is a center of intense life and effort. A heedless people, or society, or town, in which effort is relaxed and is not concentrated, quickly becomes dissipated, overcome, and absorbed by a nation or a society that goes to work, in a positive way, and controls itself. It is a way that cities sink to nothing, and that ruling classes are overthrown.[34]

When Le Corbusier wrote these words in 1924, continental Europe had just witnessed firsthand Russia's unparalleled leap from absolutism and a maximum agrarian economy to state socialism. Outside the Soviet Union, his call for order echoed a common cry for a new society built on technology, individualism, and intellectual ideals.

Le Corbusier's famous donkey polemic has an interesting history. Under his given name, Charles-Edouard Jeanneret, Le Corbusier had started work on a manuscript entitled "La Construction de Villes" (The building of cities). It was the product of an earlier time when Jeanneret was under the influence of the French version of Sitte's book, translated by Camillo Martin in 1902. Jeanneret never finished his manuscript (it was rediscovered by Allan Brooks in 1982), but he had prepared some of the illustrations, which are particularly fine examples of his early work. He had taught drawing at the arts college of his hometown, La Chaux-de-Fonds. Some of these drawings suggest the experience of a walk through Munich, for example. On the Neuhausserstrasse, the view is closed (creating what Sitte would have called a *geschlossenes Architekturbild*) because a building projects into the line of sight along a straight stretch of road. A pedestrian retracing the same route in the opposite direction, however, would see a splendid view of the Frauenkirche's two towers. During his travels in England, Jeanneret observed similar spatial qualities in Hamstead Garden City.[35] There it is: "La leçon de l'âne est à retenir." The lesson of the donkey is to be retained. In the manuscript, he urges planners to learn from the donkey how to design roads which respect and enhance the landscape and are "never tiring to ascend because of the variations in their slope."[36]

In *The City of Tomorrow*, Le Corbusier shed Sitte's influence. But he continued to represent the city as an "architectural landscape." Throughout his life he would develop typologies of buildings that support the topography of a settlement, as in the design for the Quartier Modernes Fruges proposed in 1925 for Bordeaux-Pessac or in his later studies of architectural landscapes for Rio de Janeiro and Algiers.[37] But Le Corbusier and modern movement advocates did not view, nor did they represent, such a landscape of buildings as a sequence of images but rather as a machine-made system of arteries and organisms that structure the city.

Cities have always been places for the production and exchange of goods and services. In the 1920s the modernization of production meant

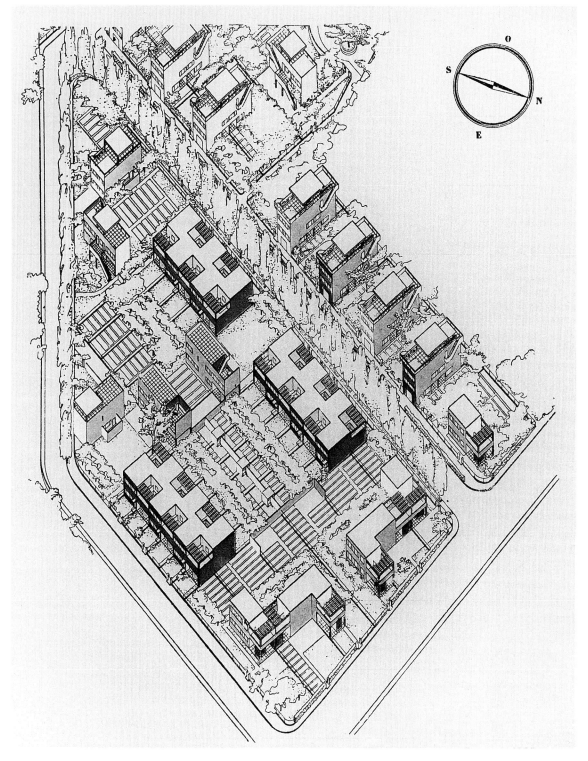

"Quartier Modernes Fruges," Bordeaux-Pessac, Le Corbusier, 1926.
© Fondation Le Corbusier, Paris.

increased mechanization, which had the effect of separating residence from workshop, production from consumption. The inhabitants of cities became commuters. Industrial production exposed the followers of the Arts and Crafts movement among city designers (essentially, Sitte's followers) to the cold blast of mechanism. Artists like the modernist sculptor Bernhard Hoetger still wanted "the individual room, not the factory made product." They wanted "personality, not norm, not schema, not series, not type."[38] But by 1928 most modernists had rejected Henry Van de Velde's 1914 thesis that the artist creates individually shaped pieces in favor of the opposing thesis of Hermann Muthesius, like Van de Velde a member of the German Werkbund. Muthesius had proclaimed concentration and standardization the aims of modern design. If products had to be standardized to be produced, then the best had to be made of the resulting matter-of-fact style, the "Neue Sachlichkeit." For city form this approach entailed abstraction and precision, spaciousness and the inclusion of nature, a fascination with mathematics and modules.

The images of new cities were like dreams where even citizens of the north could enjoy the warmth of the Mediterranean climate. The occupants of new extensions of cities would "see and feel the sun," but the old city centers would lose population, a certain criterion of city failure.[39]

The designers of new cities wanted to give all citizens equal access to the fruits of industrial production, good design for everybody. For example, the Bauhaus town planner Ludwig Hilberseimer proposed radically reducing the ground area covered by buildings in favor of green space, so that each individual could live close to nature. He also developed visions of gigantic new cities of tall buildings. For him they were a way to assert order and avoid the paralyzing effect of chaos on the individual. A population living in standardized dwelling units had predictable needs—for furniture, for appliances, and soon for automobiles. The new city encouraged consumption but not necessarily the

stability of individual ownership of land. Land in cities had been available in relatively small parcels, mainly privately held. New city designs depended on the redistribution of land.[40] Only a few modernists took issue with the overly conceptual approach to city design. Erich Mendelsohn, who had traveled and seen much of the world, including the new Russia, wrote in 1928 that world architecture needed to combine "the finiteness of mechanisms with the infiniteness of life."[41] In the journal *Urban Architecture, Ancient and Modern*, Bruno Taut discussed the new movement in a column called "Frühlicht" (Daybreak) and dismissed all concepts, old and new. In the United States, Frank Lloyd Wright lectured young architects about the overly conceptual approach to design: "Do not rationalize from machinery to life. Forget the architecture of the world, go to the building sites."[42]

The modern movement began anew in Europe when the need to rebuild cities destroyed during World War II made possible a far more sweeping application of the themes that had been developed during the 1920s. Broad straight streets were laid out and lined with homogeneous structures, where historically buildings had been diverse. In 1944 Ivor de Wolfe reacted on the editorial page of *Architectural Review* with an article called "The Art of Making Urban Landscapes." He surprised readers with a call for pluralism in urban design, an aim that requires that the architect know "how to let Bill Brown see what he is going to get." "It isn't that he is a fool," he writes; "he is quite capable of imagining complications inherent in planning, even of making sacrifices for the greater good of the greater number, but he cannot, he feels, be expected to do his part without being given an idea, a pretty clear idea, of what it is all leading up to. He wants a picture of the kind of world the physical planner will make."[43]

The new campaign started by Wolfe as editor of the *Review* was later called the Townscape Movement after the "Townscape Casebook," an editorial Wolfe prepared with the illustrator Gordon Cullen for the February 1944 issue. They wanted above all to remind readers of a picturesque tradition of arranging objects in the landscape. Cullen and Wolfe tried to solicit public support for their campaign: the public could not possibly like the "new Jerusalem, all open space and white concrete," that was being proposed by the modernists.[44] Gordon Cullen, in the introduction to his 1961 book *Townscape*, wrote, "The way the environment is put together is potentially one of the most exciting and widespread pleasure sources. It is no use complaining of ugliness, without realizing that the shoes that pinch are really a pair of ten league boots."[45] Cullen argued that design professionals needed to popularize the art of environmental design. Surely he had a twinkle in his eye when he wrote: "Until such happy day arrives when people in the streets throw their caps in the air at the sight of a planner (the volume of sardonic laughter is the measure of our deprivation) as they now do for footballers and pop-singers, the main endeavor is for the environment makers to reach the public emotionally."[46]

Although Cullen's work was criticized for reasons similar to those behind criticism of Sitte—the images evoked memories of places from the past—he had an important influence on representation in urban design because he developed methods for recording what he called the "awareness of space." His technique permits the architect to illustrate in graphic form how a person walking through a city experiences it. ■

It should be possible to combine the abstract approach to representing cities with one that shows what might be there in reality, using images to explain the concept as well as the experience of form, ideally in a nonstatic visual language understandable to the people who might live in the place represented. Such a fusion of opposing methods would be needed for completeness.

The polemic waged between authors such as Le Corbusier or Ivor de Wolfe and the various camps of sympathizers, however, indicates that divisions run deep. The images of cities shaped either by concepts or by experiences not only portray urban space but also express fundamentally different mind-sets and, possibly, political beliefs. If conceptual schemes emphasize geometric order on a large scale, they imply a need for central control—political, institutional, and economic—capable of effecting that order. But images that suggest what it might be like in a particular place are likely to be comprehensible to many people, who might in their turn object to centralized control, for reasons that may or may not have to do with a specific design proposal.

The political dimensions of representation remained important in the post–World War II era. In Boston in the 1950s the historic center was transformed by state government–sponsored renewal and the construction of urban freeways. The architect and planner Kevin Lynch and the artist Gyorgy Kepes, who had started a survey of the visual form of cities, were especially interested in Boston, realizing that the physical structure of the city was about to change. They wanted to persuade those planning the renewal to consult with local residents.

According to Lynch, his and Kepes's "first study was too simple to be quite respectable."[47] The team interviewed thirty people about the image of Boston's inner city, repeating the exercise in Jersey City and in Los Angeles, cities they believed either lacked an image because they lacked character or produced an image different from Boston's because the heavy use of automobiles in the latter two cities somehow affected residents' perception of their city.

Neither researcher had any formal training in the methodology of behavioral research, and there was no literature to guide them. Kenneth Boulding's book *The Image*, which would have given them the theoretical foundation for their inquiries, was still being written.[48] Lynch believed that the image of a city is shared knowledge, public rather than private; local residents perceive what they experience in similar ways. Lynch never concluded explicitly that subjective individual knowledge, when it is shared, becomes objective—such a conclusion belongs to the realm of epistemology—but he did conclude that if a group of people share an image of their city, if the various images are roughly identical, and if residents build up these images through much the same experiences, the value systems of the individuals must be approximately the same.

He asked residents what came to mind about their city; he asked them, moreover, to make a sketch map, to describe imaginary trips, and to recognize and locate places in various photographs. Residents described distinctive elements of Boston. Some of them took the researchers on a walk through the city, describing what they saw and how they structured the city in their minds. "At times, as we listened to the tapes, and studied the drawings, we seemed to be moving down the same imaginary street with them, watching the pavement rise and turn, the buildings and open spaces appear, feeling the same pleasant shock of recognition, or being puzzled by the same mental gray hole, where there should have been some piece of the city."[49]

Residents of Boston, the research concluded, had a relatively coherent and detailed mental image of their city—an image that had been created in the interaction between self and place. That image was essential to people's actual functioning and important to people's emotional well-being. Lynch demonstrated, moreover, that the mental image could be recorded in an image map, a novel type of map using visual language to show experience.

Inspired by Lynch's work on how urban environments are remembered, some designers in North America and in Europe began to search for their own new visual language. In the fifteen years following Lynch's publication of *The Image of the City*, new notation systems emerged, with one produced by each designer who searched for a new unified language. In retrospect, all these systems were idiosyncratic. Although graphically elegant and often artful, the notations were in code, which had to be interpreted. Some were similar to musical scores—or a language for choreographing movement and the meaning of space.[50] For designers who used notation, it became a method to predict the public image of any existing or proposed development. "Plans were fashionably decked out with nodes, and all the rest. There was no attempt to reach out to the actual inhabitants, because that effort would waste time and might be upsetting."[51]

By the early 1970s, as the search for a new language to explain experience led to other fields, especially geography and the new field of environmental psychology,[52] Lynch's work became a small part of the much larger study of human cognition.[53] For example, Stanley Milgrim asked 218 Parisians to draw a map of their city.[54] "The first principle is that reality and image are imperfectly linked. The Seine may curve in a great arc through Paris, almost forming half a circle, but Parisians imagine it as a much gentler curve, and some think of the river as a straight line, as it flows through the city." An explanation for this distorted perception may be that a person standing on one of the Seine's embankments sees the river as much straighter than it actually is. From some places the Seine indeed appears to run in a straight line.

In fact, many modern-day Parisians draw a map of Paris similar to pre-Renaisssance pictorial maps, selecting symbols to characterize the city's essence. It is interesting to note that Parisians show remarkable agreement in selecting symbols: the Seine, Notre Dame, and the Île de la Cité.

Of the 218 people asked to draw, nearly 200 noted the Seine and the city's boundaries along the *périphérique*. Listed in descending frequency, symbols that appear on the maps of at least half the subjects include the Étoile, Arc de Triomphe, Notre

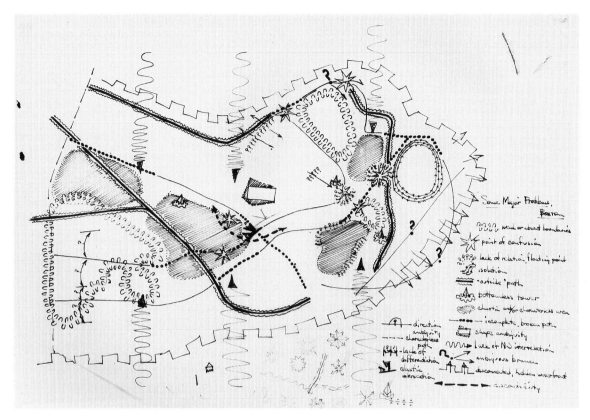

Boston Image Study: Field Analysis of Major Problems, from Kevin
Lynch, *The Image of the City*, 1964. © Institute Archives, MIT.

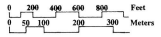

● Standing	● Standing
× Sitting	○ Standing and talking
△ Musicians, Performers	□ Standing and waiting
□ Vendors and Waiters	× Sitting

Wednesday, 19 July, 1995

Time:	13.30 P.M.
Weather:	Fine, 23° C.
Standing:	340 persons
Sitting:	389 persons
Total:	753 persons

Monday, 23 July, 1968

Time:	12:00 noon
Weather:	Fine, 20° C.
Standing:	429 persons
Sitting:	324 persons
Total:	729 persons

Dame, Eiffel Tower, Bois de Boulogne, Louvre, and the Place de la Concorde. The list goes on to include the Champs Élysée, Luxembourg Gardens, Bois de Vincennes, and the Montparnasse Station and/or tower. Parisians like to say that there is a tourist Paris but that the real Paris is something quite apart. It appears that the same places visited and remembered by tourists provide the Parisians' basic cognitive structure. When asked a question one might logically ask in view of the history of the French people—"Where would you take your last walk in Paris if you were exiled from Paris?"—Parisians gave an answer surprisingly similar to what tourists might say about the last day of their tour: a stroll on the Champs Élysée, along the Left Bank. A large number of Parisians would even join the tourists and climb Montmartre one last time.[55]

The work on Parisians' mental maps was part of expanding urban design research in the 1960s and 1970s. Researchers used focused interviews and observations, tools developed in the social sciences, to involve citizens in city design. For example, the Danish architect Jan Gehl observed pedestrians on Copenhagen's main shopping street, Strøget, in 1968, five years after this set of old streets in the town center was temporarily closed to cars on an experimental basis. On a warm summer day, 66,000 people walked down Strøget. Gehl recorded pedestrian activities at various intervals during the course of nearly thirty years, analyzing how changes of the physical spaces influenced the use of the spaces. He observed where people gathered and where they passed through quickly. His observations were used in designing permanent, expanded pedestrian networks in other cities.[56]

Lynch's experiments with the representation of cities led him away from abstract notation to more conventional pictorial diagrams. In a project called *Looking at the Vineyard*, graphics convey the character of Martha's Vineyard to a broad audience. They capture the Vineyard experience,[57] and thus they engaged many members of the community in discussion. In the Martha's Vineyard project, the visual

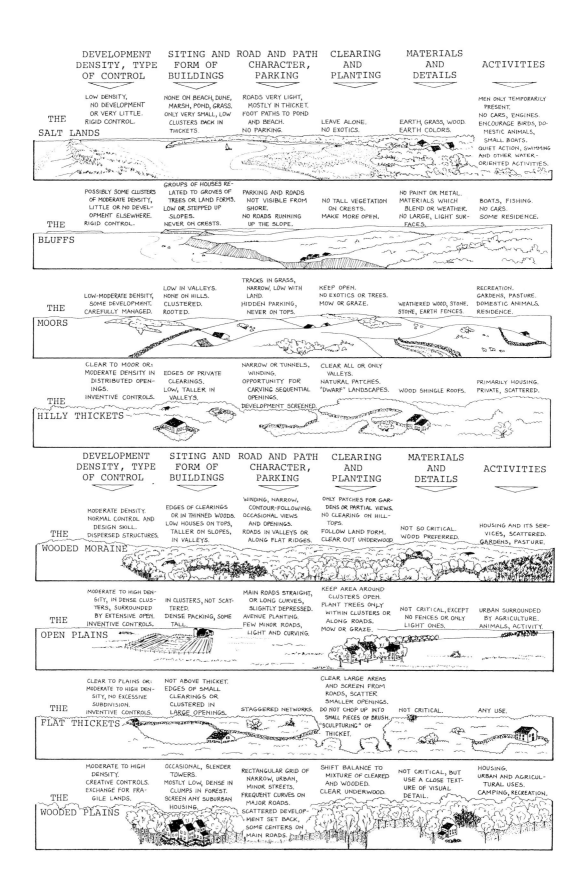

	DEVELOPMENT DENSITY, TYPE OF CONTROL	SITING AND FORM OF BUILDINGS	ROAD AND PATH CHARACTER, PARKING	CLEARING AND PLANTING	MATERIALS AND DETAILS	ACTIVITIES
THE SALT LANDS	LOW DENSITY, NO DEVELOPMENT OR VERY LITTLE. RIGID CONTROL.	NONE ON BEACH, DUNE, MARSH, POND, GRASS. ONLY VERY SMALL, LOW CLUSTERS BACK IN THICKETS.	ROADS VERY LIGHT, MOSTLY IN THICKET. FOOT PATHS TO POND AND BEACH. NO PARKING.	LEAVE ALONE. NO EXOTICS.	EARTH, GRASS, WOOD. EARTH COLORS.	MEN ONLY TEMPORARILY PRESENT. NO CARS, ENGINES. ENCOURAGE BIRDS, DOMESTIC ANIMALS, SMALL BOATS. QUIET ACTION, SWIMMING AND OTHER WATER-ORIENTED ACTIVITIES.
THE BLUFFS	POSSIBLY SOME CLUSTERS OF MODERATE DENSITY, LITTLE OR NO DEVELOPMENT ELSEWHERE. RIGID CONTROL.	GROUPS OF HOUSES RELATED TO GROVES OF TREES OR LAND FORMS. LOW OR STEPPED UP SLOPES. NEVER ON CRESTS.	PARKING AND ROADS NOT VISIBLE FROM SHORE. NO ROADS RUNNING UP THE SLOPE.	NO TALL VEGETATION ON CRESTS. MAKE MORE OPEN.	NO PAINT OR METAL. MATERIALS WHICH BLEND OR WEATHER. NO LARGE, LIGHT SURFACES.	BOATS, FISHING. NO CARS. SOME RESIDENCE.
THE MOORS	LOW-MODERATE DENSITY, SOME DEVELOPMENT. CAREFULLY MANAGED.	LOW IN VALLEYS. NONE ON HILLS. CLUSTERED. ROOTED.	TRACKS IN GRASS, NARROW, LOW WITH LAND. HIDDEN PARKING, NEVER ON TOPS.	KEEP OPEN. NO EXOTICS OR TREES. MOW OR GRAZE.	WEATHERED WOOD, STONE. STONE, EARTH FENCES.	RECREATION. GARDENS, PASTURE. DOMESTIC ANIMALS. RESIDENCE.
THE HILLY THICKETS	CLEAR TO MOOR OR: MODERATE DENSITY IN DISTRIBUTED OPENINGS. INVENTIVE CONTROLS.	EDGES OF PRIVATE CLEARINGS. LOW, TALLER IN VALLEYS.	NARROW OR TUNNELS, WINDING. OPPORTUNITY FOR CARVING SEQUENTIAL OPENINGS. DEVELOPMENT SCREENED.	CLEAR ALL OR ONLY VALLEYS. NATURAL PATCHES. "DWARF" LANDSCAPES.	WOOD SHINGLE ROOFS.	PRIMARILY HOUSING. PRIVATE, SCATTERED.

	DEVELOPMENT DENSITY, TYPE OF CONTROL	SITING AND FORM OF BUILDINGS	ROAD AND PATH CHARACTER, PARKING	CLEARING AND PLANTING	MATERIALS AND DETAILS	ACTIVITIES
THE WOODED MORAINE	MODERATE DENSITY. NORMAL CONTROL AND DESIGN SKILL. DISPERSED STRUCTURES.	EDGES OF CLEARINGS OR IN THINNED WOODS. LOW HOUSES ON TOPS, TALLER ON SLOPES, IN VALLEYS.	WINDING, NARROW, CONTOUR-FOLLOWING. OCCASIONAL VIEWS AND OPENINGS. ROADS IN VALLEYS OR ALONG FLAT RIDGES.	ONLY PATCHES FOR GARDENS OR PARTIAL VIEWS. NO CLEARING ON HILL-TOPS. FOLLOW LAND FORM. CLEAR OUT UNDERWOOD.	NOT SO CRITICAL. WOOD PREFERRED.	HOUSING AND ITS SERVICES, SCATTERED. GARDENS, PASTURE.
THE OPEN PLAINS	MODERATE TO HIGH DENSITY, IN DENSE CLUSTERS, SURROUNDED BY EXTENSIVE OPEN. INVENTIVE CONTROLS.	IN CLUSTERS, NOT SCATTERED. DENSE PACKING, SOME TALL.	MAIN ROADS STRAIGHT, OR LONG CURVES, SLIGHTLY DEPRESSED. AVENUE PLANTING. FEW MINOR ROADS, LIGHT AND CURVING.	KEEP AREA AROUND CLUSTERS OPEN. PLANT TREES ONLY WITHIN CLUSTERS OR ALONG ROADS. MOW OR GRAZE.	NOT CRITICAL, EXCEPT NO FENCES OR ONLY LIGHT ONES.	URBAN SURROUNDED BY AGRICULTURE. ANIMALS, ACTIVITY.
THE FLAT THICKETS	CLEAR TO PLAINS OR: MODERATE TO HIGH DENSITY, NO EXCESSIVE SUBDIVISION. INVENTIVE CONTROLS.	NOT ABOVE THICKET. EDGES OF SMALL CLEARINGS OR CLUSTERED IN LARGE OPENINGS.	STAGGERED NETWORKS.	CLEAR LARGE AREAS AND SCREEN FROM ROADS, SCATTER SMALLER OPENINGS. DO NOT CHOP UP INTO SMALL PIECES OF BRUSH. "SCULPTURING" OF THICKET.	NOT CRITICAL.	ANY USE.
THE WOODED PLAINS	MODERATE TO HIGH DENSITY. CREATIVE CONTROLS. EXCHANGE FOR FRAGILE LANDS.	OCCASIONAL, SLENDER TOWERS. MOSTLY LOW, DENSE IN CLUMPS IN FOREST. SCREEN ANY SUBURBAN HOUSING.	RECTANGULAR GRID OF NARROW, URBAN, MINOR STREETS. FREQUENT CURVES ON MAJOR ROADS. SCATTERED DEVELOPMENT SET BACK, SOME CENTERS ON MAIN ROADS.	SHIFT BALANCE TO MIXTURE OF CLEARED AND WOODED. CLEAR UNDERWOOD.	NOT CRITICAL, BUT USE A CLOSE TEXTURE OF VISUAL DETAIL.	HOUSING. URBAN AND AGRICULTURAL USES. CAMPING, RECREATION.

How to build compatibly with landscape elements. From Lynch, Sasaki, Dawson and Demay Associates, *Looking at the Vineyard.* © Vineyard Open Land Foundation.

language allowed local groups to understand the effect of proposed development and to agree on policies to guide it. Lynch's analysis—he also lived on the island—gave him a detailed knowledge of landforms, vegetation, climate, history, the people, and their culture.[58]

In 1976, Lynch took stock of the new type of professional representation: "A unified language appropriate to the sensory form [of cities] will be a long time developing, if indeed a unified language is possible. Meanwhile, we must deal with the many different aspects of this issue in diverse and sometimes not entirely compatible ways. Language in some form—whether graphic, verbal, gestural, mathematical, or whatever—is indispensable to thought."[59]

CHAPTER THREE

Images in Motion

Painters in Western society have learned to represent the sense of movement by studying the human body. A painter's ultimate goal might be to paint landscapes or still lifes, but the drawing of the nude would be fundamental to any exploration of rhythmic relationships—the organization of shapes, linear movement, solidity, stability, mobility, equilibrium, and expressive character.[1]

Urban designers have no equivalent educational tradition, though the work of Gordon Cullen or Edmond Bacon has taught them that movement can be read and understood as a pictorial sequence. Critics of this approach argue that reliance on serial vision has led to overly picturesque designs. That claim is true if eye-level perspectives are the dominant form of imagining a place, but if these are combined with measured drawings such as maps, designers can learn important lessons about scale in city design. A designer who compares, for example, a plan view of a place with a pictorial sequence illustrating a walk through that place has a much better grasp of dimension.

The representation of pictorial sequences came late to Western culture. Chinese landscape painters perfected the representation of movement. The art historian George Rowley has written: "For the painters of landscape scrolls the principles of spatial design are conditioned through the isolation of motifs." For Rowley, motifs are picture elements a viewer can easily grasp in one single focus. The eyes, moving through the intervals between these elements, can overcome the isolation of each motif, tying adjacent motifs together. Thus the viewer is set free to "walk" through the landscape and observe the world in motion: "A scroll painting must be experienced in time like music or literature. Our attention is carried along laterally from right to left, being restricted at any moment to a short passage which can be conveniently perused."[2]

The scroll tells a tale that can be interrupted and repeated. The walk through Venice on the pages that follow presents such a scroll, one that reads not from right to left, but from the bottom of the page to the top. At first, this direction seems counterintuitive, especially when the accompanying written text is read top to bottom. But reading images is different from reading text. For the images to have the desired effect of pulling the reader into the space, the pictures themselves must be read from bottom to top. Western art traditionally represents conditions yet to be realized, the future and things associated with it—that is, hope, expectation, and so forth—in the upper portions of pictures. The present condition or position in space or time is shown in the middle of pictures; the past, what we have left behind, is shown at the bottom. An upward movement of the eyes implies progression; a downward movement, regression.[3]

In scanning the Venice images, the reader pieces them together and gains the illusion of movement through space. Reading the pictorial sequences quickly is similar to watching a motion picture film. Like a film, the pictorial sequences transport the viewer into the scene.

▶ The walk starts on the Calle Lunga de Barnaba, in a typical Venetian alley: a dark, narrow passage about to open into a square. The pedestrian is drawn to the light beyond the passage, in the Campo Santa Barnaba. The pedestrian crosses the campo diagonally. Light reflects on the church facade and the stone pavement. Past a covered well, a bridge in the far corner of the campo gives new direction to the walk.

Beside the bridge is a shop selling mirrors. A large one on display in the window reflects the bridge and a young couple coming down the steps. The bridge arches high over the canal, reaching almost to the second story of nearby buildings. Signs announce the name of the bridge: Ponte Santa Barnaba at the Fondamente Rezzonico. At the highest point on the bridge, the pedestrian wants to take bearings.

But here the scroll technique shows its limits. The scroll continues on the obvious path down the steps into Calle de Bateche, but instead the pedestrian wants to look around. A glance to the left reveals the long straight Rio San Barnaba, with two more bridges in the distance. A Venetian might not remember the bridges' names but once oriented probably would know that they lead to another neighborhood near the large Campo San Marcherita, where an open-air market is held. The view to the right reveals the Grand Canal and perhaps the waterbus stopping at the Campo San Samuele on its way to the Rialto. The scroll, however, reveals none of this information.

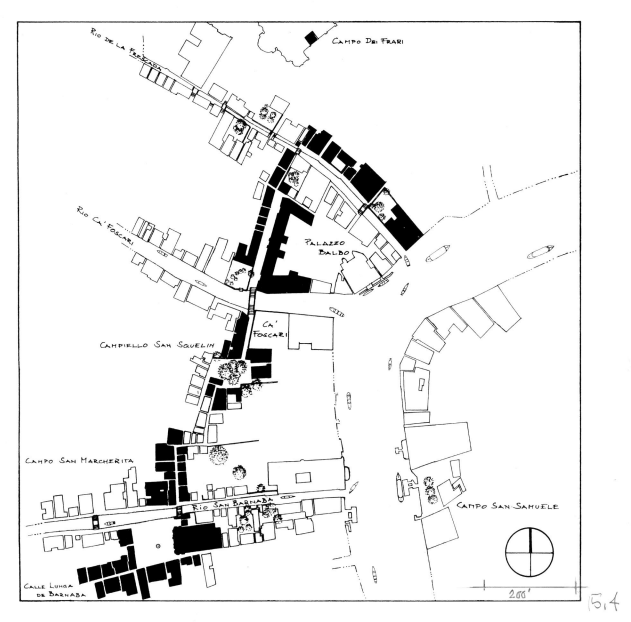

Detail, map of Venice (1 inch = 200 feet). Source: *Atlante di Venezia*, 1989.

The sequence of pictures leads down the steps and along Calle Boteche, a short, narrow street that turns right. (The walk skips a short section of the next alley.)

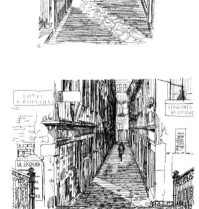

The sequence starts again at the corner of Calle Cappeler; the pedestrian turns right and—before seeing the square—senses the proximity of open space from the abundant light. A double row of trees marks a diagonal path across the Campiello del Squelin, where a bookstore sits on the square at the corner with the Calle Foscari.

Along the Calle Foscari a three-story-high wall on the right hides the garden of the Ca' Foscari; the palace itself faces the Grand Canal. The pedestrian's path parallels the Grand Canal behind the properties that face it.

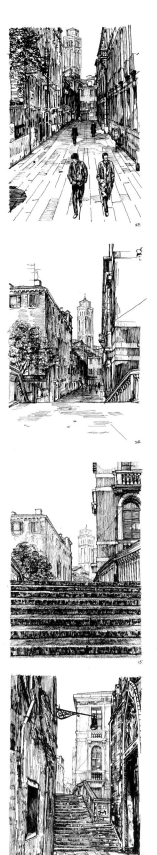

The pedestrian sees the light falling on the facade of a building beside the Palazzo Balbo, on the other side of a large bridge with many steps, suggesting a wide span. Ponte Foscari "slides" into full view as the corner building on the left recedes. From the steps of the bridge, a landmark of the Polo district comes into view: the bell tower of the church of the Frari. From the bridge itself, the pedestrian looks down a street that is very wide and straight by Venetian standards.

Standing on top of the Ponte Foscari, the pedestrian takes a bearing once more. The view to the right again reveals the Grand Canal, looking closer than it looked from the Ponte Santa Barnaba and much wider as it bends eastward, but none of these sights is shown in the limited view of the images, which lead ahead down into the Calla Larga Foscari.

Four images suffice to convey the 80-meter length of the Calla Larga Foscari, a distance that has taken up to fourteen images in earlier sections of the walk when streets were narrower and more winding. Only when the pedestrian reaches what appears to be the dead end of this street does another pedestrian, stepping out of the narrow opening to an alley, show how the route continues, into the narrow Calle de la Dona Onesta.

The contrast between the wide Calle Foscari and the narrow Calle de la Dona Onesta is impressive. Half the length of the wide Foscari, Calle Onesta nonetheless appears longer. Light falls down into it from above a high garden wall; even more light falls onto a bridge, the cast-iron Ponte di Dona Onesta, that comes into view at the end of this narrow space. Steps to it rise suddenly from the alley.

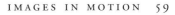

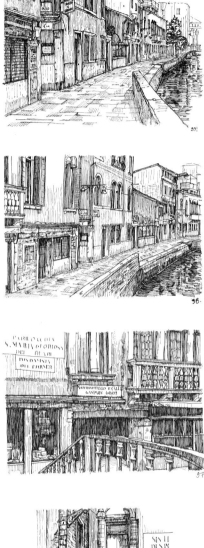

From the bridge, the pedestrian sees a bookstore on the Fondamente del Fornu straight ahead and can read the covers of the books on display. But not for long, for the walk continues with a right turn on to the Fondamente del Fornu, where a row of beautiful buildings faces the Rio de la Frescada. The Grand Canal, visible once again, looks surprisingly distant; it has curved away from the pedestrian's straight path. On the canal one of the palazzi glimpsed from the bridge over the Rio Foscari again comes into view.

I walked along this route many times on the way to and from the Giudecca. Early in my stay, when one narrow alley looked like another, the bridges stood out as spatial elements, giving structure to my movements and expressing a rhythm. I remember the experience of rising at each bridge and gaining a better view for a few moments before "plunging" back to ground level. The squares along the walk defined the beginning and end of movement. Crossing a square gave me a sense both of balance and of anticipation of the next stretch of narrow alleys to be traversed before the next bridge and the next square.

The walk in Venice measures 1,060 feet, or approximately 350 meters. It takes four minutes to walk this distance—a very short time considering the many different physical spaces encountered. In Venice, buildings, squares, alleys, canals, and bridges are all crowded together in a very small area. To explore the scale of Venice relative to the scale of other cities, I have overlaid the length of the walk in Venice on maps of other cities. The fourteen city maps that follow are all drawn to the same scale, one inch equals 200 feet, which is also the scale of the map accompanying the pictorial sequences. The fourteen city maps were selected to represent a wide range of urban scales. Some cities are finely scaled, like Kyoto or Barcelona. Others are large in scale, like Washington, D.C. Some cities have streets following regular grids; in other cities streets follow irregular patterns. The same four-minute walk applied to these fourteen city maps appears to take different amounts of time. In most cities, traveling the distance that is actually equivalent to the walk in Venice appears to take less time. In some of the cities, walking this distance comes close to the time it takes to walk in Venice. For a designer, these comparisons are important. The dimensions and placement of urban elements influence the perception of time.

| 0 | 100 | 200 | 300 | 400 | | 600 | 800 | | 1000 | | 1200 | | **Feet** |

| 0 | | 50 | | 100 | | 150 | | 200 | | | 300 | | | 400 | **Meters** |

Detail, map of the Berkeley campus (1 inch = 200 feet). Source: University of California, 1987.

The distance covered in the walk in Venice equals that of a walk many Berkeley students take daily from the corner of Telegraph Avenue and Bancroft to Wheeler Hall (along the dotted line). This walk appears much shorter than the walk in Venice.

In San Francisco, the distance covered in the Venice walk is equivalent to that of a walk from the entrance of the St. Francis Hotel, through Union Square, past the Naval Monument, across Stockton Street, and into Maiden Lane to the Circle Gallery, designed by Frank Lloyd Wright—really a very short walk.

Detail, map of San Francisco's retail district (1 inch = 200 feet).
Source: Department of City Planning, City of San Francisco, 1983.

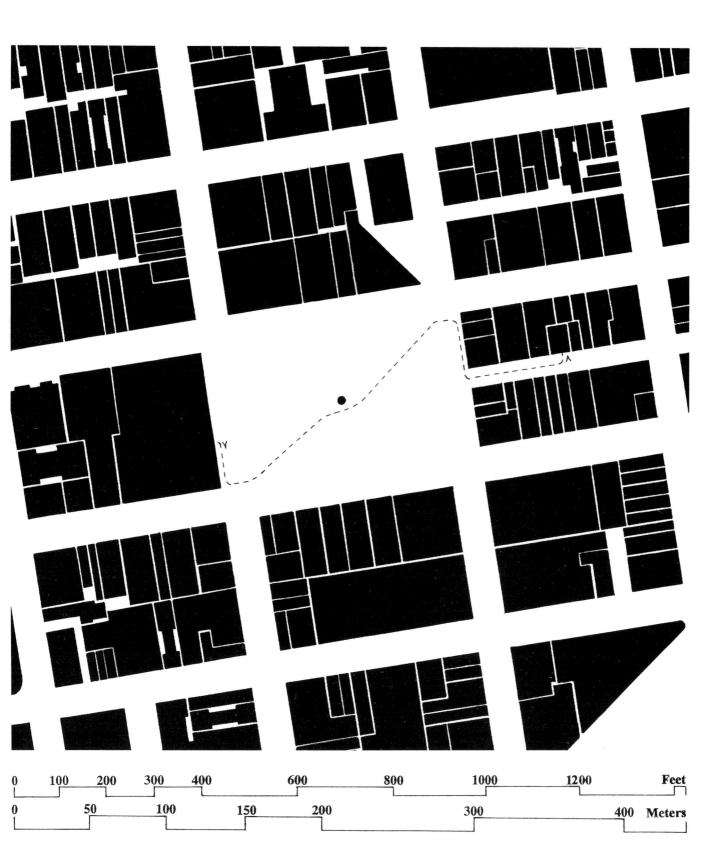

| 0 | | 100 | | 200 | | 300 | | 400 | | 600 | | 800 | | 1000 | | 1200 | | Feet |
| 0 | | | 50 | | | 100 | | | 150 | | 200 | | | | 300 | | | | 400 | | Meters |

Also in San Francisco, a walk from the Bank of America Building along California Street, past Old St. Mary's Church, with a turn into Grant Avenue to a restaurant at the corner of Commercial Street appears to take a little longer than the previous walk in San Francisco but seems shorter than the walk in Venice.

Detail, map of San Francisco's Chinatown (1 inch = 200 feet). Source: Department of City Planning, City of San Francisco, 1983.

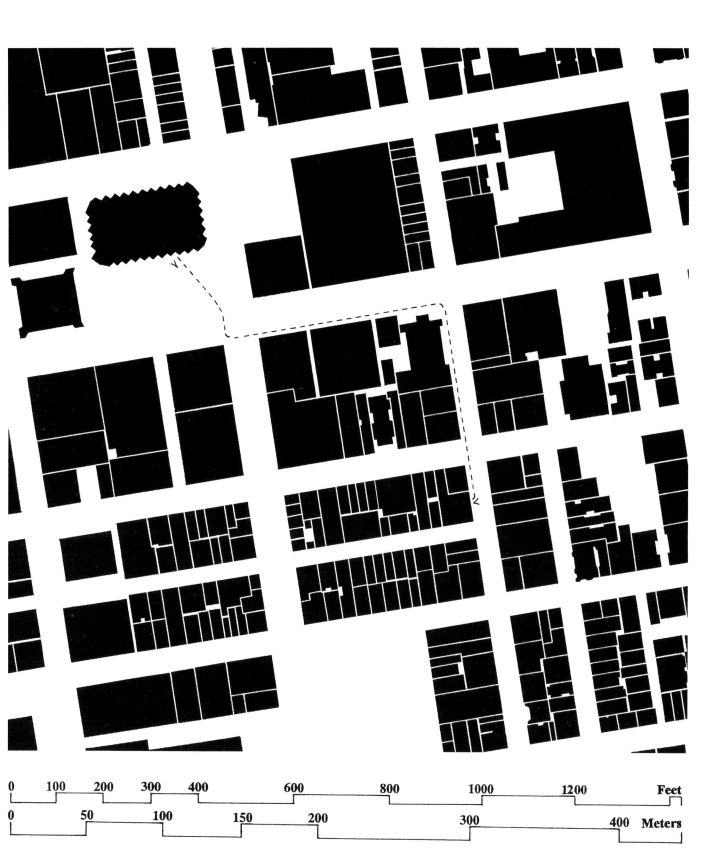

0   100   200   300   400   600   800   1000   1200   **Feet**

0   50   100   150   200   300   400   **Meters**

Map of New York City's Times Square (1 inch = 200 feet).
Source: Department of City Planning, City of New York, 1982.

At Times Square in New York, a walk begins at the foot of the old Times Tower, passes the Army Recruiting Station, stops in the median strip between Broadway and Seventh Avenue for a good look at the square, chances it across Broadway, and proceeds along to the Palace, across from Duffy Square where tickets for same-day performances are sold. This is a quick walk.

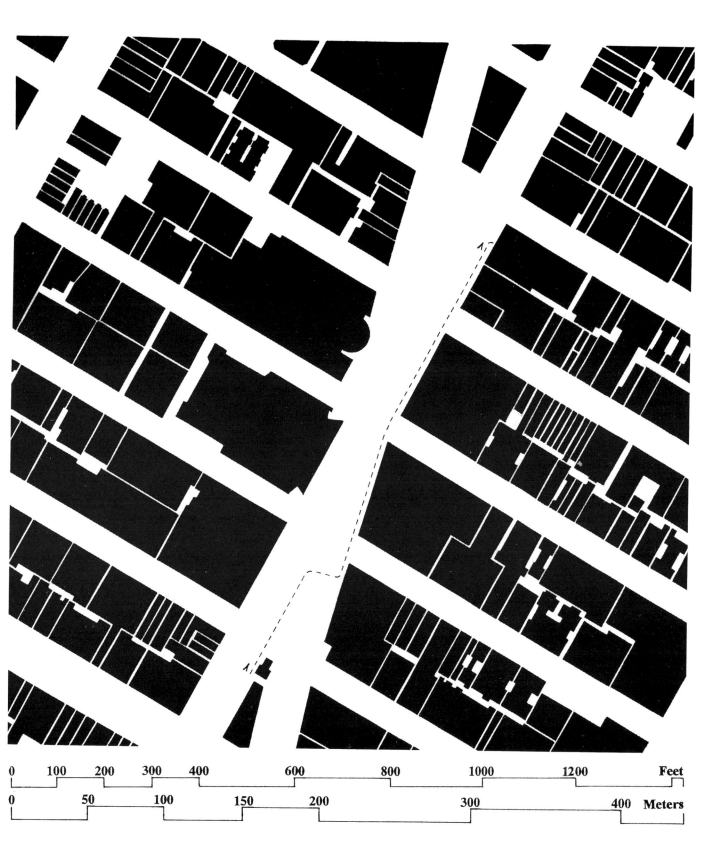

| 0 | 100 | 200 | 300 | 400 | | 600 | 800 | 1000 | 1200 | Feet |

| 0 | 50 | 100 | 150 | 200 | 300 | 400 | Meters |

| 0 | 100 | 200 | 300 | 400 | 600 | 800 | 1000 | 1200 | Feet |
| 0 | 50 | 100 | 150 | 200 | | 300 | | 400 | Meters |

Map of Copenhagen's main pedestrian street (1 inch = 200 feet). Source: Copenhagen General Planning Department; redrawn, 1989, by Allan Jacobs.

In Copenhagen, a pedestrian walks along Strøget from Nytorv, past York Passage, then catches sight of the grand old trees at the churchyard reaching into the streets at Helligaands Kirke, and walks to Amager Torv. The distance is the same as that of the walk in Venice, though it appears a little shorter.

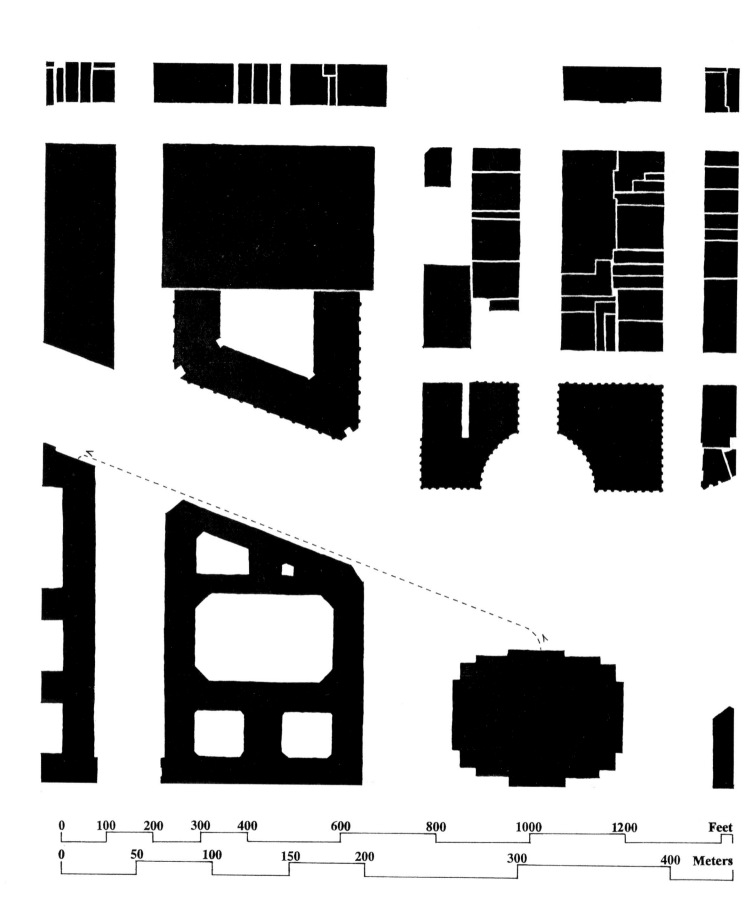

Detail, map of Washington, D.C. (1 inch = 200 feet).
Source: Allan Jacobs, 1989.

In Washington, D.C., a walk along Pennsylvania Avenue, from the National Archives to the Old Post Office, equals the distance of the walk in Venice but appears much shorter.

In an old neighborhood of Toronto, a walk equal in distance to the Venice walk takes a pedestrian along alleys from Ontario and Gerrard streets to the end of Milan Lane. Because there is much to see on this route along garages and yards in the rear of properties, this walk appears to take just as long as the Venice walk.

Detail, map of Toronto (1 inch = 200 feet). Source: Department of Public Works, City of Toronto, 1990.

| 100 | 200 | 300 | 400 | | 600 | 800 | 1000 | 1200 | Feet |

| | 50 | 100 | 150 | 200 | | 300 | | 400 | Meters |

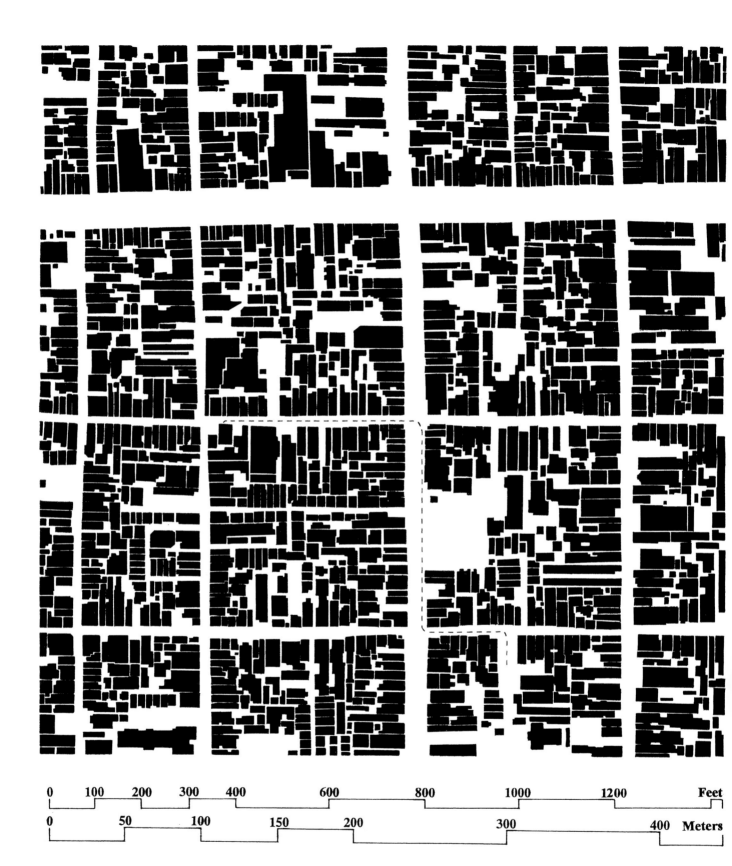

0	100	200	300	400	600	800	1000	1200	Feet

0	50	100	150	200	300	400	Meters

A walk through the old city of Kyoto, which was laid
out 1,200 years ago, starts on Aya-no Koji Street, turns
into one of the major old north–south streets called
West Side of Tohin, passes the Aya Wishi Children's
Playground, turns into Bukkō-ji Street, and almost
reaches the entrance to the neighborhood shrine
of the Suga Minister. This walk, a distance of two large
cho's, appears a little longer than the walk in Venice.

Detail, map of Kyoto (1 inch = 200 feet). Source: Kyoto City Planning
Department, 1985.

To my great surprise, the walk in Venice equals a stroll through the Piazza Navona in Rome. Although I claim to know it well, I had underestimated its size, assuming that it took only half the time of the Venice walk; but, in fact, crossing the plaza takes four minutes.

Detail, map of the historic quarter, Rome (1 inch = 200 feet). Source: City of Rome, Map of the Centro Storico, 1985; redrawn by Allan Jacobs.

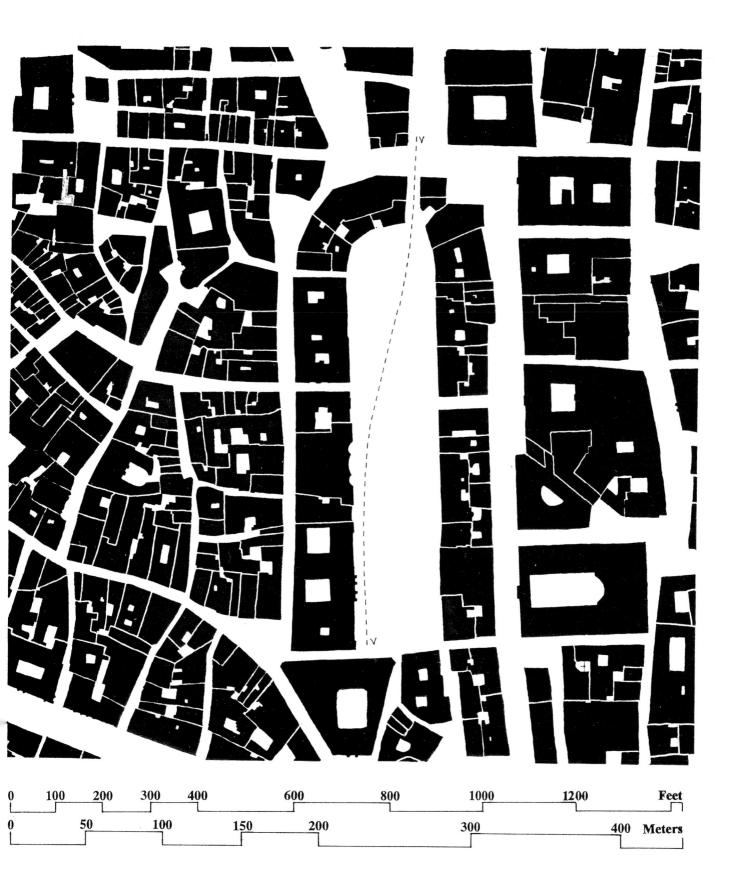

| 0 | 100 | 200 | 300 | 400 | | 600 | | 800 | | 1000 | | 1200 | | **Feet** |

| 0 | | 50 | | 100 | | 150 | | 200 | | | 300 | | | 400 | **Meters** |

Detail, map of London (1 inch = 200 feet). Source: London Ordnance Survey.

My surprise was even greater when the distance of the Venice walk was plotted out on a map of Trafalgar Square in London, from a point near the Arch of the Admiralty, past Canada House and the Venturi and Brown extension to the National Gallery, to St. Martin in the Fields. This stroll seems to cover a greater distance than the previous walks.

0 100 200 300 400 600 800 1000 1200 Feet

0 50 100 150 200 300 400 Meters

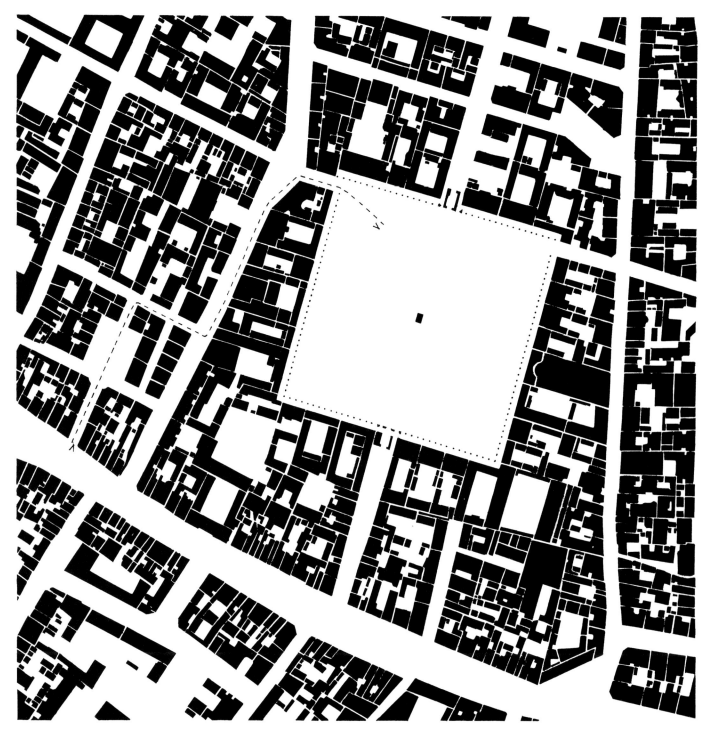

0	100	200	300	400		600		800		1000		1200	**Feet**

0		50		100		150		200			300			400	**Meters**

Map of the Marais, Paris (1 inch = 200 feet). Source: Prefecture de Paris, Edition 1969.

In Paris a walk starts at the beautiful symmetrically framed Place du Marché St. Catherine, off Rue Saint Antoine, turns right on Rue de Jarente, left on Rue Turenne, and right again to enter the Place des Vosges, where a statue of Louis XIII occupies the center of the square. The Paris walk appears to take longer than the walk in Venice.

A walk in Barcelona equal in distance to the Venice walk starts at the Plaza Reial and continues along the famous Ramblas, barely reaching the Sant Joseph Market, not quite halfway to the north end of the Ramblas, which is at the Plaza de Cataluña. The Ramblas is longer than I had remembered. I would have thought that the equivalent of the Venice walk would have reached the Plaza de Cataluña.

Detail, map of Barcelona (1 inch = 200 feet). Source: Corporacio Metropolitana de Barcelona, 1983.

| 0 | 100 | 200 | 300 | 400 | | 600 | | 800 | | 1000 | | 1200 | | Feet |

| 0 | | 50 | | 100 | | 150 | | 200 | | | 300 | | | 400 | Meters |

Map of a gated community in the City of Laguna Niguel, Orange County, California (1 inch = 200 feet). Source: Traced from a 1981 aerial photograph, Robert J. Lung and Associates.

To match the distance of the walk in Venice, a homeowner in Orange County, California, might navigate a little more than halfway around the street that loops through the neighborhood, a walk much shorter than expected.

0
100
200
300
400
600
800
1000
1200
Feet
0
50
100
150
200
300
400
Meters

Map of the Stanford Shopping Center in Palo Alto, California (1 inch = 200 feet). Source: City of Palo Alto, Stanford Shopping Center, 1994.

A shopper at the Stanford Shopping Center in Palo Alto, California, might start at the Nordstrom department store and not get very far at all. ■

0   100   200   300   400   600   800   1000   1200   **Feet**

0   50   100   150   200   300   400   **Meters**

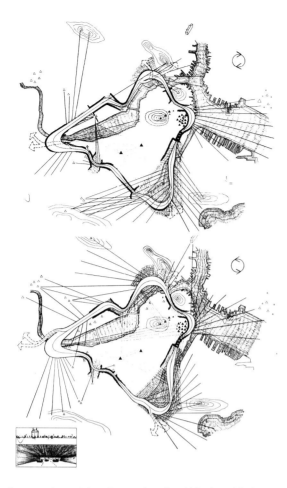

Space-motion and view diagrams, from Donald Appleyard, Kevin Lynch, and John R. Myer, *The View from the Road* (Cambridge: MIT Press, 1964).

10 PATH-EVENTS/MIN (AV)

Thinking about time's embodiment in the physical world might bewilder most of us. The failure to grasp the elements that make one walk appear longer or shorter than another has astonished some of the most experienced city designers.

I do not have answers to explain all variables that alter the perception of time, but I found some interesting hints in the writings of the philosopher William James: [4] "Our heart-beats, our breathing, the pulses of our attention, fragments of words or sentences that pass through our imagination, are what people this dim habitat" that he and others have called the twilight of our general consciousness. All of these elements have to do with rhythm. Even if we try to empty our minds, by sitting still, for example, with eyes closed, "some form of changing process remains for us to feel and cannot be expelled. Awareness of change is the condition on which our perception of time's flow depends." But there is no reason to believe that sitting still and seeing nothing suffice to arouse the awareness of change. "The change must be of some concrete sort."

Pedestrians tell the length of their walks by the rhythmic spacing of recurring elements. The Venice walk has frequent and different types of rhythmic spacing. Other environments have produced fewer types of spacing, and the visible information engages walkers less frequently. Thirty-nine drawings of unequal spacing were needed to explain the four-minute walk in Venice; far fewer drawings could explain most of the other walks. Successive acts of apperception and recognition influence one's sense of time. The walk through Venice necessitates many turns—through two squares, along several narrow alleys, across three bridges, and near a number of waterways. Pedestrians perceive change successively and adjust their knowledge—for example, of bridges—to what they have already learned. But James warns that this observation is too crude. "To our successive feelings, a feeling of succession is added, that would be treated as an additional fact requiring its own special elucidation." A walk through Venice might be followed by a walk through Mestre, the nearest town on the mainland. Or, as here, a walk through Venice might be compared to a walk in a place as far away as San Francisco, New York, or Kyoto—a comparison that requires large mental leaps in time and space. Even if these walks were known well, the sights they entail would have to be recalled; the images of Venice, in contrast, are still accessible to the reader in the pages of this book and can be looked at again. A consideration of rhythm in city design is valuable. The dimensions of the physical objects and the setting of these objects in space influence the sense of time. Designers thus have remarkable power to affect the perception of time by arranging objects in space, by setting dimensions, designing textures, selecting color, and manipulating light.

Chapter 8 discusses representations of "moving focus" as a tool in conditioning spatial design. At this point, however, I want to look at experiments conducted in the 1960s and early 1970s with moving images that capture the "View from the Road."

The construction of urban expressways made it possible to drive through cities at accelerated speeds. From these roadways, sometimes level with but frequently raised above ordinary streets, the motoring public views cities and landscapes, passing them quickly and with few interruptions. Expressways created a new image of the city. Places and their surroundings had to be relearned to the extent that walking through them differed from a drive through them at high speed. In their book *The View from the Road*, Donald Appleyard, Kevin Lynch, and Richard Myer further developed the graphic notations originally used in Lynch's *Image of the City*. The experience of a drive recorded through the windshield of a car on film in slow motion was played back at regular projection speed, which condensed the experience in time, made some passages on the roadway stand out, and showed a rhythmic spacing of bridges and overpasses. The images created for the book read like an old-fashioned flicker book (a stack of quickly made eye-level sketches riffled through rapidly, bottom to top).

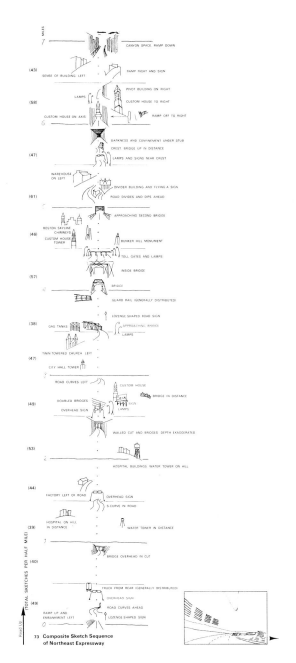

Composite sketch sequence, from Donald Appleyard, Kevin Lynch, and Richard Myer, *The View from the Road* (Cambridge: MIT Press, 1964).

A simulation camera.

In assessing their system of notation in retrospect (and a similar system used in Kevin Lynch's *Image of the City*), the authors felt their work had been impressionistic;[5] their cartoons represented the underlying structure of an environment but conveyed too little information to show what a real drive would be like.

Technological advances had not yet been applied to representation in the design of cities. The tools of the profession were still those available for print. Twentieth-century media—motion pictures, television, and computers—were rarely used as design media prior to the 1970s, despite their well-known ability to engage viewers.

The experience of watching a film involves visual, kinesthetic, spatial, temporal, and aural senses. As the scene starts, the motion captures the eye, and viewers cannot help becoming part of it. Objects pass by, allowing viewers to get their bearings. Once they have watched a few frames, they can sense the space, understand its boundaries, and gauge the distance to other objects within it.

Peter Kamnitzer used a mainframe computer in early experiments with the animation of city forms, producing a short drive through a set of computer-generated building volumes.[6] The sequence was engaging to watch, despite its obvious limitations: only ten solid objects could be simulated, each little more than a cube with a colored surface.

After the passage of the Environmental Policy Act in 1969, government funding became available in the United States for basic research in environmental assessment techniques, including funding for improvements to visual assessments understandable to the public. Concern for the environment was understood broadly to include a concern for the visual quality of cities and landscapes. Researchers began to explore ways to record qualities of the visual world that should be preserved and to measure the visual impact of proposed large-scale engineering and planning projects.

With funding from the National Science Foundation, Donald Appleyard, joined by the psychologist Kenneth Craik,[7] built the Environmental

Simulation Laboratory at the University of California at Berkeley. With the assistance of specialists from the motion picture special-effects industry and an optical engineer,[8] the team built scale models of streets, neighborhoods, and cities. They then used a computer-controlled periscopic lens, attached to a camera, to record what a person would see at eye level while walking or driving. Next they changed the model to show a future building or a new highway, and the camera repeated the journey, recording, in effect, an experience of the future.[9]

For their first project, the Berkeley team assessed the realism of a model by comparing a film of it with a film recorded at the actual site in Marin County, north of San Francisco. Model-makers created an accurate three-dimensional miniature stage set of the area, complete with a freeway, suburban neighborhood, shopping center, industrial park, and stretch of rural landscape. The laboratory hired a young filmmaker, John Dykstra, who had worked on *Voyage to the Outer Planets* with Douglas Trumbull and on *2001: A Space Odyssey* with Stanley Kubrick, to create a film that simulated the effect of driving through the model stage. In 1972 this was not a routine assignment in the special-effects industry. A continuous drive through a model landscape required a reliable motion-control system and a technician with expertise in the realistic lighting of the model stage. The use of computers in simulations was still in its infancy. The team was the first to connect a mainframe computer to the camera shutter and a large overhead crane.[10] Although the technicians demonstrated successfully how such camera recordings could be made, the main question was whether an audience watching the film would have an experience similar to that of actually walking or driving through a real environment. The main objective of the experiment was to demonstrate that the viewers who watched films of both simulated environments and the situation in the real world would report the same observations.

At first, the filmmakers were inclined to follow film convention, recording views straight ahead through the imaginary windshield of an imaginary

car, cutting to side views along the route, and returning to the view straight ahead. A filmmaker using this technique would create the film at an editing table after all moving images had been recorded. It was possible to make a continuous, straight-ahead recording of the drive through the Marin model, but would such a film be more objective than a film with cuts to the right and left?

When the team at Berkeley began the experiment, the film medium was more than half a century old. Since the early days of film, filmmakers had distinguished between objective and subjective camera recordings. Cinematographers say that the camera in the objective mode plays the role of an observer, apart from the action, selecting representative shots.[11] For film historians, the classic example of "subjective" camera recording is F. W. Murnau's 1925 silent film *The Last Laugh*. Here the camera sees the world through the eyes of a doorman, played by Emil Jannings. The camera travels down the descending elevator, through the lobby, through streets, and into buildings, like a living being. The viewer is transported into the world of the doorman. "The camera actually becomes his eye and when this is the case we say that the camera is subjective."[12] This is exactly what the Berkeley team aimed for; they wanted their film to record exactly what a person driving would see.

The team decided to shoot the entire film in one continuous movement.[13] But in using the continuous-shot technique, the team stumbled on a stubborn problem common to all media that try to capture what human eyes can see. The camera's field of vision is too narrow. The reader piecing together the individual images of the walk through Venice encounters the same problem: any framed view, still or in motion, eliminates information available to peripheral vision that might draw attention to right or left.

Before filming the model, the team conducted an experiment, producing a film of the same drive in the real world with a camera, facing forward, mounted inside a car. Disconcertingly, when the film was shown, the car seemed to move faster than its actual speed; and when it approached a turn, the direction of movement changed too abruptly. Some viewers watching the film felt a sense of imbalance and even nausea because the camera's narrow field of view deprived them of peripheral vision. Without it, they lost any accurate sense of speed. Moreover, peripheral vision helps individuals orient themselves. Drivers about to change direction, for example, can turn their head toward the new direction before actually turning the car. This is what the filmmakers did in their second recording. They pivoted the camera toward the new direction well before the driver actually turned the wheel. They called this procedure "anticipating a turn"; the term has become an industry standard.[14]

Next the team set to work to re-create the real-world drive on the model stage. A computer was programmed with the coordinate values of all points along the drive through the model terrain. The computer was then used to control a large gantry on which the periscopic lens and camera were mounted. The computer recorded the position of the camera at the end of one filming session to locate it for the next segment the following day. To match successive film recordings, the computer was programmed to film an overlap sufficiently long so that the two segments could be cut together. In most cases, the transition between segments is imperceptible when the film is projected.

After a year of experimentation, the team produced a final film. They had randomly selected a survey group of two hundred people to evaluate it. Survey results showed that the viewers understood what they saw and thought that the twenty-two-minute drive through the stage set looked realistic on film. The group had been divided into smaller audiences: one group saw the simulated tour through the model world, another viewed the film of a tour through the actual environment, and a third group was driven through the area in a van. The correlation between the responses to all three modes of presentation was high.

Each group was asked to rank qualities of the environment they saw. Viewers of the simulated world gave a high ranking to nearness to shopping, professional offices, and schools and to the resale value of homes. They noted what the neighborhood lacked: community spirit, good places for children to play, visiting among neighbors, accessible public transport, and diversity of age, social status, and lifestyle. These responses were closely aligned with those of the group that saw the real-world film of the same drive and those of the third group that experienced the real world firsthand.

The accuracy of these perceptions was tested when all three groups were asked to sketch a map of the drive, take recognition tests, and check off adjectives that described the place. Whereas very few of those who had watched either of the two films could draw a correct map of the area, those who had toured the site in person could readily do so.

Overall, the responses of people who lived in the study area or were very familiar with it differed for all three presentational modes from those of people who were seeing the place for the first time or were only marginally familiar with it. The perception of resident-participants was dominated by meaning based on their personal knowledge of the place. The team concluded that viewing the simulation film of the model was similar to a first-encounter experience of a real-world environment.[15]

Given the success of the film in the validation study, the next step for research was obvious to the team. Proposed developments could now be placed into the model and filmed to show how they would change the environment. Developments could be accurately and intelligently analyzed in their context. The Environmental Simulation Laboratory was opened in 1974 to designers, engineers, and planners, who were required by the Environmental Policy Act to disclose the effects of their projects. There they could now prepare neutral and accurate analyses that could be disclosed to the public.[16] Contrary to what might have been expected, however, the new simulation technique was not immediately put to use by the design and planning

A scale model simulation. (*The views should be read from bottom to top.*)

profession.[17] Not until 1979 was the Berkeley technique applied to major planning projects, first in San Francisco and then in other cities. The reason for the delay was cost: most planning agencies could not afford to pay the engineer, filmmaker, computer programmer, model-builders, and urban designer required to prepare a simulation at Berkeley. The costs of simulation could be justified only for very large engineering or planning projects. To gain widespread professional interest, simulations needed to be simplified and made less expensive; to achieve these goals took time. ■

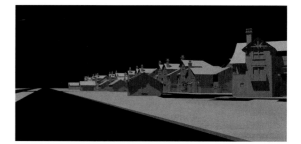

Construction of a computer model to simulate change.
From top: the existing condition; a wire-frame model; a solid model; the finished rendered model.

After the experiments at Berkeley, computer technology became more commonplace in simulations, but no less expensive. In 1978, a group at the Massachusetts Institute of Technology connected a personal computer to two videodisc machines. The discs stored a digital frame-by-frame record of a drive through the town of Aspen, Colorado. The team called their technique "movie map." A viewer at a video monitor could drive down any street in Aspen and turn in any direction at intersections by touching a menu displayed on the monitor. The computer would retrieve the location of the wanted segment on the second videodisc and would play the disc until the viewer requested a new direction, again by touching the monitor.[18]

This simulation technique was a tool for mapping cities, not for simulating environments that did not yet exist. By 1991, however, the technology for generating entire cityscapes by computer was available to design professionals.[19]

Creating a computer animation starts with defining the objects in space. Proposed buildings are drawn with the help of commercial computer programs, which also provide the three-dimensional data describing the shape and position of the new buildings. Representations of buildings surrounding the project site might exist only as conventional map drawings; these are converted into computer data. A three-dimensional computer model defines the exact location and shape of both existing and future buildings. Once the model is completed, a path is chosen for a walk or drive, a process analogous to positioning a camera and selecting where to turn, stop, or look around. Once the path of the camera and the key frame locations are defined in three-dimensional space, the computer can determine which surfaces of the structure are visible and which are obscured, from point to point on the itinerary. These are time-consuming calculations for the computer because the angles for all objects have to be checked for each frame.

The computer also simulates the lighting of the scenes, calculating sun angles to determine how much light reaches the observer and how light

Sequence of computer-generated views in motion. (*The views should be read from bottom to top.*)

A computer "library" of textures and details.

might be reflected or absorbed by the surfaces of the objects. Again, computing the intensity of light on each surface requires extensive calculations. Finally, the surfaces have to be rendered in realistic colors and textures. Computer operators, equipped with a "library" of textures for wall surfaces, pavings, and landscaping, apply these textures to the surfaces of the objects. Entire facades, with and without windows, are rendered in this fashion. Of all steps, this one requires the most skill and interpretive judgment. "The quality of images produced by most computer workstations is limited, however. Pictures can easily be recognized as computer generated, because they do not include the effects of inter-reflections among objects."[20] More important, the simulated world looks new and cartoon-like. The tarnish of everyday street scenes is missing, as are cars and people, odd street furniture, signs, and billboards, unless all this information is carefully rendered. All the computations of a scene must be repeated for each frame along a walk, of which there are many—thirty frames make up only a single second of movement.

Researchers in computer science have devoted much effort to the problem of realistic lighting and have developed the necessary mathematical algorithms for reducing the number of computations required for each frame of movement. The task of rendering details that look real, however, is not easily solved through mathematics. Realistic rendering remains a craft, even when computers are used. Moreover, without realism, the simulators could not be certain that viewers would judge or understand the images the same way they would judge or understand an experience of the real world. Without realism the simulations would not be valid. ∎

The need for better representations of urban form led to a search for new image technology, requiring specialization in disciplines outside city design. One result has been a separation between those who understand the technology and those who do not. Except for specialists, few understand how three-dimensional data are filed and interpreted or how assumptions and conventions of modeling affect the representation of design. Moreover, few know how to access the data used, in order to verify the accuracy of simulations.

Earlier researchers interested in improving visual communication in city design had a moral as well as an aesthetic rationale. They wanted to make others aware of the elements of good urban form: legibility, comfort, economy, choice, access, equity, and many more qualities valued in physical settings worth experiencing. They were dissatisfied with conventional media because these could not convey the experience of the proposed urban form.

Other researchers felt that a profession operating in a pluralistic society could not well afford to employ its own idiosyncratic graphic language. Issues of city design concern society at large. Good professional representations open up the process of design evaluation and improve the credibility of design professionals.

All of these researchers had to concern themselves with the documentary quality of their representations, which is influenced by the technology employed, the cost, the ease of application, and—most important—the relationship between those who are preparing the simulations and those who pay them to do their work. When the media chosen are not suitable, when the work takes too long to be relevant for decision making, or when the cost, confidentiality, and/or secrecy associated with the work impose a special relationship between those who commission the work and those who carry it out, then the documentary quality of representation is in question.

Researchers trying to improve representation might be tempted to believe, if the search goes on too long, that what they are looking for does not exist in pure form. Although no single form of representation thus far has offered the documentary precision researchers have hoped for, they continue to look for ways to make their images as concrete as possible. The second part of this book reports on an extended experiment with such concrete images and the issues related to the documentary quality of representation.

PART TWO

The City in the Laboratory

Humankind cannot bear very much reality.
T. S. Eliot, "Burnt Norton," 1935

Cities are shaped both by human acts and by natural forces. Human values, however complex, motivate physical changes in cities. The idea of bringing a city to a laboratory presupposes the possibility of modeling future changes and studying their consequences. Except for rare sudden natural events, change evolves gradually. How can it be depicted? An individual structure is built over a period ranging from a few months to a year; multiple changes in an urban district develop over many years, even decades. In fact, cities rarely stop changing. To show the process of this change, to discover its patterns and determine its trends, one would need to condense time. But such a representation would dramatize the pace of change. Moreover, there is no certainty that change will continue along established lines. Forecasters considering alternatives for the future need to ask whose future is in question and whose future should be represented. Who selects from the alternative futures?

These difficult-to-answer questions point to some of the risks of forecasting and representing

change. It is easier to associate the melting of the polar ice cap with the warming of the earth's atmosphere than to imagine a street in Manhattan slowly filling with water when the ice cap melts. For many of us, the metamorphosis of Broadway into a very long Grand Canal is an event that best belongs to fiction. It seems less threatening to think of the future more abstractly. Some might say that anxiety about Manhattan under water might impel necessary changes. But others would argue that we have just begun to understand the warming of the earth's atmosphere. To speculate about the results without understanding more leads only to the exaggerated scenario of coastal cities slowly sinking into the seas.

Unquestionably, those whose images show how cities will change in the future can act as advocates either of change or of the status quo. They can operate like investigative reporters, interested in getting at the truth and in writing a good story, or as diagnosticians, evaluating proposals submitted to them but leaving interpretation to others. A diagnostic laboratory for urban places—that is how the Environmental Simulation Laboratory was envisioned, and that is the role it has played vis-à-vis professional projects.

In the winter of 1987, New York City public television viewers were given the unusual opportunity to watch an animated film of a planning project that had been under discussion for several decades, sponsored by State of New York officials who were promoting a new West Side Highway in Manhattan. On this occasion, the television audience was able to experience two future scenarios: a drive along the proposed West Side Highway and a stroll along a new Hudson River esplanade. The film allowed the television viewer to experience the site's openness to sun and sky, the width of the Hudson River, and views of the Manhattan skyline and New Jersey.

The film reminded New Yorkers of a long-standing conflict about development on the West Side of Manhattan. Plans to replace Robert Moses's elevated highway were controversial long before the structure collapsed in 1974 because of old age and lack of maintenance. For two decades, the city and state governments had fought with each other and with environmental groups about adding landfill along the Hudson River. The state proposed to fill the Hudson to a line marked by the end of the river's many piers—effectively widening Manhattan by an entire city block—as a way to revitalize the Hudson waterfront, which had once been active with hundreds of transatlantic liners. The plan was to use the new real estate for a federally funded roadway called West Way and a large-scale commercial development. In 1986 an alliance of neighborhood environmental groups defeated the plan.

The 1987 television film introduced New Yorkers to the state's revised plan, one that entailed no new landfill or large development projects. During the film, viewers were encouraged to call in with questions and to participate with state officials, designers, and community groups in a televised debate. It was apparent from the public response that during the long struggle over West Way many New Yorkers had become skeptical of the state's intentions. For residents of Chelsea and the West Village, the revised West Side Highway was not very different from the earlier West Way pro-

posal. They still complained about the traffic the proposed road might spill onto their streets and objected to any on-ramps or off-ramps into Chelsea and the Village. Many were suspicious about the lack of landfill and large-scale development. They asked whether the state would keep all the space open and free of development and whether there would be as much landscaping as the film showed.

State officials saw the film footage earlier on the day the program and debate were scheduled. Because the former West Way proposal had been hotly debated, the state's motive for broadcasting this film on the revised plan was not to generate additional public debate but to appease New Yorkers, to create support for a more modest West Side Highway without landfill. Officials would have tried to block any presentation that was likely to raise controversial questions in the viewers' minds.[1]

Most viewers found scenes such as a drive down the West Side of Manhattan engaging to watch. They could not help being drawn into them. The surprise of seeing in place a new building or a structure that transforms a familiar scene, however, fades quickly. Almost immediately, the audience started to question the work. One viewer, suspicious of a medium generally reserved for fiction or advertising, wanted to know who had commissioned the work and for whom these scenes might be intended. Such a viewer reflects the adversarial response that greets most urban design and planning projects. Parties in conflict over a project rarely perceive information or a representation as neutral. They question who benefits from it and who controls it.

The physical environment is public property. Every major new building and most urban design plans spark some resistance. Decisions regarding change in the physical environment are made under public scrutiny. Nonprofessionals do not necessarily trust the judgments made by professionals. Advocacy groups have succeeded in canceling projects of well-known architects on grounds of size, character, style, and effects on the environment. The controversy is anything but passing.[2]

The debate is frequently distorted because information about a proposed project is used selectively. By selectively stressing the damaging elements of a proposal, groups in opposition try to persuade decision-making bodies and the public at large to reject it. Promoters of the design are equally selective in stressing the project's merits.

The case studies in the following chapters illustrate how the Environmental Simulation Laboratory has functioned in providing information on development projects. The basic concept is simple: the physical conditions of a city—or part of a city—are represented in the laboratory as realistically as funds permit. The process starts with careful photographing of streets and buildings to create imitative urban stage sets. Initially, these took the form of physical models, with realistic photographs pasted onto model facades; more recently, three-dimensional computer models have been used to show the geometry of building volumes and street surfaces. Photographs of buildings are scanned into computer files and "mapped" onto three-dimensional building volumes. Then an equally realistic representation of a proposed design is created. Alternatives are shown, and, frequently, the incremental and cumulative effects of a project over time are displayed. Finally, realistic eye-level views of a proposed project are produced and shown publicly.

The case studies span twelve years; they were written up and published at the time of each project. Times Square and the work in San Francisco first appeared as films made for presentation to planning commissions and to the media. The Times Square project was commissioned by the Municipal Arts Society of New York, an advocacy group involved in urban preservation issues. The other projects, the San Francisco Downtown Plan and the Toronto Plan, were commissioned by local governments, as was the work on the West Side Highway mentioned above.

For each case study, the laboratory prepared exhibits with large formal displays of models, maps, and computer graphics. Many people worked to-

West Side Highway, New York City, simulation.

gether on the projects described in the following three chapters. Each project has benefited from discussions among all those who helped. Accurate and credible representation was always the main issue of these discussions.

CHAPTER FOUR

Times Square, New York

"The internationally celebrated crossroad" was the term Adolf Ochs used to characterize the bow-tie intersection of Broadway and Seventh Avenue. After purchasing the *New York Times* in 1904, Ochs sought a new business address and acquired, at great expense, the triangular block bounded by Forty-second Street, Broadway, and Seventh Avenue, surrounded by a growing cluster of theaters and hotels including the Olympia, owned by Oscar Hammerstein, Sr. For the site, Ochs commissioned the Times Tower, Manhattan's tallest building at that time; it soon became a Broadway landmark. The subway station in the basement of the Times building became the transfer point for riders from Queens and the Bronx, who commuted to work and often stayed on for the nighttime entertainment.

On December 31, 1908, a great electric ball of light first descended from the Times Tower to mark the beginning of the new year, a ceremony repeated to this day.[1] In 1928 the *Times* added the famous "News Zipper," which spelled out wire-service news along the building's exterior shell, using a band of electric lightbulbs. Soon, in an effort to re-create Times Square's rapid pace and nightlife, newspapers

Times Square, 1985.

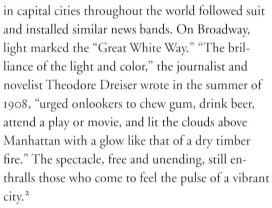

in capital cities throughout the world followed suit and installed similar news bands. On Broadway, light marked the "Great White Way." "The brilliance of the light and color," the journalist and novelist Theodore Dreiser wrote in the summer of 1908, "urged onlookers to chew gum, drink beer, attend a play or movie, and lit the clouds above Manhattan with a glow like that of a dry timber fire." The spectacle, free and unending, still enthralls those who come to feel the pulse of a vibrant city.[2]

The district's main appeal comes from the more than thirty active theaters, some more than eighty years old—gracious old structures designed to extend the dramatic atmosphere from the stage to the auditorium, from the lobby to the street. The theaters are a national treasure where virtually any kind of production can be staged. The theater business, however, is cyclical, and some theaters now remain empty many days of the year. And Times Square itself has changed. During the late 1970s and 1980s many New Yorkers stopped going there, for the area by then was only a bleak reminder of the myriad social problems afflicting New York City.[3]

With the slowdown in theater business in the 1980s, owners of theater properties welcomed the 1982 midtown planning control revisions, which proposed the expansion of the high-rise office district to the area west of Sixth Avenue that included the Times Square entertainment district. Properties on the blocks between Sixth and Eighth Avenues soon became prize real estate for office buildings.

Possible transformation of Times Square under the 1982 midtown planning controls. *From left to right:* First, a simulated view from the Marriott Hotel at Forty-fifth Street looking north up Seventh Avenue, the site that is developed in the following images; second, potential building volumes allowable "as of right"; third, potential "as of right" building volumes, plus additional floors permitted as a result of the theater rehabilitation bonus; fourth, potential "as of right" building volumes, plus the theater rehabilitation bonus, plus the transfer of "air rights" (the unused floor space above any Times Square theater).

The 1982 midtown planning controls granted additional floor space to more than twenty sites along Broadway and Seventh Avenue between Forty-second and Fifty-third Streets. Owners of each of these sites could build fifty-story office structures "as of right," that is, without zoning exemptions. These new planning controls also granted a bonus of additional floor space if a new building incorporated a historic theater into its structure. Property owners could also purchase the transfer of "air rights"—the unused development space above a building—from any other Times Square theater. The owner could add this to the "as of right" floor space granted to a site, plus the theater rehabilitation bonus, to build a new structure as high as seventy stories.

Proponents of these controls argued that the theater rehabilitation bonus and the transfer of air rights within the district would provide economic incentives for the preservation of theaters. They also argued that new construction would bring in white-collar workers who would, in turn, revitalize the district. Opponents of the new controls were skeptical on both points, with good reason. Earlier in 1982 five of Times Square's well-known theaters—the Helen Hayes, the Morosco, the Astor, the Bijou, and the Gaiety—had been demolished to make room for the new Portman Marriott Marquis Hotel at Forty-fifth Street and Broadway. When plans for this hotel were proposed in 1973, they had been praised as a crucial step in the city's redevelopment program for Times Square. But when they were completed in the mid-1980s, they failed to link pedestrians on Broadway to activities inside the Marquis Theater. Instead, the hotel turned inward on its own multistory lobby, whose third floor gives the only access to the new theater. Its decor, moreover, can hardly be compared with that of the five theaters it replaced.

The Portman, like other redevelopment projects—the replacement of the Astor Hotel by a dark office tower at 1515 Broadway, or the Claridge Hotel, which was replaced by the 1500 Broadway Tower, with its ominous facade—was intended to remove an "undesirable" element and "breathe new life" into the district. But the new skyscrapers solved no social problems. "The presence of advertising executives and lawyers at noon," wrote the *New York Times* architecture critic Paul Goldberger, "does not make this the enticing and safe environment it once was at night."[4]

In the mid-1980s, rehabilitation was also the theme of New York State's redevelopment project on Forty-second Street. Here, at the southern edge of Times Square, where five new office towers—known as the City at Forty-second Street—were proposed for construction, eight theaters were to be razed. These theaters, although run-down, included some of the city's oldest, dating from before the turn of the century, such as the Lyric, the Victory, and, most splendid of all, the New Amsterdam.

A decade later, in the 1990s, large office towers would no longer seem financially feasible for the state's redevelopment project; enough had been built in the area to absorb the current and foreseeable demand for office space. In 1995 the Disney Company would acquire the New Amsterdam Theater and fill it by staging versions of its popular musical animation films. The refurbished Victory Theater would open in December 1995, and the Lyric, combined with the Apollo, would follow. But ten years earlier the prospects of the theater business appeared dim.

Actors and producers, joined by preservationists and neighborhood groups from the West Side and East Side, questioned the integration of old theater structures into new office towers. After five theaters were demolished for the Portman, a group called Save the Theaters demanded that every remaining Broadway theater receive landmark designation. (Only five theaters were so designated.)[5] At the prompting of this advocacy group, the Board of Estimates requested a comprehensive district plan and appointed a Theater Advisory Council to study the issue. The council incited great controversy by advocating landmark status for forty-five theaters. All major theater owners were staunchly opposed to the "landmarking of an industry."[6] Gerald Schoenfeld, chairman of the Schubert Organization, argued in favor of bonuses and transfer allow-

Times Square, showing potential development under the 1982
midtown planning controls.

ances granted "as of right" and not upon discretionary review by the city. At a hearing regarding the midtown planning controls for the theater district, Schoenfeld was asked whether he could imagine Times Square surrounded by seventy-story office buildings. He replied that he had no qualms about such a future vision if it would save the theaters.

To better focus the discussion about Times Square, a model was needed. The Municipal Arts Society commissioned such a model of the Times Square area prior to a public hearing in the fall of 1985.[7] The model, 16 feet long, represented in miniature every building along Seventh Avenue and Broadway between Forty-second and Fifty-third Streets, as well as signs, billboards, cars, people, statues, and trees around the ticket booths on Duffy Square. The idea was to simulate alternatives as realistically as possible so that New Yorkers could understand the impact of all proposals.

Work commenced with a careful photo documentation of every building. To ensure accuracy, a perspective-correcting lens was used. Photographs were taken with the camera held parallel to the facades, for the desired frontal views. When printed to the scale of the model (16 feet = 1 inch) and mounted on stiff cardboard, the photographically reproduced facades looked like exact scale replicas of the existing structures. Using the same technique, large billboards and signs were photographed and assembled.[8]

According to the assessment of a real estate consultant to the Municipal Arts Society, twenty developable sites were being considered for new construction under the 1982 midtown planning controls in the Times Square area. To avoid exaggerating the potential for transforming Times Square, the team at the Environmental Simulation Laboratory selected only twelve parcels. Recently constructed high-rise buildings in midtown were photographed in the same manner as the existing buildings around Times Square, and large models were constructed to simulate the development potential under the 1982 controls.

The new buildings could be placed into the

Making the Times Square model.

From top of page: the actual conditions of Times Square in 1985; development potential under the 1982 midtown planning controls; and development potential under the alternative development controls proposed in August 1985.

model incrementally, to illustrate development opportunities over time. When three new buildings were added to the model, Broadway began to resemble Sixth Avenue, one block east. When all twelve of the parcels selected for modeling were shown developed, the result was stunning. After viewing the model, the *New York Times* architecture critic wrote—under the headline "Will Times Square Become a Grand Canyon?"—that under the 1982 midtown planning controls the identity of the place could change.[9] Indeed, these controls would have permitted an office district to replace the Times Square entertainment district. Approximately 12 million square feet of office space could have been built in the area.[10]

Anyone stepping up to the model could bend down slightly and, looking down Broadway or any side street from a pedestrian's perspective, instantly notice the startling difference in scale; the theaters tucked in between the new structures seemed to belong to a bygone era. Anyone viewing the model would also notice the large new signs, which would have to be placed on the facades of large buildings, not, as before, on rooftops at an angle where they could be seen silhouetted against the sky.

The large model effectively showed the cumulative change possible under the 1982 midtown zoning controls. The disparity in scale was stunning to designers, planners, and nonprofessionals alike. "Before" and "after" sketches, prepared in Berkeley before the model was constructed, showed the same building volumes but far understated the impact of the new buildings from a pedestrian's perspective. The model was large enough to photograph at eye level, using a conventional 35 mm camera with a close-focus lens. The model, built in 12-inch sections, permitted the camera to "walk" along Broadway as it pivoted from right to left. The model and views recorded in this fashion became a design tool for developing and testing alternative planning controls.

If the traditional brilliance of Times Square lights reflected against the nighttime sky was to be preserved, electric signs had to be visible from

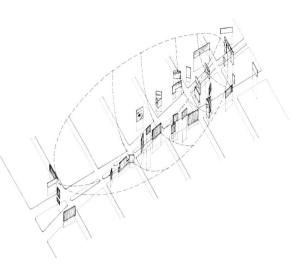

Times Square electric signs, 1985.

a distance. Thus they had to be angled against the city and the sky. The numerous stacked signs on Times Square buildings create a bowl-shaped outdoor room, a critical design element in making Times Square a gathering place for tens of thousands of people. The desire to preserve this openness to signs, light, and sky became the guide for alternative planning controls for the entertainment district.

The model of Times Square provided a stage for designing the district from the pedestrian's perspective. Lines of sight were studied and appropriate setbacks calculated. The placement of new signs and alternative building heights were tested within the realistic context of the Times Square model.[11] Openness and light could be preserved with facades five floors high, along Broadway and Seventh Avenue, and signs on the rooftops silhouetted against the sky. Taller buildings would have to step further back from the street facade, as the buildings ascended. This configuration would retain openness to the sky. Setbacks above the street facade would let light and air into the street. But this alternative configuration of buildings reduced the floor area allowed by the 1982 midtown planning controls by 30 percent.

The simulation team proposed hotels instead of office towers. The new convention center, located less than a mile from Times Square, attracts twelve major conventions each year. According to the New York Visitors Bureau, conventioneers spend approximately $1 billion annually in Manhattan, one-third of all New York City tourist dollars. Times Square seemed ideally suited for an estimated ten thousand hotel rooms needed to accommodate conventioneers.

Residential buildings were modeled for the Times Square side streets toward Eighth Avenue and the adjacent Clinton neighborhood. All new buildings formed a continuous row along the front edge of the property line, with large windows on the street level for retail stores or restaurants with individual entrances. The life inside new buildings would create life in the street.

Building a bowl. *From top to bottom:* possible building volumes under the alternative development controls proposed in 1985; zoning envelopes under the alternative development controls proposed in 1985; building volumes "outside" the zoning envelope.

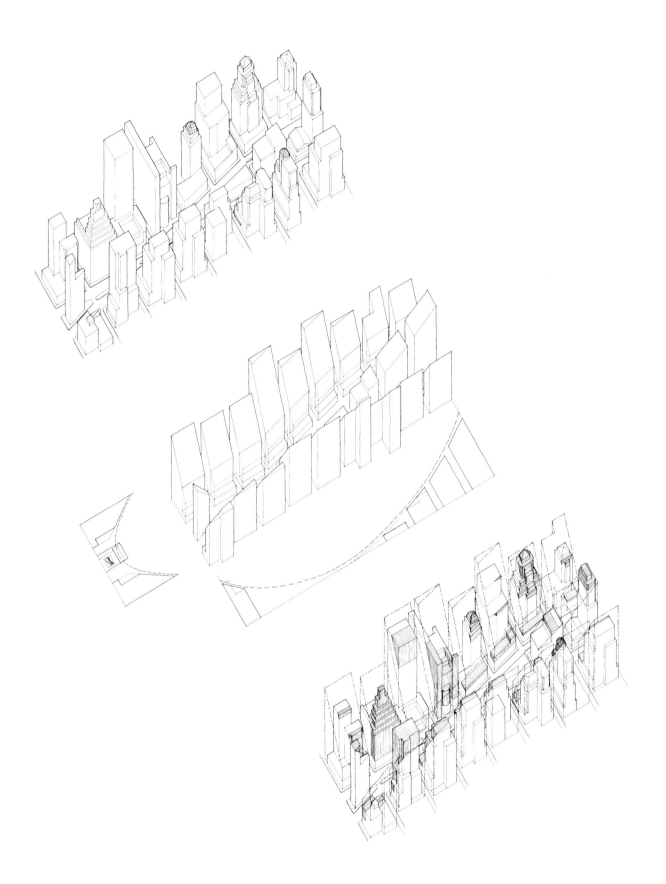

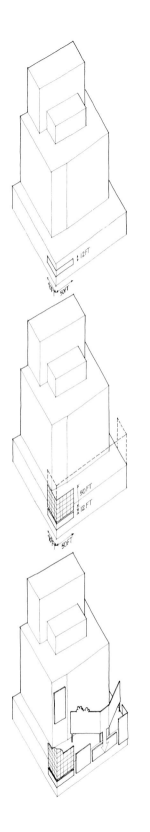

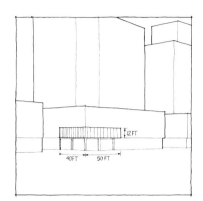

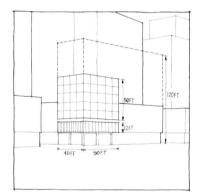

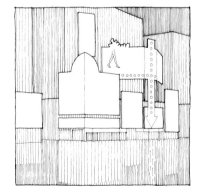

Designing and placement of signage. The top sketches illustrate the signage requirement proposed in 1985, with commercial signs related to street-level stores and restaurants, 12 feet high for every linear foot of frontage. The middle sketches show a large-format electric sign for general advertising, with a minimum of 50 feet for every foot of frontage and a maximum of 120 feet above ground level. The bottom sketches illustrate the desired signage effect.

The model of Times Square was first shown publicly at a planning commission hearing in September 1985. The Municipal Arts Society had set up the model in the front of the hearing room so that the commissioners had to maneuver around it. The model separated them from the first row, where the three heads of the theater organization sat along with their legal aides. At the urging of the theater owners, and with their help, the model was removed while they testified. But a group of actors and stage writers carried the model back in and referred to it while arguing in support of theater preservation and entertainment district zoning controls. A ten-minute film narrated by Jason Robards showed eye-level views of the Times Square model, compared the 1982 midtown planning controls and the alternative proposed by the simulation team.

This film and the model's exhibition at the Urban Center on Madison Avenue, where it went on display for four months, gave the many people who came to see it a new perspective on the future of Times Square. Midtown office workers could watch the film of the Times Square model at lunchtime. They saw the alternative scenario and had the opportunity to react, articulate their own views, and participate in public discussions held around the model.

In the summer of 1986 the *New York Times* reported on the planning department's revision of planning controls for Times Square. No building fronting on Times Square was to exceed 60 feet in height, measured at the street front; above this height, buildings would have to be set back 50 feet. Mandatory large illuminated signs would be accommodated on the roof of this 50-foot setback. The size of the signs along the facade was to be directly proportional to the sidewalk frontage of each new development, with 50 square feet of signage for every foot of Times Square frontage. Beyond the 50-foot setback, buildings could step up higher. Thus far, the city planning department's proposal directly followed the model prepared by the simulation team. But the amount of allowable floor space to be contained in each new building was still in

Simulations and reality. *From left to right:* development under the proposed 1985 alternative development controls; development under the 1986 adopted planning controls; the 1995 reality.

dispute. The city planning commission was reluctant to reverse its 1982 decision and limit the allowable floor area granted "as of right." In their view, the size of buildings had become a political issue.

The 1986 revised controls, like the 1982 midtown controls, allowed towers with a total floor area of eighteen times the square footage of the lot (18 FAR, or floor area ratio). Additional floor area was again permitted through the transfer of air rights and bonuses.[12] Consequently, the 1986 controls could produce streets with high "canyon walls," failing to ensure the "bowl of light" essential to the vitality of this large public place. To preserve the openness of Times Square to light and sky, the simulation team argued, building bulk had to be limited by sloping, angled planes. This angle would define the height of all new buildings. The maximum floor ratio under this provision would have resulted in floor space 14 times the lot area (14 FAR). But the 1986 revised controls were legislated

with the 18:1 floor area ratio unchanged.

The model lent greater specificity to consideration of both the city's official proposals and the counter-proposals, for it showed the effect of seemingly abstract rules. Floor area ratios, setbacks, and sky exposure planes, expressed in the model, became terms whose meanings more people now understood.

The Times Square project has spurred community groups in Manhattan to use modeling and animation techniques to explain the effects of city planning policies on their own neighborhoods. In 1986 a citizens' group on the Upper East Side used the technique to show what the avenues would look like if additional residential high-rises were built along the East River and on First, Second, and Third Avenues. Paul Newman narrated their story. In 1987 the Parks Council of New York City used simulation to better understand the effects of Television City, a development proposed in the mid-1980s for the site of the Seventy-second Street railroad yard. The city planners themselves, together with a task force appointed by the governor, commissioned simulations to explain the mitigated design of the still-controversial West Side Highway. Finally, the public interest in simulations led to the establishment of a laboratory in New York City modeled after the Berkeley facility; there the work continues.

Times Square at night, 1995.

CHAPTER FIVE

Downtown San Francisco

In San Francisco, the Mission Bay project had been under discussion for several decades, from the 1960s to the 1990s. The original owner of the 90-acre site, a railroad company, had offered to build housing there, but the ground was heavily contaminated and cleanup work very expensive. In 1984, when the land development branch of the railroad company argued for the inclusion of office buildings to support reasonably priced housing units, city officials questioned the proposed balance between the two kinds of land use. In the mid-1980s public discussion focused on the appropriate use of the land. Local planners used maps to explain the railroad company's proposal to politicians. They described the development, who might live there, how many people could be accommodated, and how traffic would circulate in and out. Although such discussions gave the politicians and the public a sketchy impression of the proposal, few could understand the physical scale of the "new town" or its relationship to adjacent neighborhoods and the city as a whole. The architects had not unveiled their detailed plans.

The architects brought a large model of the development to San Francisco in the spring of 1984.[1]

The buildings in this elegant off-white model were graceful, with pleasing proportions. The composition was artful and the display impressive. When local politicians and planners saw the model, they shifted their attention from the analytic reality of numbers to the more sensuous reality of shapes and surfaces. The Berkeley Environmental Simulation Laboratory also presented a third reality on a screen in the darkened conference room where the model was displayed: the slides projected on a screen showed a view of the proposed Mission Bay project against the backdrop of the city. This image had a tremendous effect on the group, including the out-of-town designers. At first the room was silent. Then someone said, "Oh, my God."

The new city, all white, was a stunning sight, looking unreal and out of place against the more colorful existing city. The slide shown first provided the most dramatic view, in that it allowed a comparison between the existing skyline of San Francisco and the new town's alteration of it. This view was also the one that mattered most to those who lived on Potrero Hill near the new town. Although other views followed, the audience seemed set against the proposal after seeing the first one.

The proposed Mission Bay project, 1984. The views (*from top of page*) are from the Upper Mission neighborhood above Dolores Park, directly south of the site; from Potrero Hill, southeast of the site; and from upper Market Street, southwest of the site.

In meetings during the week following the showing of the model and slides, local experts and politicians decided against further consideration of the proposal. Commissioners and local planners objected to the building of a new city on a scale that competed with the old. They persuaded the developers to withdraw their proposal by arguing that San Franciscans were unlikely to support the project.

To prepare the slide images of the proposed Mission Bay development, the Environmental Simulation Laboratory had superimposed the architects' model of Mission Bay on the model of San Francisco permanently housed at Berkeley, which is updated as new development occurs. The architects knew beforehand that their model would be used in the slides and had visited Berkeley to inspect the city model. They were evidently unaware of the effect that the juxtaposition of their plan and the model would have on a local audience. Certainly the model's color (or lack of it) hurt their proposal. Moreover, it may have been unfair to show the most dramatically altered view first. In hindsight, a randomly selected sequence of the views might have been more appropriate, as long as it did not confuse the audience.

After the out-of-town architects' proposal had been rejected, the city of San Francisco and the landowners each hired a team of local designers and planners. Although neighborhood groups requested simulations from time to time, city officials played down the need for such work and, possibly afraid of the outcome, argued that building heights were no longer an issue because office towers were no longer being considered for the site. Issues now under discussion related to the density of the proposed neighborhood and the inclusion of affordable housing. Simulations could have clarified some of the physical issues, but apart from idealized sketches of street views prepared by the designers, no further simulation work was commissioned for Mission Bay. ■

The model of San Francisco had already been in active use when the Mission Bay proposal was first introduced. Much of the work described in the following pages could not have been prepared without such a scale model. In 1980, when work on the Downtown Plan started, no accurate computer representation of the city existed; the Berkeley Laboratory started on a detailed three-dimensional computer model of the downtown only in 1986. Those who worked at the lab had honed their skills by manipulating and filming physical models to present future changes. Many of the model-animation procedures they used were readily transferable to computer technology once it became available.

A viewer's ability to step up to a scale model and compare the relative size of known objects with those proposed gave credence to the images created with such models. The psychological importance of such empirical tests of accuracy became clear to me when a blind man asked to visit the model of San Francisco at Berkeley. The man, in his fifties, had been blind from birth and had lived in San Francisco his entire life. The first thing he asked about was the building occupied by Lighthouse, an association of blind people. One of the staff members found the building on the model and guided his hand so that he could feel it. He then said, "Now where is Market Street?" Two spans of his hand led him to Market Street.

Then he asked about the scale of the model. When given that number, he understood distances spanned with his hand on the model. Next the man let his hand glide down Market Street, while we called out the name of each building he touched. He would frequently ask, "At what intersection am I now?" Finally he reached the end of Market Street at the Ferry Building. He touched the piers and the freeway along the waterfront. "Now where is Telegraph Hill?" he asked. When guided to it, he remarked, "Oh, the hill is so close to the waterfront. Then this must be Coit Tower [the tower at the top of Telegraph Hill]. I have been there many times. Can I go back to Market Street?" The man felt the tall buildings along Market Street in the financial

district, went back to Telegraph Hill, back again to Market Street, and back to Telegraph Hill. "Gosh," he said, "when I was a child, Coit Tower on Telegraph Hill was the tallest building in San Francisco. Now it is just a little thing compared to all those buildings on Market Street! The city has changed in my lifetime."

This man made the same comparisons as those who came to see the model at Berkeley. They would compare the scale of the new with the scale of the familiar, a comparison that would be impossible to make with projected images. Visitors can touch and see the model, examining it at their own pace; the projected images are fleeting and out of the visitors' control.

This scale model of San Francisco was funded by President Franklin D. Roosevelt's Works Progress Administration and built for the 1939 Golden Gate International Exposition. The Berkeley laboratory updated the model in 1972 to show San Francisco's growth since the 1930s. During this process, the model-builders made an animation film.[2] As they inserted buildings constructed since the 1930s, they kept a camera pointed at the model to record the changes. The cityscape on film changes little in the 1940s and 1950s. But suddenly, in the early 1960s, high-rise buildings appear. In the few minutes of film needed to show the 1960s and 1970s, San Francisco is transformed.

By the late 1970s the financial district had grown within a triangular area bounded by Market Street, Washington Street, and Montgomery Street, the city's business and banking street since the 1920s. When virtually all the usable land within this triangle had been developed, the relatively compact financial district employed approximately 280,000 people. For nearly ten years, from 1967 to 1977, the Bank of America Building was the only high-rise tower west of Montgomery Street. The construction of a new high-rise building on Kearney Street, one block west of Montgomery, seemed to signal the expansion of the downtown into Chinatown and the Union Square retail district.

Downtown San Francisco's transformation was

increasingly protested by neighborhood and environmental groups. Since the early 1960s, when the first high-rise buildings emerged on the skyline, San Franciscans have voted against the "Manhattanization" of the city. The fight that began over blocked views continued when well-known structures were replaced by high-rise development. San Franciscans complained not only that the new structures blocked familiar views but also that they clashed with the surrounding Victorian architecture. Many believed that the new taller buildings had made streets in downtown San Francisco less comfortable, producing additional shadows and cold, windy open spaces. Enough signatures were gathered to qualify anti-high-rise initiatives on six successive ballots prior to 1986, when a new Downtown Plan was finally adopted. The first three initiatives were defeated. The fourth, in November 1983, failed to pass by only 1,919 votes, or 0.2 percent of the electorate. This narrow defeat signaled the need for a new plan acceptable to neighborhood and environmental groups as well as the downtown real estate and business community.[3]

In 1979, to represent the consequences of future downtown development, the Berkeley team modified the San Francisco model, first inserting buildings allowable under existing planning controls and then projecting future development. Working with maps prepared by real estate professionals to show land under assemblage, the Berkeley team projected the construction of 10 million square feet of new development and then an additional 10 million.[4]

The discussion of growth rates in the early 1980s did not cover the possibility that such projected development was unrealistic, even in the fifteen-year period the planners assumed. (The planners in turn were responding to development pressures resulting from the deregulation of the savings and loan industry and from an influx of capital from Hong Kong after stalemated negotiations over the future of the British colony.) But more office space was already under construction in suburban locations than in downtown San Francisco as corpora-

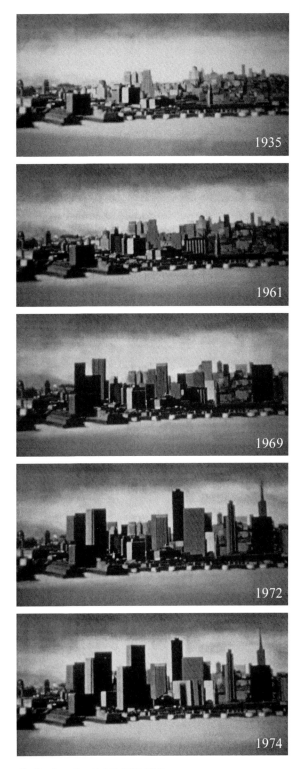

The San Francisco skyline, 1935–1974.

A San Francisco planner checking proposed height limits against the model.

tions restructured their administrative functions. The new development of suburban offices did not go unnoticed, especially when the corporations that built such offices sold their downtown headquarters buildings, contributing to a vacancy rate that reached 25 percent by the end of the 1980s. The actual growth of new downtown office space would slow to a trickle. From 1985 to 1995, only 2 million square feet of downtown office space would be constructed.

In the early 1980s few people anticipated such low figures. At that time, four new hotel towers near Union Square were on the drawing board, all taking advantage of the height limits of up to thirty-four stories. In Chinatown, where only one 1960s apartment building had reached the sixteen-story height limit, several more were proposed. And at the edge of Chinatown, in the office core area, 8 million square feet of office space were under consideration. The planning department, in response to public concerns about accelerated development, proposed lower height limits, a reduction in allowable floor space, and the transfer of air rights to protect historic structures. They contracted with the Environmental Simulation Laboratory to illustrate their proposals.

The best way to explain the effects of these new planning proposals visually was to show potential development incrementally as well as cumulatively on the model. The laboratory team positioned the camera at a number of locations in the model and took pictures at eye level, first of the existing views, then of a series of incremental changes under 1974 planning controls, and finally of changes under alternative controls. These images, recorded on film, could be shown slowly if an individual project was to be analyzed or at greater speed if the cumulative effect was at issue. Repeated screenings of these film clips enabled planners and planning commissioners to analyze the patterns of growth and the effect of new planning controls.

The most telling views were those of downtown streets in the retail district near Union Square. Lined in the early 1980s with buildings 70 to 100

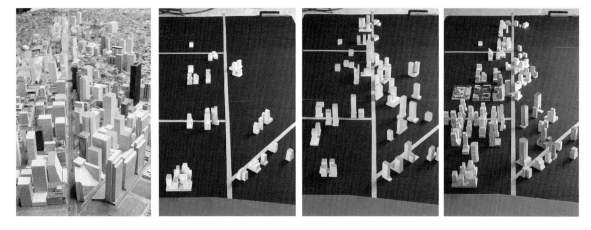

The San Francisco downtown model, with the view centered on Market Street. *From left to right:* the status quo (1985); the addition of 10 million square feet of office space under the 1974 planning controls; the addition of 20 million square feet of office space under the 1974 planning controls; the addition of 20 million square feet of office space under alternative planning controls.

feet high, they were to be changed by the construction of new hotels. Planning controls allowed such buildings to rise to 360 feet. Similarly, in Chinatown, buildings could rise to 160 or 240 feet where structures of 50 to 70 feet stood. In the Tenderloin, an area west of Union Square where existing structures rarely exceeded 90 to 100 feet, buildings could rise to 240 or 320 feet.

The city planners agreed to lower allowable building heights west of the financial district to a scale compatible with that of the surrounding districts. The "hill policy" of a 1974 San Francisco Urban Design Plan offered no guidance; it was, in fact, partly responsible for the problem. To create a downtown "hill" of closely placed high-rise towers, the plan's controls set the heights to gradually taper down, from 500 or 600 feet to 30 or 40 feet, as in nearby neighborhoods. In the Union Square area of this "hill," there was no room for a gradual tapering between the financial district, the retail district, and Chinatown.

The Berkeley team constructed detailed displays of downtown streets near the financial district to study the transformation of scale as it might be perceived by a pedestrian. Existing buildings were fairly uniform in scale. Although they do not necessarily have the same length and height, their measurements fall within a range that allows pedestrians to perceive them both as a series of units and as a whole.

To demonstrate how building heights should be set to keep the scale of proposed buildings compatible with the character of a district, the Berkeley laboratory created a sequence of views showing hypothetical buildings gradually increasing in height. Planners watching the sequence agreed on the desirability of a range of allowable heights if the facade length could also be limited. One idea was to limit the facade length to a range of existing dimensions found in a given district. The planners could not agree on how to define such a range, however, fearing that new development would tend to ignore the lower height and frontage measurements. The best solution the planners could think of was to correlate the two ranges, limiting buildings with long facades to lower heights and allowing those with short facades to reach the upper boundary of the height range. Legal advisers, however, declared that such a limit to property owners' rights could be judged arbitrary.[5]

As the laboratory continued its work, it now engaged in producing analysis relevant to official policy making, a subtle but important change in role—important because thus far the laboratory had simply responded to the need of city planners to test their ideas. Now the laboratory was charged to find a basis for urban planning standards. The team at the Berkeley laboratory generated ideas and tested them.

The laboratory produced representations showing what it was like to walk along sidewalks in the retail district. The best graphic method was to produce fish-eye pictures taken at sidewalk level, looking directly up into the sky above the street. Such circular images capture all information in a 180-degree angle view. Despite the distortion, the fish-eye image places the viewer, as in the real world, in the middle of things, surrounded by buildings roofed by the sky. The images provide a good analytical tool. A set of images comprising a walk from the financial district into the retail district along one particular street suggests how buildings define that street and shows how much sky they obscure or leave unobscured. On "skymaps" produced by the laboratory, streets in the retail district had ample sky, and buildings appeared light colored; but

streets in the financial district had very little sky, and the buildings there looked dark. The amount of sky obscured could be measured by superimposing a circular grid. A count of grid squares on the overlay reveals that streets in the retail district have a 75 percent view of the sky at midblock, whereas streets in the financial district have only 10 or 15 percent. Further, when the arc of the sun was superimposed on retail district streets and compared with a similar superimposition on financial district streets,[6] sidewalks in the retail district were shown to have ample sun. At lunchtime the sun reaches the northern sidewalk on east–west streets six months of the year, and along north–south streets sunlight is available year-round (six hours in summer, four hours in fall, and two hours in winter). In the financial district, the sun is blocked at lunchtime on all east–west streets; north–south streets receive less than an hour of sunlight year-round.

When the analysis of sunlight and the measurement of open sky were presented to the planning commission, members discussed them and agreed that sunlight for pedestrians was an asset in the retail district and contributed to its economic vitality. They believed that retailers as well as the public would support a reduction of allowable building heights there if these heights would allow sun on sidewalks. The team at Berkeley was charged with calculating building heights that would preserve sunlight. These computations, taking into account the width and direction of individual streets, provided the rationale for a reduction of individual development rights not only in the retail district but also in the adjacent Tenderloin.

The work had just begun at Berkeley when the Department of City Planning requested additional analysis. Of immediate concern to the planners was a proposed 132-foot-high condominium project that threatened to shade a small playground in Chinatown—the Chinese Playground. The playground was especially busy on weekday afternoons between two and four o'clock, when many children left to attend Chinese language school.[7]

Fish-eye lens images were taken of the Chinese

Playground. A montage of hypothetical buildings 160 feet high—the allowable building height—was added to pictures of sky above the playground. The resulting images showed how much sky and sun were obscured by the proposed development. Then, with the same hypothetical 160-foot buildings in place, a sun-path diagram was used to measure sunlight hours at the playground. The photo studies showed that sunlight during afternoon hours would disappear if such buildings were constructed. The planning commission, at an emotional meeting, passed a resolution to lower building heights around the Chinese Playground effective immediately. A year later, in 1983, the Board of Supervisors (San Francisco's equivalent of a city council) upheld the resolution and reduced the maximum height of buildings around the playground from 160 feet to 50 feet.[8] Subsequently, the planning commission ordered sun-access studies for all open spaces in downtown San Francisco.

With official policies now based on the need for a comfortable climate, further research was needed on the relation between climate and the use of open space. The Department of City Planning began by conducting a user survey of twelve downtown open spaces. In response to open-ended questions about what attracted them to the open space they used, downtown office workers most frequently mentioned sunlight.[9] Because of the survey's limited scope and qualitative emphasis, it did not offer enough evidence to support lower building heights near all public open spaces. What was needed was a systematic modeling of the relationship between building form and the four variables that influence microclimatic conditions: sun, wind, humidity, and temperature.[10] The laboratory team needed to analyze these variables for all seasons and measure the effect that building form has on sunlight availability and wind velocity.

Four additional large models of downtown areas were constructed to measure sun and wind conditions. The resulting data were correlated to a computerized model of the human body's thermoregulatory system. The team made assumptions

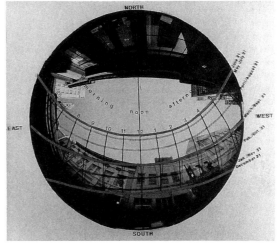

(*Top*) Measuring sunlight on streets in downtown San Francisco; (*above*) Polar grid above Kearney Street and the arc of the sun above Commercial Street.

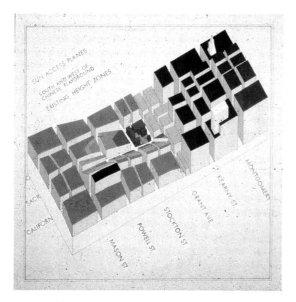

Diagram of the Chinatown playground, with surrounding height limits set to allow for sunlight.

about the clothing people would wear during a given season and how actively they would move about. Seasonal maps confirmed the initial hypothesis: areas that receive direct sunlight are comfortable more than 50 percent of the time; those in shade rarely are. Although windy shaded places are especially inhospitable, reducing wind speed is usually not enough to make them welcoming.[11] The research team confirmed what San Franciscans had long known: direct sunlight and shelter from the wind are necessary for comfort outdoors.

By the time the Berkeley laboratory team's findings were published in 1984,[12] work on the Downtown Plan had entered a critical stage. Citizens' groups and some members of the Board of Supervisors viewed the plan as too friendly to development. Others, including the mayor, were concerned about its restrictions on development. Advocacy groups decided to break the stalemate by taking the issue to the voters in an initiative on the 1984 primary election ballot. The initiative proposed to amend the city charter to protect sunlight in public open spaces, a measure that, as many voters knew, would also prevent the building of high-rise offices along the western flank of downtown San Francisco, alongside public parks. Seven months after the defeat of the previous initiative, 64 percent of San Franciscans voted to preserve sunlight in parks and squares. The environmental groups had scored their first victory in a growth-control battle that had lasted for two decades. ■

The city of San Francisco had been taken into the laboratory to test the cumulative effect of new development on its physical form. Those promoting downtown development believed the Berkeley studies had supported the limitation of downtown growth; the planners believed the analysis supported a more careful monitoring of the cumulative change likely to result from proposed development. The findings created a great stir in the development community. The dean of the College of Environmental Design at the Berkeley campus of the University of California, where the laboratory is

located, received calls from San Francisco architects complaining that the work of the laboratory was "detrimental to the profession." These callers claimed the Berkeley team had played into the hands of the foes of growth.

Those eager to limit growth believed the work at Berkeley did not illustrate forcefully enough the detrimental effects of downtown development. They saw the laboratory as an extension of San Francisco's Department of City Planning, whose leadership, in their opinion, opposed growth limitations. The laboratory was caught in the middle, exactly where it should have been.

Clearly, the studies and images produced at the laboratory fueled the political battle over growth. The planning commission valued the laboratory's research because it answered their needs. Aware of the community's growing opposition to downtown development, commissioners knew that the Board of Supervisors would approve a new plan only if it addressed the opposition's concerns.

San Francisco planners watch the setup of a model for testing in the wind tunnel.

Given this heated political debate, it was important not only that the laboratory produce accurate information but also that it be open to anyone who wanted to stop by and see "science at work." And indeed, many San Franciscans made the thirty-minute trip to Berkeley to watch the laboratory team.

The Urban Design Committee of the American Institute of Architects convened a meeting at the Berkeley lab. The urban designers gathered around the model with members of San Francisco's planning commission and planning staff. Opponents of downtown development also came to see the scale-model studies. The planning staff was well prepared for the discussion, having requested simulations for several alternative height regulations. The urban designers on the planning staff had studied these, checked their assumptions, and tested alternatives.

Prior to the meeting, the architects had argued for higher buildings in specific locations. As the AIA members and the commissioners studied the model together, however, they reached a consensus. All parties—developers, planners, architects, and development foes—had challenged the assumptions made in the model studies. But once they saw the model, they conceded that the studies accurately represented the proposed new planning controls.

Planners, like others under political pressure, sometimes alter their views. After seeing film clips of the model, the planning director, who had agreed to new increased height limits and defended their appropriateness, decided that several buildings possible under the new plan were too high. The team at Berkeley learned to expect such turnabouts. Visitors to the laboratory often made very specific comments. Indeed, the model prompted focused discussions among visiting groups about complex planning and design issues. The motive for the trip to the Berkeley laboratory to see the large-scale model of San Francisco was often a healthy mistrust of images. All the groups had seen selected views of the model: on television, on the wall of the meeting room at the planning commission where slides were projected on TV monitors, or in photo-graphic prints. The key actors from both sides of the planning controversy were suspicious of manipulation of these images. They had to come and see for themselves and listen to the reactions of others they brought along.

San Franciscans on either side of the downtown controversy accepted the city's master plan premise that high-rise buildings should be concentrated in a well-defined area to contain office development and protect the surrounding neighborhoods. The question still to be answered was where to draw the boundary around the area to be developed.

The laboratory's experiments with the effects of tall buildings on the city's micro-climates had suggested the western edge of the financial district as the boundary. It was clear, however, that development was likely to grow to the south, near the Transbay Bus Terminal. Areas surrounding bus terminals are often disreputable. For years, the real estate community resisted any development near the Transbay Terminal. Even though, unlike typical bus terminals, this one served those who commuted to the financial district from suburban towns in the East Bay, the stigma remained.

To direct investors away from sites in the core of the financial district, where land had become scarce, the city offered to transfer the development potential of those sites occupied by historic structures to a new special district around the Transbay Terminal, where intensive use of properties would be allowed. Even with incentives, however, developers showed little interest in this district; but with other directions for downtown development blocked, they had no choice.

In the mid-1980s few San Franciscans challenged the effect of large-scale development on the streets in the South of Market area or asked what urban design criteria should apply to a building proposed for this district. There was little public opposition to policies that encouraged very large new buildings. Moreover, South of Market city blocks measured longer and wider, making it easier to assemble parcels of land that could accommodate structures with larger floor areas than elsewhere.

Model of the San Francisco skyline, showing existing conditions in 1985 (*left column*) and potential conditions under the 1985 Downtown Plan (*right column*). The views (*top to bottom*) are from Treasure Island, Potrero Hill, Dolores Park, the Western Addition, and the Bay Bridge.

But the transfer of air rights used in the South of Market area raised questions about the effect of tall buildings, in particular the disparity between such towers and the area's predominantly small-scale commercial structures. For years a tall building would dominate the surrounding area.[13] Over time, however, the financial district would spread southward and more small-scale buildings would be replaced by new construction, changing the character of the Transbay Terminal district.

The "hill" policy of closely placed high-rises sloping down to the height of buildings in surrounding districts suggested a solution to this development issue, but first the "hill" had to be designed. Anyone walking to and from work in the financial district would move from open streets on the periphery of downtown with ample sunlight and views of the Bay, the Bay Bridge, and downtown to more confined streets with greater activity and greater density—with the order reversed on the way home.[14] To study how pedestrians would experience new development with the progression of density characteristic of the "hill," the district around the Transbay Terminal was modeled in the laboratory. Scale models of typical street sections were built to study the effects on pedestrians of being surrounded or contained by buildings as they cross the district. Although the width of the streets in the South of Market district is constant, building heights vary considerably. On Second Street, half a mile south of Market Street, buildings measured 40 feet in height, equal to half the street width. A quarter mile south of Market Street, building heights increased to 80 feet, equal to street width. Finally, in the block just south of Market Street, building heights from 100 to 400 feet exceeded the width of streets. If new construction followed this pattern, the street sections of the Transbay Terminal district furthest from Market Street could maintain a streetwall of 40 feet. Building towers would rise above this streetwall, but only after a setback of 50 feet. Both the height of the streetwall and the tower height would increase gradually, block by block, toward Market Street.

The proposal was studied, and after much discussion with the development community, the planners suggested a preservation zone along two of the streets in the Transbay Terminal area south of the downtown core, along New Montgomery and Second Streets, but no additional controls to decrease streetwall dimensions with increased distance from the downtown core. Instead, the planners proposed unified streetwall heights and bulk controls that limited the streetwall to 1.25 times the street's width. In the Transbay Terminal area, this would produce buildings with a streetwall about 100 feet high on all streets and towers set back and capped with a decorative top. Prototypes of buildings under proposed controls were modeled and then inserted into both the larger San Francisco model and more detailed models of downtown streets. ■

Testing the visual form of cities, as in the laboratory experiments discussed in this chapter, is relatively easy. But questions surface when these tests are evaluated. With no widely accepted standard for the visual form of the city, many interpretations of good form are possible. The San Francisco "hill" policy is a widely accepted standard against which new developments can easily be tested and evaluated. But this is a local standard, rooted in the experience of San Francisco's topography and location on a peninsula with many hills overlaid with a regular grid of streets lined with small buildings. In another city such a downtown "hill" might be irrelevant. In Denver, an ordinance that limits the height of buildings near parks and open spaces is based on an imaginary view from the open space toward the ridge line of the Rocky Mountains. The best-known building height ordinance is that of Washington, D.C., where structures must be lower than the base of the Capitol dome.

Urban designers have tried to promote similar ordering principles in other cities. In New York, in reaction to towers such as the World Trade Center, designers have argued that Manhattan should be shaped like a mountain ridge, with high buildings stretching along the center of the island from

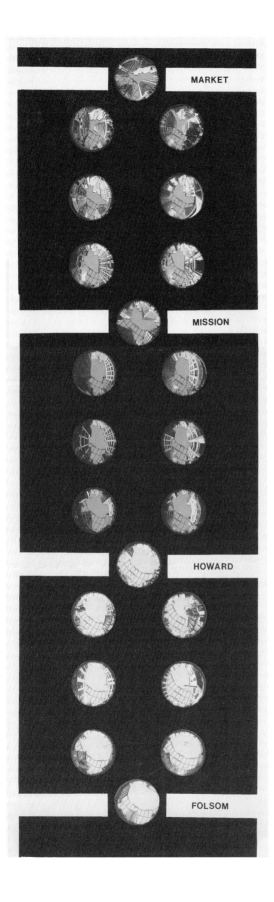

Sky exposure map for Second Street, from Market Street south to Folsom, 1983.

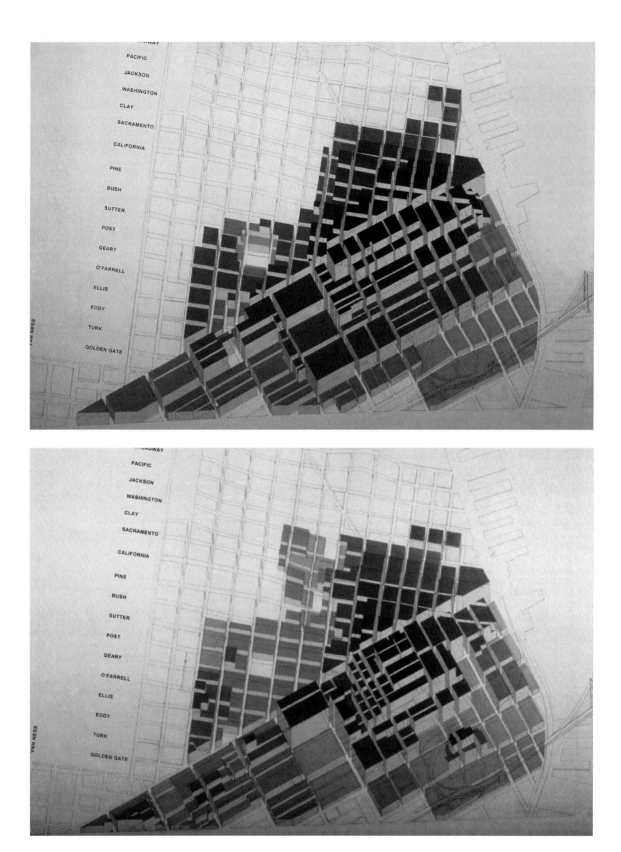

Central Park south through midtown, with a saddle south of the Empire State Building, before height again increases south of Soho toward the southern tip of Manhattan. If adopted, this ordinance would prevent outright a structure like Television City, the "tallest building in the world." But a Manhattan ridge line is only remotely related to New Yorkers' daily movements. Many would admit that such shaping might be more pleasing to those who see Manhattan from the bay, from the East and Hudson Rivers, or from New Jersey.

Residents value a city form shaped according to natural topography because it allows them to cope with change. People interviewed in San Diego, California, about the physical form of their city, expressed affection for the oceanside setting, the bay, and the canyons that open toward the bay. According to one resident, nostalgic for an earlier cityscape, "The north side is ugly, and the accelerated building in the valley floor is plain tragic. And there are the areas of parked cars waiting to be sold, where once there was greenery and birds and peace and quiet. Imagine hearing spring peepers in the city. We used to!"[15]

Planners in San Diego have tried to direct the city's development away from the valleys to protect them as elements of the city's visual structure. Although they have not always succeeded, their work enjoys public support. In his review of literature on the perception of, and response to, anticipated or experienced change, Erwin Zube notes that "a greater obligation will be placed upon those in the planning and design professions to ensure change does not outrun the ability to comprehend and cope with it."[16]

I have focused on natural images that influence the aesthetics of a city's structure. Helmut Wohl usefully relates aesthetic vision to a coherent point of view and to trust, "perhaps the deepest criterion for the measure of coherence that a point of view represents. Aesthetic vision provides both an ideal and a standard of that wholeness which a point of view imparts on reality."[17]

Opposite: Downtown "hill" shaped by the 1974 planning controls (*top*) and by the 1985 Downtown Plan.

CHAPTER SIX

Downtown Toronto:
Urban Form and Climate

City planners in San Francisco drew on the knowledge of a relationship, as old as the experience of living in cities, between urban form and a city's climate. During the Renaissance, both Leon Battista Alberti and, later, Andrea Palladio reported the observation of Tacitus that parts of Rome became hotter during the summer—and less healthy—when streets were widened during the reign of Emperor Nero.[1] Palladio recommended that cities in cool climates have "ample and broad" streets so that these cities would be "much wholesomer, more commodious, and more beautiful." But cities in hotter climates would be more healthful with narrow streets and tall houses to provide shade. Palladio and Alberti were inspired by the writings on city planning and climate of Vitruvius, who, in recommending the laying out of colonial cities at the time of Emperor Augustus, suggested orienting streets away from the direction of prevailing winds as a protection against their violent force.[2] Vitruvius's writings were studied in Spain's colonial office and incorporated into the Law of the Indies, proclaimed by King Philip II of Spain in 1573 and sometimes applied to city building in the New World.[3]

Thomas Jefferson, upon returning from England and France in 1800, complained about the constantly gray skies of England and noted the "collective psyche of the English men who tended to be suicidal due to lack of sunlight in the North." In America, skies are usually blue, he observed, but people suffer from high humidity during the summer months. He designed a checkerboard city plan where black squares represented built-up city blocks and white squares indicated gardens crossed diagonally by roads. He anticipated that cool air from the shaded garden squares would cause a natural airflow between them and the hotter city blocks.[4]

The health benefits of direct sunlight and air circulation became the focus of research by the medical profession around the turn of the century. The findings on the relationship between sunlight and bone diseases or tuberculosis, for example, and on ventilation as a factor in health had a major effect on the practice of architecture and urban planning worldwide.[5] But subsequently, local climate conditions have had less influence on the form, spacing, and style of buildings. The architect Bruno Taut observed correctly in 1937 that his fellow modernists disregarded local differences in climates: "The modern buildings built up high in the north [of Europe] have the same appearance as those built along the Mediterranean Sea."[6]

Each decade has brought new building styles; changes in functional and structural requirements have changed building dimensions, but modern cities have rarely been shaped by a concern for climate. In downtown Toronto, where winters are cold and summers hot and humid, buildings resemble those of downtown Los Angeles, where winters are mild and summers moderately warm. In arid Phoenix, Arizona, street dimensions and the spacing between tall buildings are similar to those in the Shinjuku district of Tokyo, where summers are also hot but much more humid. In all these cities, urban form has adversely affected the local climate: streets and squares have become windier, hotter, or colder.

Although the relationship between a city's form and its climate has been intuitively understood, intuition cannot predict how specific future buildings will affect climatic conditions. No comprehensive mathematical model exists that relates proposed structures to the comfort of pedestrians on sidewalks or in public open spaces –that is, the thermal conditions that affect their physiological well-being. A combination of experimental and computational techniques is necessary to make comfort predictions.

Six variables affect thermal comfort outdoors: sunlight, wind, humidity, ambient air temperature, activity level, and clothing. Depending on local climate and weather, a person might prefer to sit or walk in sunlight or in the shadow of buildings, might enjoy a breeze, or might take shelter from the weather in buildings or under arcades. Cities can be built to provide these choices.

In 1990 planners in Toronto were searching for a rationale for setting new building height limits and density controls near the city's downtown. The Environmental Simulation Laboratory was commissioned to carry out modeling experiments on the effects of urban form on microclimatic conditions there.[7] The laboratory examined the effects

Bioclimatic charts for Toronto, Vancouver, Phoenix, and New Orleans. *To read the bioclimatic chart for Toronto*, note that lines in the lower right portion indicate the range of average monthly maximum and minimum temperatures and humidity. The comfort zone in the center indicates comfortable temperature and humidity conditions for a person dressed in a business suit, taking a leisurely walk in the shade.

Except for July and August and a few days in September, Toronto's temperatures are too low for a comfortable leisurely stroll. During most of the year, pedestrians in business clothing are comfortable only in direct sunlight. Lines below the lower edge of the comfort zone indicate how much sunlight they need. For example, to compensate for midday temperatures of 50°F (10°C) in April, the equivalent of 350 watts per square meter of radiation is needed. Direct sunlight produces such amounts when the sun rises high enough above the horizon, as it does at midday in April and September in Toronto. On July and August days when midday temperatures rise above 77°F (25°C) and the humidity measures above 55 percent, people in Toronto seek shade and a light breeze. A breeze of 0.5 meters per second, as shown above the comfort zone on the chart, compensates for the heat and humidity.

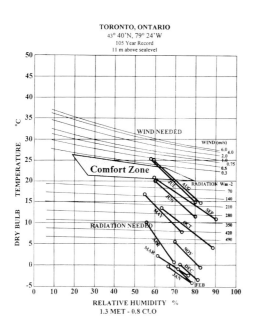

TORONTO, ONTARIO
43° 40'N, 79° 24'W
105 Year Record
11 m above sealevel

RELATIVE HUMIDITY %
1.3 MET - 0.8 CLO

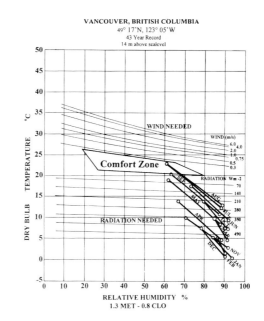

VANCOUVER, BRITISH COLUMBIA
49° 17'N, 123° 05'W
43 Year Record
14 m above sealevel

RELATIVE HUMIDITY %
1.3 MET - 0.8 CLO

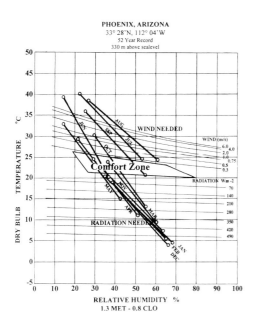

PHOENIX, ARIZONA
33° 28'N, 112° 04'W
52 Year Record
330 m above sealevel

RELATIVE HUMIDITY %
1.3 MET - 0.8 CLO

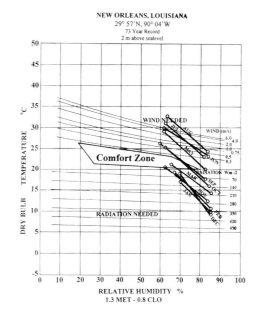

NEW ORLEANS, LOUISIANA
29° 57'N, 90° 04'W
73 Year Record
2 m above sealevel

RELATIVE HUMIDITY %
1.3 MET - 0.8 CLO

Source: Edward Arens, Dept. of Architecture, U.C. Berkeley

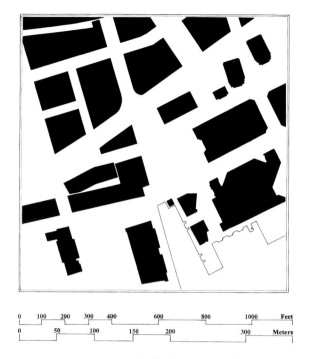

0 | 100 | 200 | 300 | 400 | 600 | 800 | 1000 | **Feet**

0 | 50 | 100 | 150 | 200 | 300 | **Meters**

Existing (1990) and proposed building footprints, lakefront.

of buildings on wind conditions at street level and evaluated pedestrian comfort in relation to sun and wind conditions. Rather than focus on individual buildings, members of the laboratory team looked at the cumulative effects of area-wide development, comparing existing conditions with those of development permissible under existing Toronto planning controls as well as under controls reflecting the laboratory's recommendations.

The challenges Canadians face are greater than those faced by populations in cities of comparable latitude in Europe and Asia. Toronto, located at 43 degrees 40 minutes north latitude (the same position on the globe as the Cantabrian coast of Spain; Marseilles, France; and Florence, Italy), has a six-month winter, from November to April, when the average daily maximum temperature hovers around 35.5°F (4.5°C). During May and June the weather is generally fine, with average daily maximum temperatures around 68°F (20°C). Pedestrians can expect comfortable conditions if it is sunny. In July and August, when the average maximum daily temperature rises above 85°F (29°C) and the humidity measures above 55 percent on most days, people in Toronto seek shade and light breezes to stay cool. They find such conditions in the parks or on the shore of Lake Ontario. Fall is world famous in Canada, but short.

The effect of buildings on climate conditions was first noticed when in the late sixties the first stage of the Toronto Dominion Center, now called the Downtown Center, neared completion. The buildings, designed by Mies van der Rohe and modeled after the Seagram Building in New York, were the first in Toronto's financial district to give up an orientation to the street. They stood on corporately owned plazas open on all sides, where the towers created a harsh microclimate. On windy days pedestrians had to brace themselves against the wind, whose force the towers exacerbated.

With the Toronto Downtown Center came the underground mall, essentially a suburban shopping mall, connected to the subway system. This allowed nearly every downtown building to be reached through an underground network of tunnels and passages, giving access to shops, restaurants, and the city's clean and efficient subway system. Some office workers can leave home, arrive downtown by train, and walk underground through a well-lit, heated shopping mall right into the underground lobby of a high-rise building without ever setting foot on a sidewalk exposed to sky. The windchill factor reported on the radio is rarely experienced firsthand; the insulated clothing remains in the trunk of the car.

Cafés serve lunch underground. After the evening rush hour, the underground stores start to close, and sections of tunnel are locked until the next workday. The population of office workers appears to be well served by the underground network. Its convenience might help explain why 61 percent of Torontonians take public transport to work, a percentage second in North America only to that of Manhattan.[8] The convenience comes at a price, however. Much of the street life has disappeared from Toronto's downtown streets.

In 1990 planners were asked to design an extension of the business district in a former railroad yard between downtown and Lake Ontario. Doubtful about lining the new streets with buildings that would only drive Torontonians underground, they proposed that streets could function as an important pedestrian link between the existing downtown core and the lakefront. The planners envisioned a concentration of housing immediately east of downtown, with stores along streets that would entice people to walk to work downtown. In a third area, a cluster of office towers that had sprung up near the intersection of the two subway lines would soon encroach on a low-rise neighborhood and a colorful historic district with evening entertainment. Maps of these three areas show differently scaled urban form; as a consequence of these differences, local climate conditions also vary. Streets lined with small four-story buildings are more comfortable than streets with tall buildings. Large models of the three areas were constructed in the laboratory for wind tunnel studies and shadow analysis.

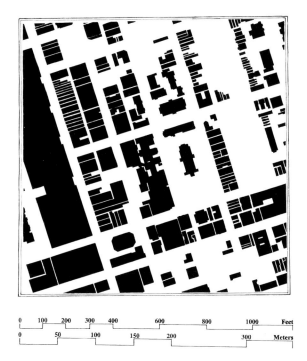

Existing (1990) building footprints, east downtown.

0 | 100 | 200 | 300 | 400 | | 600 | | 800 | | 1000 | Feet
0 | | 50 | | 100 | | 150 | | 200 | | 300 | Meters

Existing (1990) building footprints, midtown and Yorkville area.

The wind tunnel studies confirmed what had been measured in other cities. Streets 66 feet wide lined by buildings up to four stories high produce shelter. Winds on such a street have from 25 to 50 percent the strength of winds in the open countryside. For example, on Yorkville Avenue near the intersection of Bel Air Street in Toronto's Yorkville district, the average wind velocity is one-quarter to one-half that of the wind at the weather station in the open countryside outside of the city; that holds for all wind directions. The rows of buildings along this street rarely exceed four stories.

Two blocks east of this intersection, near Bloor and Yonge Streets, wind velocities are from 94 to 150 percent stronger than those at the weather station. On this corner, winds from the northwest, accelerating between high-rise towers, are deflected downward toward the sidewalks on Bloor Street, chilling pedestrians as well as exerting force on them. Along this section of the Bloor Street sidewalk, a modest wind of 8 mph—as measured at the weather station—is accelerated to 12 mph, a speed that drives rain laterally, raises dust and paper, and disturbs people's hair. If the wind at the weather station exceeds 20 mph, as it does during the cold season, pedestrians on the street here have difficulty walking because an average wind of 30 mph includes gusts in excess of 44 mph, a wind-speed criterion commonly considered unsafe.[9]

Although standards for wind protection are still new in North American cities, models exist for developing them.[10] If they were applied consistently, they would change the form of cities so that high buildings would rise less abruptly. In general, building heights would gradually increase from neighborhoods to city center. In the aggregate, the contour of buildings downtown would resemble that of a hill, as in San Francisco, with the highest structures in the center. Where height zones abut, the greatest height allowable would be less than half that of the zone where greater building heights are permitted.

These desiderata grew out of the wind tunnel experiments done at the Environmental Simulation

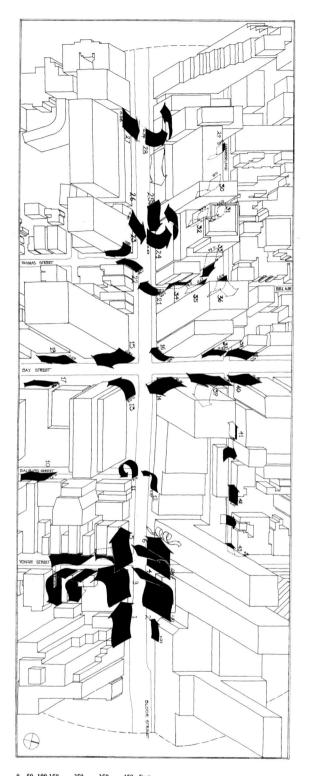

Wind velocities along Bloor Street, existing conditions.

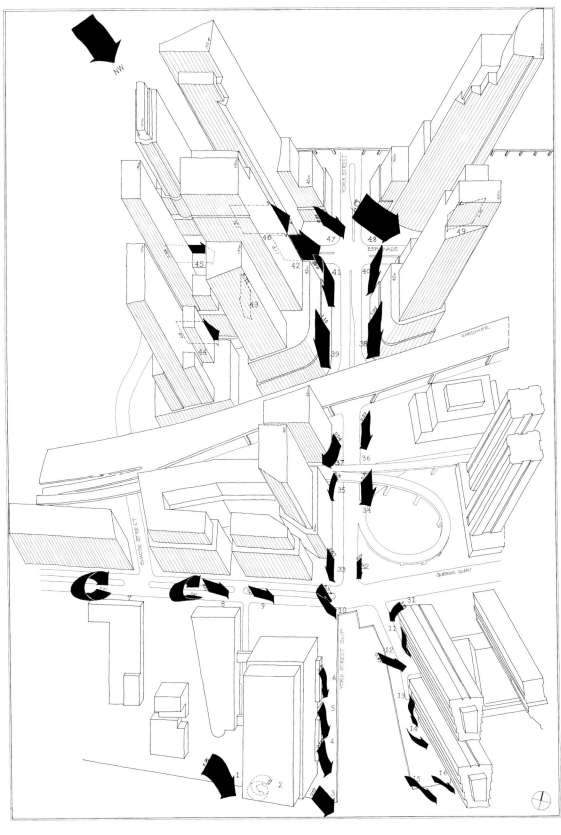

Laboratory for San Francisco and New York City and were confirmed in the testing of the three Toronto areas. They are useful to city designers. But few opportunities exist to build a compact downtown of high-rise buildings on empty land. In most cities tall buildings are scattered among lower buildings.

Wind, sun, humidity, and temperature at any particular sidewalk location can be predicted from weather records, from calculations of the shade produced by buildings at specific times, and from wind tunnel measurements. To relate such a prediction to human comfort requires that people's activity level and their clothing be taken into account as well as the time they are likely to spend outdoors. With these data, comfort probabilities can be calculated, using a computer model of the human body's thermal response to the environment, which predicts comfort/discomfort for any given hour.[11] Such a computation would indicate, for example, the thermal comfort of a person in a business suit strolling along the sidewalk on Yorkville Avenue near Bel Air Street on a sunny spring day at lunchtime. With air temperature at 63°F (17°C) at the local weather station, humidity a moderate 55 percent, and winds from the west at 20 mph, sidewalk wind tunnel measurements show a wind speed of 8 mph, or 40 percent of the 20 mph measured at the weather station. A person walking in a business suit would be comfortable.

The same pedestrian on a stretch of sidewalk with two high-rise towers instead of a row of four-story buildings would be in the shade; and wind tunnel measurements indicate that the two towers would accelerate the northwest wind to 22 mph. If temperature, humidity, activity level, and clothing stay the same, the pedestrian would be chilled, and even an additional layer of clothing would not be enough for comfort. This computation, repeated for all lunchtimes during each season, yields the percentage of time when pedestrians are likely to be comfortable or uncomfortable.

The methods used, in combination, to study the effect of buildings on Toronto's climate included

Opposite: Wind velocities in the lakefront area under potential development.

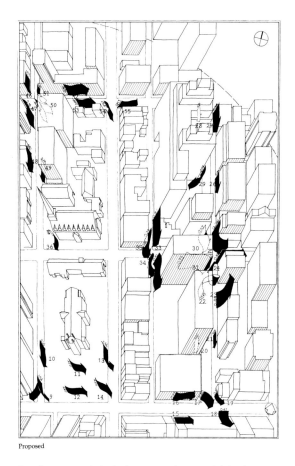

Proposed

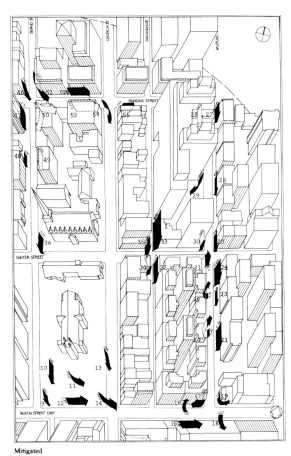

Mitigated

East downtown, wind velocity maps, under potential development (*left*) and mitigated development (*right*).

modeling existing and potential development for wind tunnel experiments and mathematical modeling of the human body's thermoregulatory system. An important step in the research was to prepare seasonal maps that noted the exact location where wind and comfort measurements had been taken. The research team analyzed these maps and then changed the model to show potential development under existing planning controls on selected sites. Measurements were repeated at identical locations on the model and analyzed. The team then modeled a set of future buildings with setbacks above street facades to reduce sidewalk wind velocities and to permit sunlight into streets and open spaces. They tested the reconfigured buildings in the wind tunnel, modeled human comfort conditions, mapped the new results, and compared existing conditions with the two alternative futures. The maps made it possible to analyze all comfort variables more closely and allowed the team to determine which of the variables had the dominant influence on comfort.

Winter sunlight, for example, is beneficial but does not produce sufficient warmth for pedestrian comfort; even sunny sidewalks need protection from strong winds. Such sheltered sidewalks are normally comfortable even in winter for an energetic pedestrian in warm clothing. In spring and fall, strolling or sitting on a bench outdoors is comfortable only in direct sunlight, which is clearly the dominant variable in Toronto.

"Not an intellectual bombshell," concluded William Whyte in his film *The Social Life of Small Urban Spaces*, after studying the effect of climate and other variables on the outdoor behavior of people in midtown Manhattan. Although people in Toronto, if asked, could have given the information obtained by laborious modeling and mapping, that work has a distinct advantage. It enables the laboratory team to predict how new buildings, individually and cumulatively, would change microclimate conditions. A politician voting on master plan revisions with higher or lower height limits, more or less floor space, could understand the implica-

tions for climate conditions. The models and the maps have become a design tool for downtown Toronto.

Toronto can have comfortable streets year-round. Many streets in the inner city are comfortable, while streets in the financial district are rarely so. High-rise buildings proposed for the former railroad yards contain larger floor plates than the Toronto Downtown Center. In both renderings and models, the proposed buildings evoke such older high-rises as those on a section of King Street at the Imperial Bank of Commerce, built in the 1920s. In fact, though, the buildings proposed for the former railroad yards are much taller and bulkier.

Modeling has shown that to keep the streets of this area comfortable, the total floor area for each building should not be fifteen times the lot area, but rather ten times—and it should never exceed twelve times the lot area. Such a reduction in building bulk would make possible the design of buildings that would not create strong winds on sidewalks. Given the large-size city blocks, moreover, towers could be shaped to allow for three hours of sunlight at midday from March to September on at least one sidewalk of all streets between downtown and the lakefront. ■

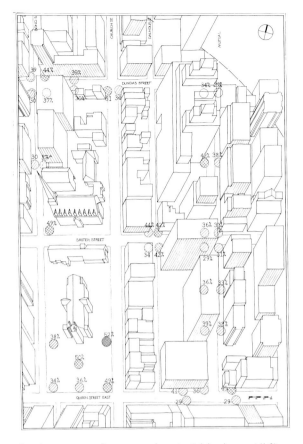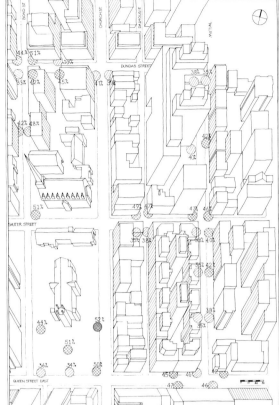

East downtown, comfort maps, under potential development (*left*)
and mitigated development (*right*). The hatching inside the circles
indicates duration of comfort in percentage of time on a typical
spring day. The darker the hatching, the greater the duration of
comfort.

The modeling in the Environmental Simulation Laboratory has helped to establish height limits and bulk controls for buildings.[12] The team recommended that allowable heights for new construction be set to produce three, five, or seven hours of sunlight daily from March to September. The three-hour period was considered the minimum for midday comfort on commercial streets in central Toronto. Elsewhere downtown the five-hour time window was proposed for all major pedestrian connectors, shopping streets, and historic or tourist areas. Finally, seven hours of sunlight were proposed for all residential streets on the edge of downtown. All three windows of time were centered on noon, September 21. For example, a building on a north–south street 66 feet wide would have a street facade 90 feet high; above that height, the upper floors would be set back along a 60-degree plane. Along streets 100 feet wide, the street facade would rise to 124 feet.

Such dimensions are abstract even when shown in diagrams. Before planning commissioners, council members, and senior city planners were ready to advocate changes to height limits publicly, they had to see "visual evidence" of the proposed changes. Computer modeling techniques were used to combine views of models used in the wind tunnel experiment with views depicting existing street conditions. The first showing of the simulated street views caused quite a stir. Few had been able to imagine what it would be like to stand on one of the streets proposed for the former railroad yards and look at development permitted under recently negotiated planning controls. Upon seeing the simulation, the planners hastily computed the floor area ratios shown and checked building heights. What the laboratory team had produced was accurate.

Simulations of the northern section of downtown Toronto showed a large parcel of land at the intersection of two major streets. Here a building with a bulk eight times the lot area was shaped in two different ways: under the existing planning controls and under mitigated controls. Generally,

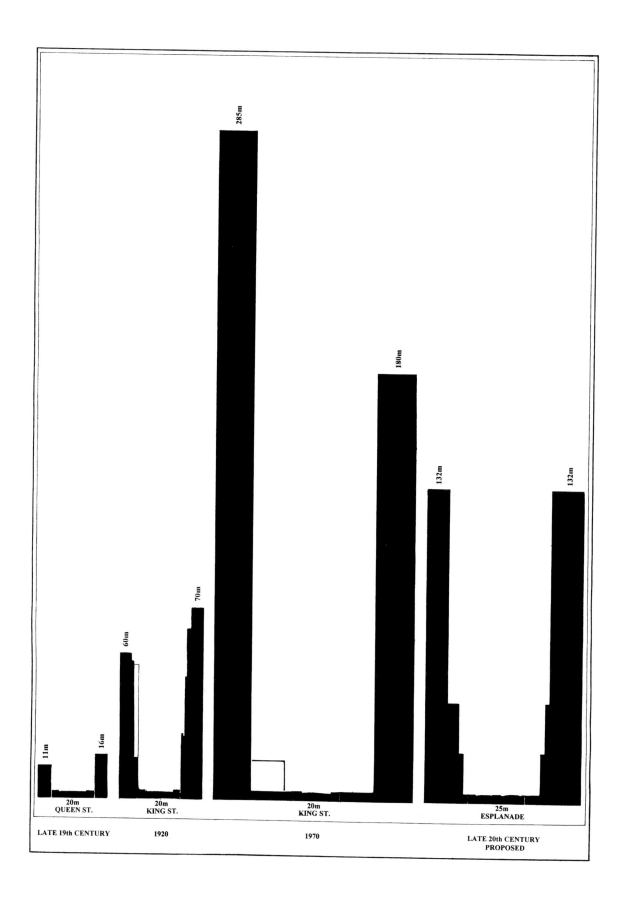

buildings designed to mitigate—that is, to shelter sidewalks from wind and to preserve sunlight—would have a somewhat higher streetwall and a lower tower height. As a result, the allowable floor area ratios in this area could be reached on large parcels of land but not on small lots.

After studying the analysis, Toronto planners recommended revising the building height limits and bulk controls. Districts in Toronto allowing buildings up to 93 feet high were generally less affected by these recommendations than districts where higher structures were permitted. Likewise, districts with an allowable building bulk of four to six times the lot area were less affected than districts with higher floor area ratios.

The research was completed in December 1990. Toronto's city council held hearings on the recommendations, combined with hearings on various other aspects of a new plan for the center city area. In the spring of 1993, in voting to amend the general plan, the council adopted portions of the recommendation, omitting height limits and bulk controls in the railroad yard near Lake Ontario and on many streets east and north of the financial district, but implementing them along all main streets leading from the city's core to the neighborhoods. The council also adopted wind protection standards and wind tunnel testing consistent with the laboratory's recommendations for all downtown Toronto locations. ■

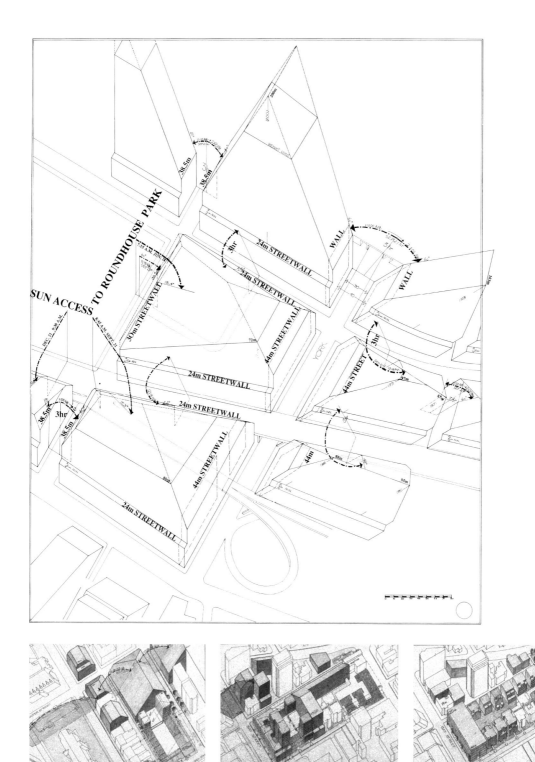

Comfort controls and allowable building height envelopes. *Top of page:* lakefront area; *above, from left:* east downtown, midtown zoning envelope, and midtown potential building configuration.

Visitors to Toronto are impressed by the city's many beautiful neighborhoods. Mature trees on neighborhood streets create a "roof" that improves the microclimate, especially in summer. The same effect could be achieved along downtown streets.[13] Sun access controls would provide direct sunlight in spring and fall, when sunlight is needed for comfort and when trees lack foliage. In summer Torontorians could walk in sun or shade, depending on weather conditions. On wide sidewalks, like those along University Avenue, double rows of trees could be planted. Walking and sitting under rows of majestic maple trees would be comfortable even on hot, humid days, and the heat exchange between shaded and sunny areas would create light breezes.

Arcades paralleling sidewalks along the new commercial streets in the former railroad yards could shelter pedestrians from snow and rain and provide an alternative to the extension of underground walkways. The sidewalks could be wide enough to accommodate pedestrians who prefer sunlight, and the arcades would be attractive places for outdoor restaurants. High-density residential buildings in the railroad yard and along the lakefront, office towers, the city's largest sports facility, and the main commuter rail terminal—all these would bring great numbers of pedestrians to the sidewalks near the lakefront. It could be an opportunity for a city design with streets for all seasons.

The effort to determine physical dimensions for cities is based on a principle of urban form: cities provide shelter so that economic, cultural, and social activities, public and private, can be conducted. The work in Toronto helped define how high and large buildings could be built without adversely affecting the climate at street level. Authorities in Toronto, as in other cities, resisted rules that might threaten the city's economic well-being. But commissioners and council members approving higher and bulkier structures would now understand how these might make streets less comfortable. They would also understand that the cost for Toronto's tunnel network (or other northern

Visual simulations of the former railroad yard area. *From top of page*: existing (1990) conditions; under potential development; under mitigated development.

Visual simulations of Bloor and Yonge Streets. *From top of page*:
existing (1990) conditions; under potential development; under
mitigated development.

cities' skywalks) would be prohibitive and could be justified only for the most heavily traveled connections. Council members, who can ultimately limit the development of private property, recognized the importance of comfort controls because these were articulated in the systematic terminology city authorities are accustomed to using in discussions of economic forecasts based on statistical inference.

In Toronto, a city where development projects have been negotiated one by one, few planners remember the rationale for any limit on building heights and density; a rationale drawn from the city's natural climate, however, could offer the foundation for a coherent public view of what downtown Toronto should be like.

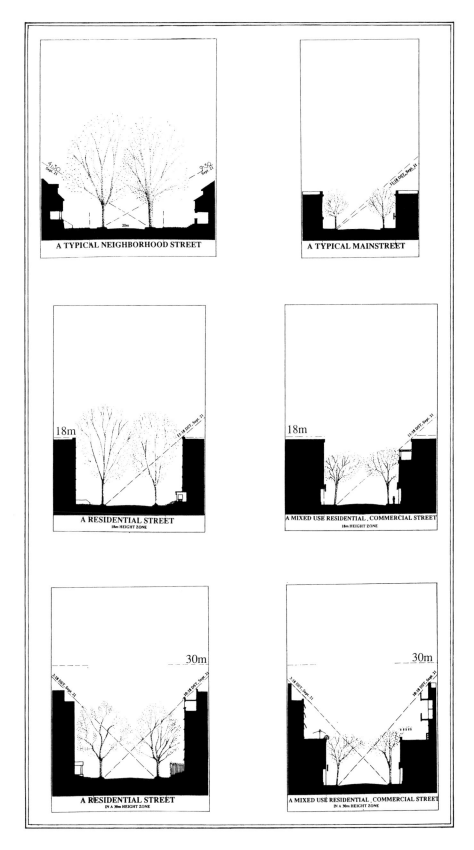

Typical street sections in height zones of 90 feet (30 meters) and less.

Within the image:

A TYPICAL NEIGHBORHOOD STREET

A TYPICAL MAINSTREET

A RESIDENTIAL STREET
18m HEIGHT ZONE

A MIXED USE RESIDENTIAL , COMMERCIAL STREET
18m HEIGHT ZONE

A RESIDENTIAL STREET
IN A 30m HEIGHT ZONE

A MIXED USE RESIDENTIAL , COMMERCIAL STREET
IN A 30m HEIGHT ZONE

PART THREE

Reality and Realism

Of course, the problem is as old as the shadows on Plato's cave. It is incessantly proposed anew because we are never at ease with any definition of reality and its derivated rules.

Carlos Fuentes, "Velasquez, Plato's Cave, and Bette Davis"

In the fall of 1786 Johann Wolfgang von Goethe took a leave from his administrative duties at the court in Weimar and traveled to Italy, seeking inspiration in the great works of antiquity. Although he knew the literary tradition, he had been unable to integrate it with firsthand experience. Andrea Palladio had journeyed through Italy and Provence two hundred and fifty years earlier for similar reasons. During his journey Palladio prepared the drawings for the *Quattro libri*. Goethe and Palladio believed that if they could see ancient architecture, they would understand the "power and moral force" of ancient Rome.[1]

On arriving in Vicenza, Goethe sought out the buildings of Andrea Palladio, which he found without difficulty. He especially admired the Teatro Olimpico and the Villa Rotunda. Goethe obtained "a little book with copperplates [of Palladian drawings] produced by someone with an expert knowledge of art," which he studied carefully. "You have to see Palladio's buildings with your own eyes to realize how good they are. No reproduction of Palladio's designs gives an adequate idea of the harmony of their dimensions: they must be seen in their actual perspective."[2] Still in Vicenza, Goethe purchased from a local architect named Scamozzi another book on Palladio that showed drawings of the house Palladio built for himself. Again Goethe commented on the difference between plan and reality: "There is far more to it than one would imagine from a picture."[3] In Padua he found and purchased an English edition of Palladio's *Quattro libri*, with copperplate engravings. Eager to see Palladio's church, Il Redentore, Goethe traveled to Venice, equipped with guidebooks and drawings of Palladio's work.

After an extended visit, he went to Assisi, hoping to find the Temple of Minerva, a structure dating to the time of Augustus that Palladio had greatly prized. Reputedly well preserved, the structure had been used as the Church of the Madonna della Minerva since early Christian times. When he found it, Goethe wrote, "Lo and behold! There it stood, the first complete classical monument I have seen. A modest temple, just right for such a small town, yet so perfect in design that it would be an ornament anywhere."[4]

Despite the awe with which he described the classical architecture of the temple, Goethe noted in comparing the temple to Palladio's representation "how little accepted tradition is to be trusted. Palladio, on whom I had relied implicitly, made a sketch of this temple, but he cannot have seen it personally for he puts real pedestals on the ground which give the columns a disproportionate height and make the whole a Palmyra-like monstrosity instead of the great loveliness of the real thing."[5]

Today, a visitor to Assisi standing in front of the Minerva temple would agree with Goethe. Its dimensions and proportions as Palladio drew them look different from the reality. Excavation has confirmed that the ground level immediately in front of the temple is unchanged from Roman times, and no records exist to explain Palladio's alterations to the gable of the temple. Indeed, scholars since the early nineteenth century, most recently the historian Heinz Spielmann,[6] have confirmed Goethe's observations. Spielmann found that virtually none of the dimensions of Palladio's ground plan and elevation matches the reality. For example, the ratio of the height of the gable triangle to the length of the gable above the architrave is 1:3 in reality but 1:4 in Palladio's drawing. Moreover, although Palladio's drawing shows the height of the temple equal to its width, in reality the temple's facade is 1.5 times wider than it is high. The peristyle, the column dimensions, and other facade details are differently scaled, so that the imposing building Palladio drew has none of the "great loveliness" Goethe saw.

Spielmann, after comparing other buildings that Palladio drew with the remaining fragments, characterizes Palladio's work as a "platonic projection of what he intended to find in the architecture of Roman antiquity."[7] Rather than replicate classical models, Palladio used his knowledge to develop an ideal system of construction, the first universal and

A pedestrian approach to the Temple of Minerva from the south side.

consistent theory of building form in modern times. But he never explained that he had re-created the Minerva temple according to his own system. Thus Goethe, looking, if not for reality then for at least a true representation of what classical Roman architecture from the time of Augustus was like, was inevitably disappointed.

Goethe encountered a common problem: the creator of an architectural image intentionally distorts it for reasons that are not always apparent. As the critic Charles Jencks has written: "The contradictions between the statements and buildings of architects has reached impressive proportions. In a way, this situation is comic. The contradiction has been apparent to everyone except the architect. In a way it is pathetic because the architects don't seem interested in reducing the credibility gap."[8]

That Palladio's imagination had embellished the temple's proportions would also have been my conclusion, had I not viewed the site with my own eyes. Depending on the viewpoint, Palladio's proportions have a basis in reality. Goethe, like Palladio (and like visitors today), approached the Minerva temple from either the southeast or the southwest. Since Roman times the temple has been located on the town square. Because Assisi sits high on a steep slope, the square is long and narrow, with the two roads leading to it cut like ramps that reach the square on its two narrow sides. If Palladio and Goethe had entered the square from the southwest, the temple would have come suddenly into view diagonally across the square at an oblique

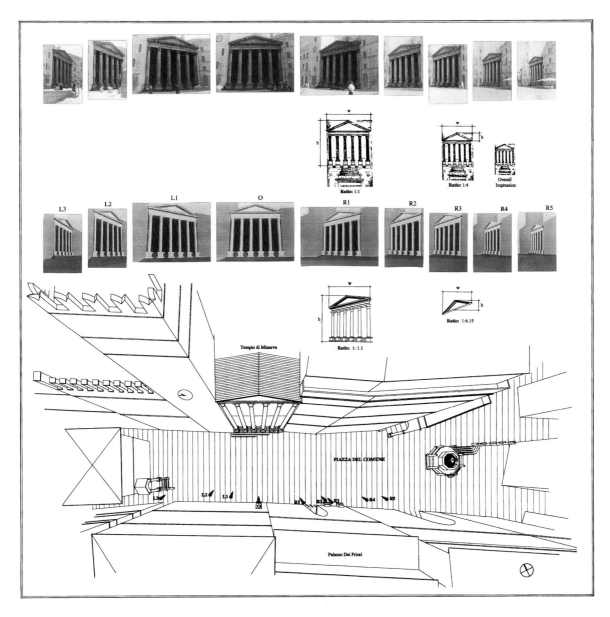

Plan view of the main square of Assisi, Piazza del Comune.

Steps of the Temple of Minerva.

angle. Had they approached the temple from the southeast, they would have seen it sooner, but still on the diagonal. In any case, the visitor who sees the temple for the first time has to agree with Goethe that it is "just right for such a small town, yet so perfect in design that it would be an ornament anywhere."

Knowing about Goethe's response to Palladio's drawing, I began to question his judgment. The proportions of the temple are relative to the location in the square from which the temple is viewed. The entire temple is never seen in an axial view, from the front, as Palladio drew it (and in the way he used classic proportioning for the design of his villas). To obtain that axial view, directly opposite the facade, I had to step into the doorway of a small café, but even then I was too close to see the entire facade in one glance. The square is too narrow. Depending on my position on the square, I perceived the temple's proportions differently. There are in fact locations in the square from which the temple height and width appear even and from which the ratio of height to width of the gable triangle is 1:4, exactly as Palladio drew it. From another point close to the temple, the height of the two center columns relative to their distance measures exactly as Palladio drew it. Visitors who approach the temple more closely lose the sense of the whole facade. The temple becomes too large; because of its apparent size, the proportion of parts to the whole can no longer be judged.

A computer model of Assisi's square and temple puts to rest the issue Goethe raised about Palladio: the architect drew the temple's Roman design with great sophistication when he adapted it to demonstrate his new theory of good building form. But there is no evidence, no proof, that Palladio used model studies or perspective drawings to manipulate the dimensions of the Minerva temple for his purposes. However abstract and diagrammatic the facade he drew, Palladio may well have known the temple's dimensions and how they would be experienced. The example from Assisi is a fitting introduction to a discussion of reality and realism because the relationship between the two is characterized by limitations and contradictions. To think about that relationship is to think about the workings of the human mind. Although historians associate Palladio's mind with a rational approach to design, he was also apparently an empiricist.

If Palladio was right, so was Goethe. The steps between the column pedestals in Assisi gracefully connect the temple to the ground, and they are visually important, however little use Palladio had for them in his "new" order.

CHAPTER SEVEN

Representing the Experience of Places

The visual representations I have been describing re-create constructed and natural forms so that images can be experienced as substitutes for the real world—as it is and as it might be. The goal is to create images that permit observers to report as they would on the same situation in the real world. But the experience of a place can be represented only in part—and the representation itself can easily emphasize the distance between design and reality. Ideally, decisions about places should be made where construction is proposed; but in actuality decisions about the design of large-scale projects or plans are generally made far from the site of construction: in the studio of the design team, the meeting rooms of clients or government and financial institutions, and during hearings held in courtroom-type settings where public votes are cast on a design or plan.

This chapter discusses some of the technical limits to good visual representation, looking in particular at the following issues: correct viewing distance of images; representation of physical dimensions in space; representation of colors, shapes, and textures; and representation of movement. The first two topics are best explained with the help of Euclidian geometry; the third and fourth apply the laws of physics to the realm of art.

Viewing Images

Brunelleschi's experiment with the painting of the Baptistery in Florence suggests that he understood how to convey a match between image and reality by controlling the distance of the mirror from the painting. (See Chapter 1.) Had he held the mirror further away, a person looking through the hole on the back of the painting would have judged the space between the Baptistery and the cathedral greater in the painting than in reality. Holding the mirror too close would create the opposite impression: the Baptistery would have appeared larger than in reality, and the space before it narrower than in reality. The overall size of the picture and the viewing angle determined where Brunelleschi held the mirror. It is commonly understood that optical lenses distort dimensions of objects in an image; the wider the viewing angle, the greater the apparent distortion. Similarly, the representation of the three-dimensional world on a two-dimensional surface, using Brunelleschi's convention of linear perspective, also results in distortion, whether on a television screen or a computer monitor.

If a 35 mm still camera equipped with an adjustable zoom lens is focused on an object so that what is visible through the viewfinder is identical in size and distance to what is seen by the human eye, the ring on the adjustable lens will register a focal length of between 62 and 65 mm. The viewing angle at that focal length measures between 27 and 30 degrees, horizontally. This narrow field of view corresponds to that of the eye focusing on an object. If the head is kept still while the eyes move over a scene, in reality, the field of view is wider, similar to what a 35 mm focal length would capture. When the zoom lens is set to this focal length, the scene in the viewfinder appears further away and smaller than it is in reality. If exposures are taken at both the closer and the longer focal length and prints of equal size are produced, anyone remembering the actual scene will conclude that each picture must be viewed from a proper distance, nearer for the print taken at closer focal length (35 mm) and further away for the print taken with

Tables for determining the field of view of various camera formats and for determining correct viewing distances. These tables were created by Kevin Gilson, Environmental Simulation Laboratory, University of California at Berkeley.

Field of View (measured horizontally, H, and vertically, V, in degrees)

Lens Focal Length in mm	1/2" Video		2/3" Video		16 mm		35 mm		60 mm
	H	V	H	V	H	V	H	V	H/V
12	37	28	57	45	45	35	113	90	136
15	30	23	47	37	37	28	100	77	127
20	23	17	36	28	28	21	84	62	113
25	18	14	29	23	23	17	72	51	100
28	16	12	26	20	20	15	65	46	94
35	13	10	21	16	16	12	54	38	81
44	10	8	17	13	13	10	44	31	69
50	9	7	15	11	11	9	40	27	62
60	8	6	12	10	10	7	33	23	53
70	7	5	11	8	8	6	29	19	46
80	6	4	9	7	7	5	25	17	41
100	5	3	7	6	6	4	20	14	33
150	3	2	5	4	4	3	14	9	23
200	2	2	4	3	3	2	10	7	17

Viewing Distance of Images (for images recorded with a 35 mm camera format, measured in inches and centimeters)

Image Width		20 mm		28 mm		35 mm		50 mm		65 mm		80 mm		100 mm	
1	2.54	0.56	1.40	0.78	1.98	0.97	2.46	1.39	3.53	1.81	4.59	2.22	5.60	2.78	7.06
5	12.70	3	7.62	4	10.16	5	12.70	7	17.78	9	22.86	11	27.94	14	35.56
6	15.24	3	7.62	5	12.70	6	15.24	8	20.32	11	27.94	13	33.02	17	43.18
8	20.32	4	10.16	6	15.24	8	20.32	11	27.94	14	35.56	18	45.72	22	55.88
10	25.40	6	15.24	8	20.32	10	25.40	14	35.56	18	45.72	22	55.88	28	71.12
14	35.56	8	20.32	11	27.94	14	35.56	19	48.26	25	63.50	31	78.74	39	99.06
18	45.72	10	25.40	14	35.56	18	45.72	25	63.50	33	83.82	40	101.60	50	127.00
24	60.96	13	33.02	19	48.26	23	58.42	33	83.82	43	109.22	53	134.62	67	170.18
36	91.44	20	50.80	28	71.12	35	88.90	50	127.00	65	165.10	80	203.20	100	254.00
50	127.00	28	71.12	39	99.06	49	124.46	69	175.26	90	228.60	111	281.94	139	353.06
100	254.00	56	142.24	78	198.12	97	246.38	139	353.06	181	459.74	222	563.88	278	706.12

With Future Development

Photo of the proposed 1,946-foot Television City Tower viewed from a distance of 1,300 feet with a line indicating the upper limit of normal vision.

Right: Six views of the proposed Television City Tower from a playground at the Amsterdam Housing Project, a distance of 1,300 feet, panning upward from a horizontal viewing axis in 15-degree increments.

the longer focal length (65 mm). In each case the prints must be viewed so that the "angle subtended at the eye is equal to the angle subtended at the lens by the object."[1]

For example, a print enlarged to 10 inches horizontally, from a 34 mm negative exposed by a lens adjusted to a focal length of 35 mm, has to be viewed from a distance of 10 inches. The same size print taken with a focal length of 65 mm would have to be viewed from a distance of 18 inches. From a distance of 10 inches, the first print cannot be taken in at a glance. If the viewer moves the print further away to see the entire scene, the perspective is distorted. If the print is viewed from a distance of 10 inches, the eyes wander across the scene and upward to take in the top of the print. This eye movement is identical to that of a person standing where the picture was taken. The upward glance is important to give a sense of the object's dimensions relative to the viewer.

The notion of a correct viewing distance in linear perspective is troublesome because such a distance is not observed—indeed, cannot be observed—in practice, for example, in viewing television and computer screens.[2] Thus judgments about dimensions and the scale of objects can be erroneous, as an experiment demonstrated. At the Berkeley simulation laboratory, a scale model was made of the 1,946-foot Television City Tower proposed for Manhattan's Upper West Side and buildings in the surrounding neighborhoods and Central Park, showing how the new structure's height would exceed that of everything around it. The same building in electronically composed photographs of the model appeared much lower.

Professional photographers know that they can achieve a realistic perspective when they include in their images a continuous set of reference points, ranging from foreground to middle ground to background. But tall buildings lack such reference points: only sky surrounds them. In photographs of the proposed tower the viewing distance of observers was carefully controlled. Large prints made for a public exhibit were mounted at eye level, and a red

line was taped horizontally over each view, as a reminder that such a tall building cannot be taken in without an upward movement of the eyes and sometimes the head. To see the building from the middle of Central Park, one mile away, required a 10-degree tilt of the head. To see it from a playground near the foot of the structure required a 75-degree tilt. Without the line indicating the upper limit of vision, these pictures would have created a misleading impression.

The application of the red line also gives credence to the writings of the aesthetic theorist Hans Maertens, who in 1877 "promulgated a series of rules about the proper size of a building or monument in relation to its surroundings."[3] Maertens developed tables, based on the experiments of the physicist Hermann Helmholtz, indicating how a "building should be placed" in order to be seen from a distance equal to the height of the object above eye level. According to Maertens, a 45-degree angle would be best to see the details, a 27-degree angle best to appreciate the entire building, and an 18-degree angle best to take in the setting in which the building is located.

The Castle in Central Park, about a mile from the proposed Television City Tower, would have provided a good 27-degree view of the building. From the terrace of the Boathouse Restaurant, a distance of 6,175 feet (with the top of the tower 18 degrees above the horizon), the tower no longer dominates the view, and the eye takes in the setting. A viewer is out of the "visual reach" of this single structure; the trees hold the eye.

View from the Castle in Central Park, 4,525 feet from the proposed Television City Tower.

View from the terrace of the Boathouse Restaurant, 6,175 feet from the proposed Television City Tower.

REPRESENTING PHYSICAL DIMENSIONS
IN SPACE

Brunelleschi's experiment with linear perspective marked a turning point in visual representation because his perspective defined the location of objects in space; but just how were the objects defined? Historians have not conclusively answered this question. Brunelleschi, as some suggest, could simply have traced the view of the Baptistery on the surface of a mirror, positioned at the main portal of Santa Maria del Fiore. Then, after he had traced the outlines, he could have transferred the images to the wooden board he used for his painting.

Alternatively, he could have used the laws of geometry documented by Euclid to construct a perspective. He could have projected from a central point (his eye) lines dissected by planes—the picture plane and other planes: portions of facades, ground, and roof surfaces. Had he constructed the view in this way, he would have had to survey all plan dimensions and building elevations to compute the ratio between actual dimensions of objects and the reduced dimensions of these objects on the picture plane. No trace or mention of such a survey by Brunelleschi exists.

Today, in a process analogous to that of the mirror, we can trace the outlines of the structure from a photoprint or projection, or we can construct an eye-level view from the planimetric and altimetric information (plan and height dimensions) of a cartographic survey of the area around the Baptistery.

A detailed database can be developed using aerial photogrammetry and computerized modeling of the data read from such photographs: the outlines of buildings, the height of building corners and cornice line, the dimensions of roof overhangs, the measurements of recessed entrances or windows, the alignment of curbs and sidewalks, the placing of tree trunks and the extent of tree canopies—in short, everything visible to a camera mounted under a low-flying airplane. The camera taking pictures for a photogrammetric survey points downward, exposing two negatives simultaneously through two separate optics.

With the help of a computerized viewing instrument, the coordinate values of any visible point on these photo pairs can be related to reference points and recorded as files of numbers. The points are logged in sequence, describing, for example, the corners of a roof polygon, or a facade, or a sidewalk. Objects obscured by neighboring objects are generally visible on photo pairs taken during the same photo session along either the same or an adjacent flight path, or they can be added from data supplied by a detailed ground survey.

A forerunner in the development of accurate and detailed geographic information systems was the work that resulted, in 1986, in the *Atlante di Venezia*,[4] a survey of the historic center of Venice. On one day, May 25, 1982, photographs were made from an altitude of 1,000 meters along fourteen flight lines. Information from these photographs was read and digitized into points, lines, and closed polygonal figures. The data were organized into building units or vacant units. Ground surveys completed the data gathering where buildings obscured narrow walls and canals. The planimetric data were accurate to within ±10 cm. Once it had been established as a database, the spatial configuration of Venice could be shown on digital maps.

A by-product of the numerical readings of the aerial photographs is a set of full-color aerial photomaps of Venice.[5] Single tiles are visible on many roofs, as are pigeons and the individual paving stones on which they sit along the canals and the lagoon. One photograph shows Campo San Barnaba, the place where the walk described in Chapter 3 began.

One of the participants in the Venice cartography project comments that the photomaps "induce us to reflect upon the changes made over time, be they fast and sudden or slow and gradual."[6] Her next sentence, however, startles the reader: "The maps produced from the survey are not objective." Although the photomaps treat all information equally, showing important buildings with the same precision as other elements of the

Campo San Barnaba, Venice (near lower left corner), from *Atlante di Venezia*, photomap. © Marsilio.

urban fabric, this detailed treatment is a tool of power for those who promote an awareness of the past, for new works must fit in:

> But the power wishes to render itself explicit, to manifest itself through knowledge, rather than giving precedence to policies, and public works. The survey and its maps broaden the discipline of town planning, which has struggled to identify its own field of action and is split between a restrictive school, concerned with

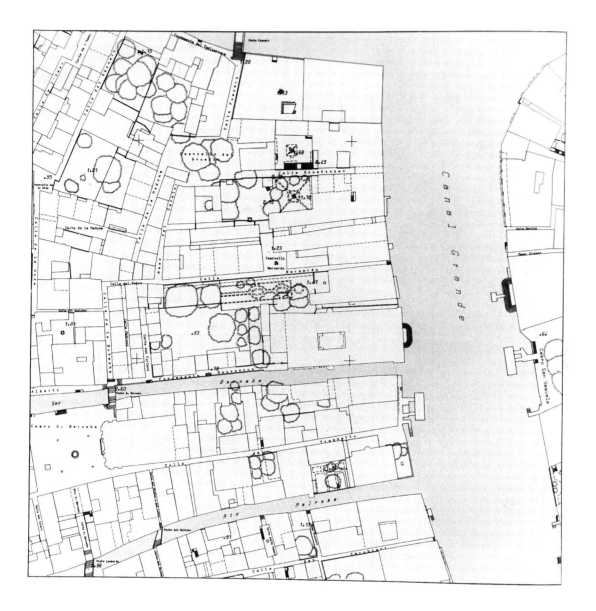

Campo San Barnaba, Venice, from *Atlante di Venezia*, Plan view.
© Marsilio.

quantitative aspects, which seeks to define the highest standards for building practice, use, and density, and the school of urban art, which conceives the city as made up of formally complete pieces.[7]

The head of planning writes in the *Atlante di Venezia* that "the new spatial urban information system does not wish to be neutral toward town planning and its way of operating in recent decades."[8] It does not seek to be neutral when it proposes that planning begin with the representation itself. The new system, updatable in almost real time, suggests and promotes "the systematic control of the whole, alongside, and no longer separate from, individual checks of the parts." The survey is overtly a tool of power because it is "both self-aware and open to verification."⁹

The new representational technique is met with professional optimism. The photomaps (and the numerical computerized information that made them possible) offer a greater capacity than previous representational techniques for dialogue with ordinary citizens, with scholars, and with the promoters of physical change. Like all representations of reality, they stimulate reflection and provide information that resonates differently for individual observers.

An aerial photo survey of San Francisco was conducted in 1986. As in the Venice survey, the downtown section was flown on one day (July 26), and data were read into files describing fourteen subareas of downtown San Francisco.¹⁰ The survey was commissioned by administrators of San Francisco's sun-and-shadow ordinance (described in Chapter 5).

The data were organized in vector files, representing buildings, and grid files for open space. The display images represented buildings as wire frames or solid objects, and open spaces as a mesh of 1-square-foot cells.¹¹ The cells became the basic unit in the account of existing and potential shadows on open spaces. San Francisco planners, like their Venetian colleagues, were enthusiastic at the prospect of an accurate, detailed, and updatable three-dimensional database for their city.

The new database has given the San Francisco planners greater power, but the proponents of change have not accepted this new power lying down. Whenever the application of the database has produced findings contrary to the interest of developers, they have challenged the accuracy of the computer modeling. In some cases, developers have commissioned their own databases. Verification and control of information have remained subjects of discussion among professional consultants, real estate developers, and city government. The database and the associated spatial urban information system are vulnerable because the cost of updating and maintaining the system has been great and funds more difficult to secure than those for the initial project. In seven years the system has outgrown the hardware and software capabilities of three different computer operating systems. Moreover, only one person in the San Francisco planning department is qualified to operate it.

The Venice survey and the work in San Francisco exemplify a larger concern for accurate geographic information systems. These systems combine digital maps and databases into graphic systems that can be shown on maps. For our purposes, however, a detailed spatial information system is only the first step in creating realistic eye-level views. True, we can now select a viewpoint and a direction anywhere in Venice or San Francisco and produce a computer-generated perspective view. This image, however, shows a highly abstract array of lines, points, or solids in space. The section that follows discusses the work required to make a perspective view a recognizable image of reality.

Details, computer model of San Francisco.

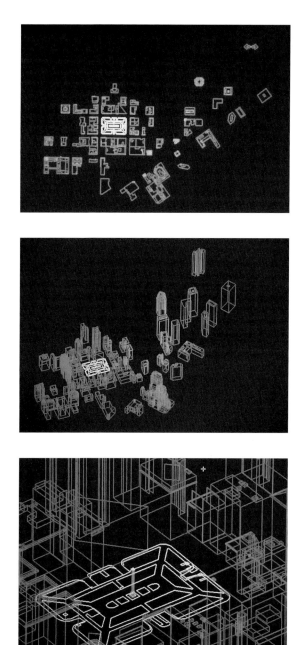

Representing Colors, Shapes, and Textures

In the five hundred years since Brunelleschi, painters have developed combinations of techniques to use in representing the three-dimensional world on a two-dimensional surface. These include color mixture, texture of application, and tonal modeling of form. The results have been five hundred years of naturalistic art.

Discoveries in the science of color and the physics of light have influenced painters throughout this period as much as scientists were influenced by the art of painting.[12] After the invention of photography, when color printing techniques were being developed, a number of scientists, including Hermann Von Helmholtz, David Brewster, and Ogden Rood, focused on observations made with colored light. "Different colors are placed side by side by lines or dots, and when viewed at such a distance that the blending is more or less accomplished by the eye of the beholder, the tints mix on the retina and produce new colors."[13] Instead of mixing colors on the palette, artists applied the strong pigments directly, so that for the first time (and in accord with Newtonian theory), they were able to paint with light.

For example, "grass in nature is not one single green but many greens with shades of yellow, blue, red, purple and brown tints. When applied in dots and viewed from a distance the modulated green resembles grass."[14] Paintings done in this manner appear to vibrate, shimmer, or glisten. Each color is at its maximum intensity but always in harmony with its neighbor, influenced by it and influencing it in turn. The art historian Martin Kemp cites Eugène Delacroix's fresco in St. Sulpice as the first picture executed in this technique.[15] Georges Seurat perfected the method in *Farm Women at Work*, painted in 1882. Seurat's novel technique involved painting interwoven brushstrokes as well as a series of small dots, dashes, and separate strokes of intense color. Mixing colors ceased to be haphazard or intuitive. The new technique provided the quantitative foundation for all coloristic effects in representations, because the dots of paint, or brushstrokes, are precise with regard to location, color, and tone; all three variables can be expressed numerically.[16]

With the invention of photography, the optical lenses that captured, on plates, mirror images of reality were called the "pencil of nature." "The discovery of the Photographic Art," wrote the English inventor William Henry Fox Talbot, "will enable us to introduce into our pictures a multitude of minute details which add to the truth and reality of the representation, but which no artist would take the trouble to copy faithfully from nature."[17] In early photographs the colors of nature were translated into monochromatic tones. The same experimental physics that inspired the painters Delacroix and Seurat became the basis for color photography.[18] As early as 1868, the French pianist Louis Ducos du Hauron applied for a patent for color processing, which formed the basis of all later methods. Instead of projecting three positive transparencies, tinted for each of the primary colors, red-green and blue-violet in register on the same surface, Ducos du Hauron suggested the use of a glass screen covered with minute colored dots or lines.

The Lumière brothers, among others, picked up Ducos du Hauron's idea and in 1907 manufactured in their Lyons factory plates coated with microscopically small grains of potato starch dyed green, red, and blue. A thin emulsion was applied. When the plate was exposed and reexposed to light, the resulting transparency gave the effect of a Seurat "pointillist" picture.

An enlarged view of a modern color computer display gives the same impression. The pixels, like the dots in a pointillist picture, can create representations in the tradition of naturalistic art. The direction and intensity of light on the colors and textures of surfaces are computed and represented. But the images produced have an artificial quality. Objects look new, untarnished, and bright.

An alternative way to represent the colors, shapes, and textures of surfaces in urban settings

Georges Seurat, *Farm Women at Work*, 1882. © The Solomon
Guggenheim Museum, New York.

View to the east from the Cathedral of Notre-Dame, Paris, before
1858, signed "Bisson frères." The Bisson brothers, Louis Auguste
Bisson, an architect for the city of Paris, and his younger brother
Auguste-Rosalie, a heraldic painter, were known in France for the
quantity and perfection of their work. Their father had established
the photographic firm Bisson Père et Fils soon after the invention of
the daguerreotype in 1839. This photograph was originally called
"Panorama de Bercy" after the large complex of wine warehouses,
known as the Entrepôt de Bercy, visible in the upper left. © Centre
Canadien d'Architecture, Montreal.

employs photography.[19] Building facades and ground planes are photographed with a special lens that produces orthogonal images. The photographer places the camera on an axis perpendicular to the facade of a building so that vertical edges in the scene register parallel to the edges of the framed view in the viewfinder. Several photographs are required to record the entire facade of long or tall buildings. The images—in color—are then scanned by a computer and converted into digital image files. (In the future this work might be done directly by digital image recorders, but for now, good professional lenses are expensive, and images recorded conventionally, in analog fashion, produce better results.)

Where necessary, several images can be assembled, side by side, to produce a single image of an entire building facade. A graphic spatial information system serves as a guide for image assembly. For example, a wire-frame volume of a building is called up from the database, and the photo-realistic texture is "mapped" onto a polygon representing the exact dimensions of a building facade. Objects that obscured the complete view of a facade when the photographs were taken—parked cars, mailboxes, and so forth—are electronically removed, and duplicated elements of the facade from the digital image file are applied where information was obscured. But the resulting image represents only a portion of the data gathering, because a view generated from what has been digitized would show buildings standing on an undifferentiated ground plane.

In urban views, significant details are generally located in the foreground. The digital image files need to include ground surface textures, trees, signs, people, cars, and much more. All this information has to be photographed, scanned, and modeled for exact placement in the computer model. The technology enforces economies: although it is possible to display eye-level views of a city at will—by freely choosing a view location, a direction, and an angle and expecting the computer to generate a complete image—some planning is required.

A computer image in the pointillist tradition.

Construction of a three-dimensional computer model of the San Francisco Embarcadero. *From top to bottom:* a plan view; a wire-frame model; a rendered model; a view of the redesigned Embarcadero roadway from the southeast; and a view of the Ferry Building from the south.

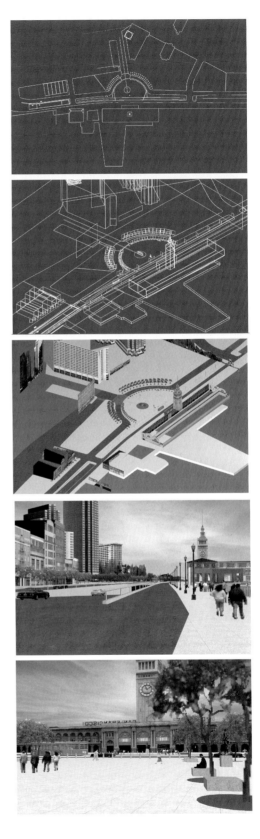

From most vantage points, only a small fraction of the entire model can be seen. In other words, only a subset of polygons and image files is potentially visible from an observer's position.[20] Some objects, moreover, appear in the distance, others close by. Those in the distance could be displayed at a lower resolution (with fewer lines or pixels); in addition, the complexity of distant building models could be reduced without changing the quality of the image. In the field of computer science, these "shortcuts" in image rendering fall under the heading of "visibility precomputations." The programmer, before rendering an image, requests from the computer an estimate of all polygons and image files visible from a single location or locations and selects for rendering only those files and polygons that are relevant for a particular view location.[21]

Because all surfaces are not visible from a given perspective, the computer model resembles a stage set showing only the buildings and surfaces visible from the chosen location. Additional polygons and rendered facades can be downloaded for other views.

Representing Motion

When an image displays motion, all objects in it are set free. The image, no longer static, draws observers into the scene, giving them a greater mastery over what is shown, because they cannot help being part of the image. As the image moves, observers take their bearings, defining their position in space. New information is revealed constantly. The light falling on surfaces changes rapidly.

Viewers of moving images make more reliable judgments about dimensions and proportions than viewers of still pictures because relative sizes are revealed as nearer objects rotate or shift in front of other objects further away.

Motion appears smooth and continuous if a set number of frames per second is displayed. For example, video technology displays images at a rate of thirty images per second. A real-time display of movement through space then requires a rapid recalculation of the changing images. But, unlike visitors to a video arcade or users of a flight training simulator, viewers of moving urban images are not interested simply in avoiding collisions as they move through space. They interact differently with the moving images. They might move slowly, like pedestrians, or more quickly, like drivers; they may stop, look about, fix on a detail, or otherwise analyze the scene. If trees line the street, they might judge the canopy the trees create or calculate the trees' spacing or height. Repeated movement through the scene gives them the chance to consider adjustments: to the pavement, the street furniture, or even the design of buildings on the street.

The viewers' ability to move through space at will in real time is less important than their ability to select from a library of objects they can add to the model in repeated viewings. They might instruct the computer to follow a script that would define the range of design solutions under investigation and the timing of their appearance on the screen or monitor. The script would determine movement sequences that represent a future experience—a stroll along a sidewalk or diagonally across a square. Other view directions can easily be added

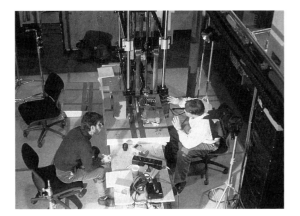

Robotics at the New York Simulation Center.

later in the analysis; but there will always be a finite number of view directions and movements.

At the time of this writing, the detailed information necessary for photo-realistic movement displays exceeds a computer's real-time rendering capability. A wire-frame display of buildings, or a display of buildings rendered as simple solid objects, can easily be brought into motion at a real-time frame rate where each frame, for example, is computed and displayed in one-thirtieth of a second. The problem emerges in adding all the necessary photo-realistic details that permit observers to judge the simulated scene as they would an actual scene. The computer animation of photo-realistic imagery remains slow—each frame of movement requires anywhere from a few seconds to several minutes of computing time. The exact time depends on the visual complexity of the scene and on the equipment used. Therefore, the process requires a recording device connected to the computer that records (on tape, film, or disc) single frames of movement.

Because foreground information in an animation changes more quickly in relation to the viewer than background information, which is more easily predicted by visibility preprocessing,[22] conventional real-world video or film recordings can be superimposed on computer-generated backgrounds, obviating the need to compute and render detailed information frame by frame. The superimposition of scenes recorded live in a studio on scenes generated by computer first began to be perfected by cinematographers for films like *Star Wars*.[23]

The techniques I have described belong to a specialized subfield of the design profession in which the work is both costly and time-consuming. Indeed, because setup time far exceeds the time available for design, designers are prey to a sense of unreality, taking for real what has been produced at high cost after many hours of work. Designers can keep the cost of representations and animation under control by doing as much of the work as possible themselves. Many graphic techniques exist that communicate the experience of places. The

drawings of the walk through Venice in Chapter 3
or photography of models such as Times Square in
Chapter 4 illustrate alternative approaches.

The advantage of using computer technology
is the ability to transform an image of a place developed in the designer's mind into a representation
that looks and feels real and can be experienced as
a substitute for reality. Although slower than the
human mind and often with too predictable a
result, computer image technology creates a record
that can be checked and verified. To be useful as
a design tool in this creation of design, the conceptual mode of conceiving places and the experiential
mode must be integrated. In that integration lies
the strength of computer image technology. The
data files storing information about a place can
be used to display both abstract and concrete
images—the subject of the next chapter.

CHAPTER EIGHT

Representation and Design

The schematism by which our understanding deals with the phenomenal world is a skill so deeply hidden in the human soul that we shall hardly guess the secret trick that nature here employs.
Immanuel Kant, *Critique of Pure Reason*

Erich Gombrich quotes Kant in *Art and Illusion* when he writes about the limits of likeness in representation. Gombrich argues that seeking meaning in representation comes before seeing order. Originating with Kant, Gombrich's argument is based on the evolution of the human mind and senses: the mind asks first what a representation means; only when it discovers meaning is it ready to study the order of things in the representation.[1] Designers begin with specific meaning for a design and experiment with ways to support this meaning through order, changing the lines and shapes of a drawing to convey what it would be like to be in a space or move through it. The designer enters into a "dialogue" with a representation, a complex process of reasoning with architectural form, the reality of a site, and the purpose of the design. But images have a visual logic of their own: plan drawings call for square angles and the correspondence of objects (things want to line up, axes are important); perspectives require clear vistas framed by objects in the foreground that make the necessary but arbitrarily chosen frame less important; bird's-eye views and axionometrics have a tendency to miniaturize what is represented. Every type of visual, numerical, and verbal representation follows its own logic, "talking back" to the designer and clouding the relationship between representation and reality.

Computer graphics have enabled designers to integrate the various forms of representation. A designer can use numerical data files to display two- and three-dimensional images, including animations, in work reminiscent of the sketchbooks of artists in the Renaissance, when modern graphic conventions were invented. Few sketchbooks reveal as much of the complex reasoning process as those of Leonardo da Vinci. He frequently rotated the object of his design to study all its relationships and represented the same design in an aerial view, or a quickly drawn axionometric view, followed by a precise plan view or a section, and followed again by another oblique view from above. He made extensive use of perspectives and frequently placed the viewing point above eye level. The design, seen from above, discloses not only appearance but also geometric order.

This chapter addresses questions relating to Leonardo's methods and those of Enlightenment artists working to perfect graphic conventions discovered during their time. These conventions have not changed with computers, but designers are now experimenting with integrated forms of design imagery and with movement. Can a designer overcome the limits of any single representation by simultaneously working with many? Can many representations of the same design enable a designer unequivocally to evoke a future reality? Ideally, this is what a good professional representation does. Or does the persuasiveness of a *virtual* reality only further remove the designer from reality?

I begin with movement. The power of the moving image is likely to influence the way designers think about form, site, and purpose, as the team at the Berkeley laboratory learned in filming scale models and animating virtual models.

I remember setting up to film a model of a street design proposed for San Francisco. The street was defined by the curbs and sidewalks, hedges, fences, buildings, and trees that lined it. The elements of the model were put in place according to the logic of plan views. Then the camera was set up to film from the perspective of a person moving along the street. Three layers of information in space were discernible in the viewfinder image: the trees along the curb, the fences or hedges at the property lines, and the entrance porches and steps leading to front doors. To convey the sense of depth in the scene, however, the elements of the model had to be rearranged. My hand experimented with the three layers as my eye watched through the viewfinder. The trees were adjusted so that two framed each view. As the camera moved back and forth along the street, the cinematic effect of the framed views became obvious. Each was similar to the previous one yet somewhat different.

Next my hands also rearranged elements in the middle ground and background of the model, and soon the model had little resemblance to the way

it has been set up when elements corresponded to the plan view. Model elements no longer lined up, spacing between trees was uneven, and trees on one side of the street did not align with trees on the other side. The rearranged model followed a different logic, but nothing about it appeared contrived when it was projected as an animation on a screen. With each pair of trees a perfectly balanced framed view unfolded. Designs opened up to the eyes of passersby like opulent window displays on a shopping street. Each turn of the camera would make viewers look at a new arrangement, keeping them attentive and expectant. No one was ever bored watching the film. Viewers kept their eyes on the screen. The imagery was somewhat "sweet"; the design was overstated. The first viewer to point this out was Sven Ingver Anderson in Copenhagen. He was polite: "I know why you have to do this. You want to explain a new concept of a street; therefore you have to overstate your design." In fact, there was enough design on this one street to suffice for three. The street was designed for film, and the representational medium had taken control, so that design decisions were made to support the film's picturesque effect. When images can be at once so real and so distorted, reality itself becomes a more urgent concern.

In 1994 another model kit was made to create animations. This time, though, the model resided in the memory of a computer. It showed a hypothetical residential community near an existing commuter rail station. The California Department of Transportation wanted to test people's responses to medium to high residential densities appropriate near such rail stations. The older residential communities near such stations in the San Francisco Bay Area include amenities such as stores, but these communities have limited use in a study of people's acceptance of new construction. Therefore, a simulation was needed. Images of new communities of varying density had to be produced and animated so that selected groups could view and respond to simulated walks through them.

The potential amenities of such locations had to

be shown, and viewers had to be given a realistic impression of the simulated community's density, a sense of what it would be like to live there. Density figures, the number of people living on a unit of land, are highly abstract. Indeed, the architect Amos Rapoport and others have argued that perceptions of density are a function not simply of the number of people per unit area but also of the physical and social environment.[2] For example, natural greenery in a neighborhood—tree-lined streets and separate front yards—might make a visitor judge an area's density lower than it actually is. Conversely, people on sidewalks, cars parked along the street, or the absence of individual entrances might lead the visitor to judge the density higher than it really is.

The basis for Rapoport's argument is the association between density and crowding, "a subjective experience of sensory and social overload." Few of Rapoport's assumptions had been tested empirically, however. The commission from the Department of Transportation provided an excellent opportunity to test some of the variables influencing people's perceptions. If Rapoport's observations are correct, and a relationship exists between density and the feeling of "sensory and social overload," designers might not be able to manipulate residents' perceptions by simply disguising density. But the feeling of "overload" might be counteracted by designs with a separate entrance for each home, facades that express privacy or individuality (for example, bay windows), private gardens, and such residential amenities as a park at the end of a street, stores within walking distance, and the train station itself.

Previous experience with models and other representations made the design team mistrust any single form of representation. All forms known to designers should be used, from the conceptual, abstract, and diagrammatic plan drawings of housing types to compute square footage, to facade drawings, scale models for study purposes, and computer models, to highly realistic rendered computer models and computer animations. The

designers expected to learn from each representation. A design decision represented in one form could be checked and modified in another.

One member of the team kept a log of all design decisions. The designers began by looking at existing row houses, which support a population density similar to the one transportation planners expected near commuter rail stations, from twenty-four to thirty-six units per acre. They decided to add one plan for lower density and one for higher density: freestanding single-family homes, twelve per acre, are close to the lower limit needed to support rail transit;[3] local transportation planners had set a goal of forty-eight units per acre for the Bay Area transit station. The designers produced plans for four densities, with lot sizes determined by density but with identical floor areas for homes at all four densities. All buildings faced residential streets of identical design, 30 feet wide, with a 5-foot-wide sidewalk on either side. When the building footprint drawing for the computer model emerged, dimensions could be entered into the database.

The articulated design of building facades addressed Rapoport's issue of sensory and social overload.[4] Individual entrances, small front porches raised a few steps, bay windows, and varied roof lines were sketched (using conventional graphic methods), studied, and discussed. The discussions focused on style, a catch-all term designers use for the appearance of architecture. Although the usual concern of designers to develop a personal style that makes their work recognizable was of little importance to the Department of Transportation experiment, a consistent and plausible style had to be chosen. However viewers felt about the style during the experiment, keeping the architectural style constant would equally bias their perceptions of all four densities. As the computer model took shape and volumes appeared, the designers could position themselves in the model and look down streets or into backyards from upstairs windows.

"Shop drawings" were made for digitizing and transfer to the computer model. Before the transfer, the laboratory team settled on four variations for

Four alternative residential densities, in plan. *From top to bottom:* twelve dwelling units per acre; twenty-four dwelling units per acre; thirty-six dwelling units per acre; forty-eight dwelling units per acre.

Opposite, left: Four alternative residential densities, facade drawings. *From top to bottom:* twelve dwelling units per acre; twenty-four dwelling units per acre; thirty-six dwelling units per acre; forty-eight dwelling units per acre.

Opposite, right: Four alternative residential densities, scale models. *From top to bottom:* twelve dwelling units per acre; twenty-four dwelling units per acre; thirty-six dwelling units per acre; forty-eight dwelling units per acre.

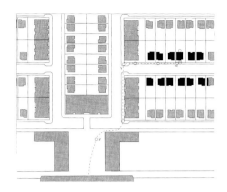

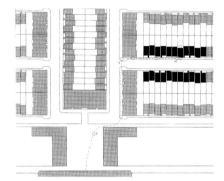

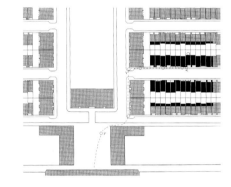

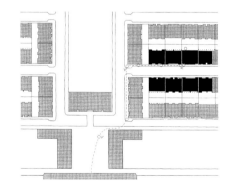

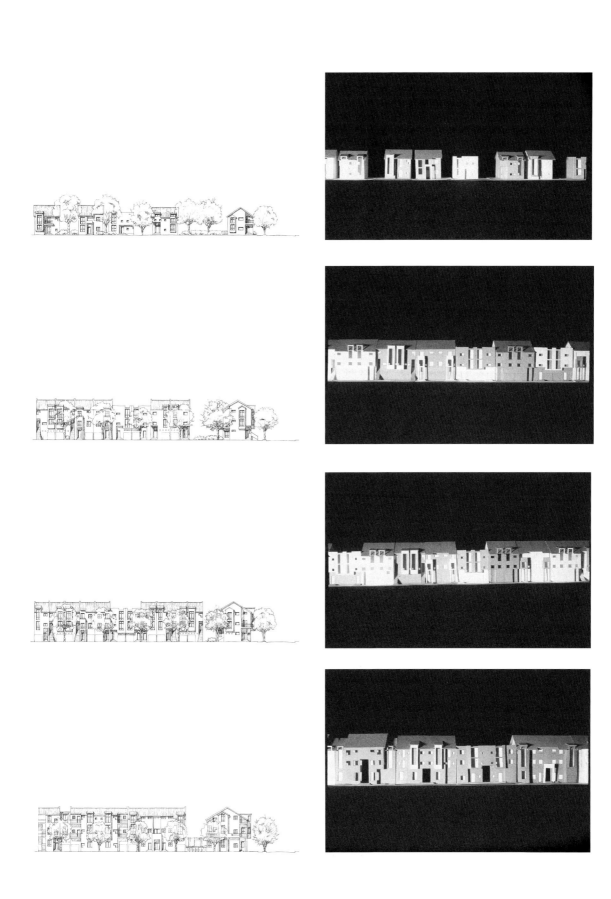

each building type. But when the facade drawings were in place on the computer screen, a decision was made to express each building more clearly as an individual structure.

The transfer from drawing to computer had caused an important change in the appearance of the designs: the "softness" of the drawings was replaced by "starkness." The computer light illuminating the model shapes made the buildings look exact and "hard." The street looked brand new, the colors artificial; everything seemed perfect. Real building edges are less precise, their surfaces less uniform; windows sit differently in a facade plane. But there is no easy way to add imperfections to the model because the lines that give shape to volumes are created by strings of numbers. The appearance of the designs reflects the exact geometry of the vector files. Interestingly, the scale models of the street facades made by hand did not suffer from this artificiality. The hand-cut edges of the cardboard and the surface of the paper reveal their imperfections when viewed close-up. The design team, concerned about the artificiality, expected viewers to react to it, favorably or unfavorably—probably unfavorably because people's impression of a brand-new place, built all at once and obviously designed by only one team of people, is often negative.

All four "walks" through the models started with a view from the upstairs rear window into the backyard, followed by a look down the street from a front window. Then the imaginary visitor would walk out a front door, turn right, look down the street, and head toward the intersection. A "stroll" through the two higher-density neighborhoods would take the visitor past a park at the end of a residential street and into an adjacent street, past a café and a convenience store to the square in front of the station, with additional commercial spaces and outdoor seating. The two lower-density neighborhoods would have no park at the end of the street (but rather additional homes facing the adjoining street), no café (only a convenience store), and, on the station square, fewer commercial places. The visitor would see more people walking toward the station in the two higher-density neighborhoods, fewer people in the lower-density neighborhoods. The number of parked cars would also differ accordingly. The computer model, designed as a kit with exchangeable components for variables (density, people and cars, stores) and constants (streets, station, and architecture), appeared ideal for the experiment.

A total of 176 respondents, with educational and social backgrounds reflecting those of Bay Area residents, saw the simulated walks through the four alternative densities. (The percentage of residents living with families is higher in the region than in the sampling, however.) In each of the eight separate showings in eight different Bay Area towns, the sequence of the density presentations was changed at random.[5] We asked the respondents to rate the four communities from desirable to undesirable and to rank them in order. On the whole the respondents felt at best neutral about what they saw. They preferred detached two-story homes in a neighborhood without a park but with medium-size private gardens. While most of them preferred the lowest density, twelve units per acre, ratings did not regularly fall off as density rose. Thirty-six dwelling units per acre had the second highest average rating, followed by the highest density, forty-eight units per acre. The second lowest density, twenty-four units per acre with a small private garden but no park at the end of the street, consistently rated lowest. People were willing to accept higher densities in communities with amenities— a transit station nearby with stores and services. That result encouraged the planners at the Department of Transportation. But all four densities seemed to produce some feeling of sensory overload, despite the designers' attempt to make the homes look and feel like private places.

The architecture chosen for the experiment was disliked beyond the expectations of the designers on the team. When respondents were asked to list one thing they disliked about the neighborhood, between 28 and 37 percent described the architecture as sterile, cold, characterized by too

Animation sequence, twelve dwelling units per acre
(*read from bottom to top of each column*).

Animation sequence, twelve dwelling units per acre
(*read from bottom to top*).

Animation sequence, twenty-four dwelling units per acre (*read from bottom to top*).

Animation sequence, thirty-six dwelling units per acre (*read from bottom to top*).

Animation sequence, forty-eight dwelling units per acre (*read from bottom to top*).

much concrete, too modern, stark, boxy, and too much the same. But when asked to list one thing they liked, 27 to 38 percent of the respondents mentioned the architecture, describing it as clean, neat, quiet, and friendly. The look of newness elicited both positive and negative responses equally.

Respondents expressed their "sensory and social overload" in finding the neighborhoods too dense, too crowded, too cramped, and too confined, with too little privacy and houses too close together. Such judgments applied (31 percent) even to the lowest density, twelve units of freestanding homes per acre, the percentage rising with increasing density: to 42 percent for twenty-four units per acre, and 50 percent for the two highest densities.

The respondents understood the meaning of the images. The simulated walk-through gave them a good sense of the spatial configurations of each density: 19 percent correctly matched the density with the walk-through that simulated it, and 64 percent identified at least two out of four density settings in the correct rank order, a difficult task given the similarity of the architecture, but apparently made easier by the simulated walks.

Many respondents commented on the cleanliness of the simulated neighborhoods as well as their newness. Whether they responded favorably or unfavorably to the cleanliness, they could not very well expect it in reality, any more than they could expect to find a real scene without imperfections. The designers managed to sprinkle dead leaves on the grass but did not render aging surfaces. They repeatedly used the textures they knew how to use from a "library" of textures developed over time. Rendering is a craft, if not an art. The computer applications make this craft no easier—in fact, they make it more difficult. The available technology uses crude algorithms to simulate direct light and ambient light. Without realistic light, surfaces look unreal, space has no depth, and the perception of scale is distorted. It remains to be seen whether new applications will move designers closer to reality or further from it, toward the realm of myths, invented things designed to impress— images that create an idealized world where we might like to live, but which is far from reality.

Responses to simulations of communities with four different levels of density (dua = dwelling units per acre).

	Like				Dislike			
	12 dua	24 dua	36 dua	48 dua	12 dua	24 dua	36 dua	48 dua
LANDSCAPE ARCHITECTURE	nice backyard trees plants greenery landscaping foliage wide streets beautiful backyard yard is excellent vegetation trees on street street design **45**	trees greenery nice yard green yard lots of grass vegetation shrubbery ivy plantings landscape trees as fence friendly streets friendly streets **42**	trees greenery nice yard green yard street peaceful design good use of plaza size of the streets parking between trees **36**	trees wide streets nice backyard grass greenery landscaping planned parking **28**	trees on road not enough trees backyard is tacky lack of greenery no crosswalks no streetlighting **20**	not enough greens streets too narrow no streetlighting too much asphalt parked cars lack of scenery **21**	parking problem few trees bareness of park **11**	lack of green lack of trees trees in street parking no greenery no dirt too much parking not enough art **26**
ARCHITECTURE	clean neat quiet nice housing friendly front garage "modern architecture" architectural design lots of windows looks very good has an identity nice town **50**	clean neat quiet architecture color of houses no graffiti large sidewalks looks great more personal homelike interesting building design wood fence front access good effort with minimum resources big houses BART square **67**	clean neat friendly quiet cleanliness similar architecture backyard view front access good beauty of the building organized modern peaceful looks safe **53**	clean quiet neat nice view from window interesting architecture large windows seems homelike appears safe active neighborhood clean place to live BART square **50**	sterile sameness no personality lacks individuality colors of the buildings too much concrete concrete too boxy square architecture no large windows architecture lacking design lacks creativity **65**	sterile sameness too much concrete too quiet architecture not secure plaza boring design too antiseptic it's a concrete box too square warehouse type look too industrial windows too small unsafe at night **59**	sterile too much concrete bland architecture sameness lacks character cold looking looks like a future slum looks like a project blocklike buildings houses rather drab garage—if close to transportation **48**	sterile concrete architecture looks boring all houses look the same too urban looking office bldg. look architecture too plain condescending Europa garage in **49**
LOCATION	close to BART proximity to BART near shopping close to shops park near house **21**	close to BART close to shops convenient market close to transportation easy transit access housing near BART **30**	close to BART shops park nearby convenient shopping center near transit housing near BART park at end of road services walk to amenities good for family **41**	near park BART proximity to BART near transit services convenient shopping shopping center close to plaza garden school coffeeshop at station coffeeshop **46**	isolated no stores lack of services auto oriented **14**	no shops no stores too close to BART **11**	no buses no night life **9**	lacked stores close to park **7**
DENSITY	large yard backyard spacious low density open space open space on corner house separated detached housing single family residences individual private garage private yard yard spread out space in yard comfortable density roomy **65**	backyard private yard big yard privacy personal green space low density economical use of space **32**	park backyard small yard private yard open space fenced yard large park public park open park more people a lot of people spacious economical use of space **46**	park big backyard backyard spacious open spaces room between buildings detached housing landscaping for privacy **33**	no park no backyards no front yards density too dense houses too close together too close lack of privacy little privacy high density housing too many homes car traffic presence of cars **52**	homes too close together density no parks too dense crowded too crowded small yard too close institution like prison like tall buildings housing connects little open space congested compact claustrophobic no playground no children's park more planting and space need more people **73**	houses too close together density very small backyard backyards too dense houses too dense compact crowded too crowded no privacy no open space high density boxed yards lack of space itty bitty living space prison-like houses connect too many neighbors more people no other parks **80**	no backyard buildings too close together crowded density too dense lack of privacy institutional prison-like all tall buildings like an apartment type of residence itty bitty living space not enough space trapped feeling buildings too dense too many cars too many neighbors no play area no park impersonal yard **80**
VIEW					**1**	no view **3**	poor view **2**	poor view **2**
NOTHING	nothing none **7**	nothing nothing nothing nothing **14**	nothing do not like area **7**	nothing nothing don't like very much **15**	liked everything like everything nothing ——— **15**	nothing really everything I didn't **12**	nothing liked everything **17**	none **7**
TOTAL	**188**	**185**	**183**	**175**	**167**	**179**	**167**	**171**

Who Watches the Watchers?

Representations of design take on importance in political discourse when they give evidence of someone's intent to change an environment. This chapter focuses on representations as decision-making tools that are also intended to influence decision making. In fact, although decision makers require graphic representations of design proposals, there is little professional consensus about their presentation, nor is there a clarity of purpose. A greater ability to conceive and imagine design can lead to a greater ability to misrepresent that design in the adversarial arena of planning approvals.

Decision makers, planning commissioners, mayors, and council members regard the representation of urban design proposals as public property, testimony belonging in the public domain. Good representations should be understandable and open to evaluation by those who will be affected by design. Representations should be complete, accurate, engaging, detailed, and true to the sense of those who will experience the designs once they are built. But the thoughts of those viewing visual information may differ greatly because viewers examine what they see in relation to their own concerns.

During the preparation of the San Francisco Downtown Plan (described in Chapter 5), a group of city planners looked carefully at film clips of the San Francisco model that forecast how the city might develop. They first analyzed film sequences of existing conditions and then, looking at the same area, compared the development allowable under the current plan with that allowable under a proposed revision of the plan. The film of the model enabled them to distinguish lasting from changing patterns of development.

For the planners the film was like a test. Prior to the screening they questioned whether the modeling would show the intent of the proposed plan: to balance the city's need for growth with concerns for historic and environmental preservation. After viewing and re-viewing the film, they agreed that the proposed plan would indeed produce lower and less bulky buildings, as it was meant to do, since it had been prepared in response to a citizens' initiative calling for lower downtown building heights.

Although the planners were pleased, the planning director asked to see the film clips yet again. After calculating the new buildings possible in the two alternative futures, he realized that more buildings could be built under the proposed plan. The director's staff confirmed his observation. The planning director requested a third showing, which confirmed his initial suspicions. Although the buildings permissible under the proposed plan would be shorter and less bulky, the plan did allow a greater number of buildings as well as greater total floor space than possible under current laws. The proposed plan would produce more floor space because in it the planners had increased the amount of downtown land available for office buildings. They had redrawn district boundary lines to include an area previously not available for development of high buildings. The planning director exclaimed, "But how was this possible? You people told me we downzoned everything."

Clearly displeased with the outcome, he challenged the accuracy of the Berkeley model. He was also worried that if the film clips became public and others made observations similar to his own, the film would take on a political charge.

The planning director sent his staff to Berkeley to count and measure all potential buildings in the model. After all assumptions made in the modeling were checked, the planners confirmed the accuracy of the representation. (In such situations, there is rarely an acknowledgment of right or wrong.) Nonetheless, the planners insisted that in subsequent showings the film clips must compare equal amounts of growth in the alternative futures shown. Such a representation would not have been entirely truthful without an amendment to the proposed plan to limit the amount of buildable floor space. Although later a citizens' initiative limited the annual permissible floor space, the proposed plan was not amended at this point.[1] The additional land the plan made available for development more than compensated for the height restrictions placed on existing downtown properties.

But the San Francisco planners were justified in challenging the images that represented the city's future. Anyone preparing and using images in decision making must ensure that the representations are open to scrutiny and independent tests. More-

over, because representations are readily understood by people who would otherwise have no access to information about development, those commissioning and preparing the representations must be concerned about their accuracy. To use simulations selectively risks undermining the credibility of the representations. It is a form of distortion. Clients commissioning work—whether private developers, government officials, or community advocates—often expect to control the information they purchase. But when such control threatens to subvert the credibility of representations, it is right to ask who exercises it.

For example, a community group in Louisiana filed suit in federal court to block the construction of an interstate freeway across scenic lake country near Shreveport.[2] The group argued that the state had not fully examined the visual impact of the proposed freeway and had not explored alternative routes. The judge ordered the state to comply with its own law mandating the disclosure of visual effects in all environmental impact reports. A reluctant state transportation agency commissioned simulation work from the Berkeley laboratory. Had the agency then tried to use the information selectively, the simulators could have asked the court to step in as referee. In the event, such action was not needed.

Most requests for simulation work come from architects and developers, at times reluctantly. For example, a developer and his architect presented a proposal for a new shopping mall that would be "scaled like a European village" to the city council of Lafayette, California, a small suburban town east of San Francisco. When a council member wanted to know more about the European village analogy, the council asked the architect to prepare a new presentation, including a simulated walk through the proposed mall. The council, which would have to approve or deny a permit for the project, was the referee. Whenever the architect and the developer tried to influence the portrayal of the mall, the simulators were obligated to point out that the work was done for the benefit of the city council of Lafayette. The simulators refused to revise the model at the client's behest.

To dramatize the information can itself amount to distortion. Civitas, a group on New York's Upper East Side, fought the construction of thirty- to fifty-story apartment towers along the avenues in its neighborhood. The group requested simulations illustrating the cumulative effect of such buildings. After viewing the simulations, group members were optimistic that their protest would be heard by politicians. To assert their position more forcefully, they asked the actor Paul Newman to narrate a film script prepared by the Berkeley laboratory. Newman, who lives in the neighborhood, refused to read the script prepared by the simulators, which he said was "too clinical." He asked a writer friend of his to rework the narration.

The simulators pointed out that a dramatic narrative would distort the simulation work.[3] They insisted on the right to approve the Newman script, which was rewritten several times. As it turned out, Newman's appearance in the film, narrating in front of the camera, dramatized the simulation. Such an experience suggests the need to explain to prospective users of simulation the principle of neutrality: not a neutrality of values—that would be neither possible nor desirable—but a neutrality of position. A neutral stance toward the parties in a dispute is best maintained by insisting that all representations be treated as public property. Work carried on at public universities, moreover, is subject to freedom-of-information laws: anyone can ask to see what work was done.

Neutrality is a protection; it is also a responsibility. Before the 1985 San Francisco Downtown Plan was enacted into law, in a period when building review decisions were made at the discretion of the planning commission, a developer in San Francisco encountered community opposition to a thirty-eight-story tower at the edge of the financial district, in view of many homes on Nob Hill. In defending the size of the project, the developer's architect announced that the new building would make a graceful visual transition between down-town and the smaller-scaled neighborhood on the hill. But the president of the planning commission, unconvinced, requested that the developer commission simulations of the proposed building. After viewing them, he voted against the proposal. At a public hearing minutes before the vote took place, he read the following statement: "If this planning commission allows the natural contours of the city to be destroyed, if we allow these high-rises to march right up the hill, we'll be guilty of the biggest crime that any planning commission in any city has ever perpetrated."[4] He urged his fellow commissioners not to approve the building.

Knowing that the planning commission depends on simulations when it makes decisions, developers have tried to exploit the trust between the simulators and the commissioners by offering to compensate the simulators to mediate between proponents of development and decision makers. For their part, decision makers have called on the simulators privately asking how to vote on a proposed project. To protect their credibility, simulators must insist that they act as providers of information, not policy advisers. Neutrality is so important that simulators should never become involved in negotiation, arbitration, or decision making.

Even though simulators have their own opinions about the merits of a project, the goal remains clear: to elicit from viewers an observation that is the same for a simulation as for the real-world situation. Ideally, simulations should be previewed before they are shown to the public. During the preview, the simulators can explain their assumptions in portraying a proposed project, and, if necessary, viewers can remind the simulators of important elements that have been left out or details that have been overlooked.

The roles of project proponents, opponents, design professionals, and decision makers sketched out in this chapter follow predictable patterns. The exchange of information begins with the place as it exists in the real world, with all its physical and social dimensions. The proposed change for this place is represented in words, images, and numbers,

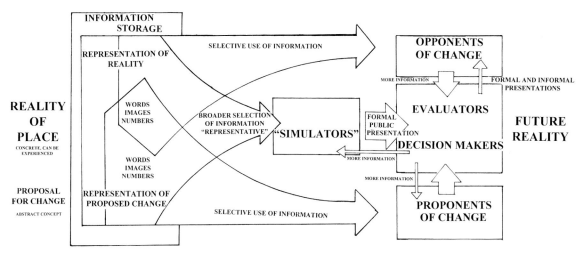

DESIGN COMMUNICATIONS MODEL

Design communication model.

to emerge in the form of representations in the studio of the designer. Over time, maps and models representing the proposed changes appear on drafting tables, computer screens, and word processors. New realities are created. Proponents get ready to present information to evaluators and to decision makers of all kinds, generally mayors, council members, or planning commissioners. But the information presented is a selection of all available information. Proponents show the proposal to its best advantage, and negative impacts on existing conditions are played down or omitted from presentations. Opponents of the proposal are just as selective in their choice of information, highlighting the negative and acknowledging little, if anything, about the benefits of proposed changes. Both proponents and opponents will use their information to persuade the evaluators to adopt their position, for or against the project.

Experienced decision makers, of course, are not easily confused by the predictable behavior proponents and opponents are likely to display, but decision makers might not know how to distinguish facts from deception, especially if the information is of a technical nature, presented without sufficient discussion about assumptions. The decision makers depend on simulation. In contrast to the proponents and opponents, simulators need to take a broader view of all the information available to produce simulations that are representative both of the place as it exists in reality and of the changes proposed. Under potential attack from proponents and opponents, the simulators must produce information that is open to accuracy tests, and they have to avoid being perceived as a party favoring either side in the dispute. To protect the documentary quality of their representations, they must maintain a neutral position.

However obvious these principles might appear, they need to be explained to the many users of the laboratory's services each time work is commissioned. ■

The benefit of the laboratory experiments I have described here lies in creating a concrete experience on which to base decisions. The development of representational techniques, moreover, advances the field. But the concomitant difficulty is to be objective about these techniques, to acknowledge their flaws.

Among these flaws is lighting. Far too frequently the represented world has a blue, sunny sky. The direct sun that shines and the direct light that illuminates the streets in the simulations evoke a different mood from that of indirect or diffused light.[5] More experiments are needed to assess different lighting conditions and their effect on decision making.

Another flaw in the representational techniques is that buildings are shown before their designs have been worked out in detail. The designers in the laboratory have had to invent plausible building facades and forms. Because other designers generally have strong feelings about any interpreting of what is plausible but not fully developed, simulators need to invent a range of plausible designs showing different design intents. Simulations represent building dimensions (height, bulk, facade length, and streetwall continuity) long before any specific building design proposal has been reviewed. It defeats the purpose of urban design plans to make these decisions only after an architect has

been commissioned for the design of an individual building. Decisions made late in the process would be dictated by individual concerns. Thus, representations should be done at least twice: early in the process, when the overall desired character of an area is under discussion and cumulative effects rather than individual building designs are at issue; and later, when individual buildings are discussed and simulations that detail building designs are relevant.

Simulation techniques that are geared to representing an existing environment faithfully will treat a new building unfavorably unless it fits in. Clearly, this creates a bias in favor of designs that follow existing dimensions and proportions and against those that stick out. Would the design of the Guggenheim Museum have been treated unfavorably by a technology that produces realistic eye-level views, had it been applied when the museum was proposed? I would hope not, but I do not know. Frank Lloyd Wright's building fits well into the 200-foot plan dimensions of existing city blocks and into the streetwall along Fifth Avenue, where some blocks are taken up by the remaining freestanding mansions at the east side of Central Park.

Across the park from the Guggenheim, a simulation of the Columbus Circle project revealed that the relatively small size of the Skidmore, Owings, and Merrill design was a better fit than the very large Moshe Saftie design. Although the crystal shape of Saftie's conception was not objectionable, the immense volume was problematic. A view from Lincoln Center, looking south on Broadway, shows the large building as it was proposed in 1985; it came about as a result of trades in development rights sanctioned by the city of New York. The height and volume were then dictated to the architect by the developer.

Although professionals who work in a tradition of design do not necessarily think of the biases in their work, other professionals outside the tradition clearly do. The laboratory work belongs to an urban design tradition that has responded to

Moshe Saftie, proposal for Columbus Circle, 1985, viewed from Lincoln Center, looking south on Broadway.

an overly conceptual approach to developing and explaining designs and a lack of regard for the human dimension that inevitably results from this approach. The tradition of urban design concerned with the experience of cities had its roots in nineteenth-century English landscape architecture, for example, Humphrey Repton's famous Red Books, filled with before-and-after perspectives of landscape design. In these books, the eye-level view was more important in the design development than the plan. From its beginning in landscape architecture, the tradition surfaced again in urban design through the writings of Camillo Sitte, Joseph Stübbe, and Raymond Unwin. Chapter 2 discussed the development of this design tradition. Gordon Cullen sketched in this tradition, and Edmond Bacon photographed a stroll through a Greek village. The movement matured through the writings of Kevin Lynch on the mental structure of cities.

Urban design plans and some regional plans, like the work done at the Berkeley laboratory, reacted to such traditions as the modern movement in town planning, which tried to convey an architecture of lightness, spaciousness, openness, clarity, purity, and honesty in conceptual diagrams emphasizing structure, chiefly spatial structure. In the renewal areas and in the new towns, these projects resembled fields of huge sculptures—exactly what they had looked like as white conceptual models.

Later, the neorationalists preferred aerial perspectives or axionometric views to explain their projects because only a view from above would show their design intent: the transformation of an urban morphology through physical elements or prototypes. The contextual movement used figure-ground plans. Each movement favored its own particular graphic expression.

To suggest comprehensive ways to preserve or improve a city, the designers of urban places first have to describe an existing city. For that task a visual language is needed. But that language is developing slowly. The technology has not slowed this development, but the lack of knowledge about the elements of the language and how they should fit together has done so. Mastery requires that quantifiable information be combined with sensory information—for example, the geometry of form with the perception of form; statistical information about climate with a person's feeling of comfort; or the dimensions of buildings and streets with a person's perception of time. The language will become richer when additional combinations are added. This is possible by measuring, in one form or another, the phenomena of the visual world.

The search for a visual language of design has not been futile. Such a unified language has to be capable of expressing both structure and experience. The best cities have both.

NOTES

INTRODUCTION

1. Spiro Kostof, *The Architect* (New York: Oxford University Press, 1977); see the introduction.

2. Donald Appleyard experimented with visual simulation while working with Kevin Lynch at MIT in the mid-1960s. He founded the Berkeley Environmental Simulation Laboratory in 1968. He discussed many issues addressed in this book in "Understanding Professional Media: Issues and a Research Agenda," in *Human Behavior and Environment*, ed. Irwin Altman and Joachim F. Wohlwill, vol. 2 (New York: Plenum Press, 1977).

3. Kevin Lynch made a major contribution to the improvement of visual communication in urban design. His book *The Image of the City* (Cambridge: MIT Press, 1960) has influenced many architects and urban designers and convinced them of the need to explain their designs and plans in ways that relate to people's experience of cities.

4. Lewis Mumford wrote similarly in the introduction to his *Technics and Civilization* (New York: Harcourt, Brace, 1934).

5. Margaret A. Hagen, ed., introduction to *The Perception of Pictures*, vol. 1 (New York: Academic Press, 1980), i.

6. James J. Gibson, "A Prefatory Essay on the Perception of Surfaces versus the Perception of Markings on a Surface," preface in ibid.

7. Donlyn Lyndon, "Caring about Places," *Places* 1, no. 4 (1984).

CHAPTER 1

1. Rudolf Arnheim, "Brunelleschi's Peep Show," *Zeitschrift für Kunstgeschichte* 41 (1978): 57–60.

2. See Samuel Y. Edgerton, *The Renaissance Rediscovery of Linear Perspective* (New York: Basic Books, 1975), who estimates 1425; Martin Kemp, *Geometrical Perspective from Brunelleschi to Desargues* (New York: Oxford University Press, 1985), who gives the date as prior to 1413; and Michael Kubovy, *The Psychology of Perspective in Renaissance Art* (New York: Cambridge University Press, 1986), who cites a source setting the date between 1401 and 1409.

3. Antonio di Tuccio Manetti, in John White, *The Birth and Rebirth of Pictorial Space* (Boston: Boston Book and Art Shop, 1967), 116.

4. According to Manetti, "some three braccia inside the middle door of Santa Maria del Fiore," in ibid., 114.

5. Ibid.

6. See Leon Battista Alberti [1402–1472], *Della Pittura* (1435).

7. Edgerton, *Renaissance Rediscovery of Linear Perspective*, 40.

8. Quoted in ibid., 42.

9. Manetti, in White, *Birth and Rebirth*, 114.

10. L. A. Mannheim, ed., *The Focal Encyclopedia of Photography* (New York: McGraw-Hill, 1969), defines "focal length" as the distance from the plane in which the lens forms an image of objects at infinity to the node of emission.

11. See David Hockney, "On Photography," lecture at the Victoria and Albert Museum (New York: André Emmerich Gallery, 1983).

12. James S. Ackerman, *The Architecture of Michelangelo* (London: A. Zwemmer, 1964). The model mentioned here was included in an exhibition titled "The Representation of Architecture: The Renaissance, from Brunelleschi to Michelangelo," Palazzo Grassi, Venice, March–November 1994.

13. Leonardo's map of Imola, commissioned by Cesare Borgia, is preserved, together with field notes and sketches, in the Royal Library at Windsor Castle, Codex Atlanticus, no. 12284.

14. Howard Saalman, *Medieval Cities* (New York: George Braziller, 1968).

15. "Leonardo's transit consisted of a circular, dial-like surface with its circumference divided into eight parts corresponding to the eight winds, each further subdivided into eight degrees. At the center of this disc was a magnetic compass. With the addition of a movable right vane, also pivoted at the center, the transit was identical in all its essentials to a modern surveying instrument" (John Pinto, "Origins and Development of the Ichnographic City Plan," *Journal of the Society of Architecture Historians* 35, no. 1 [1976]: 40).

16. Leonardo's measuring wheel, an odometer, is described and illustrated in the Codex Atlanticus, fol. 312V-a and fol. 14-a, dated 1497 and 1500, respectively. Alberti describes the forerunner of Leonardo's invention in the *Ludi matematici*, chap. 18. It is derived from a similar instrument described by Vitruvius in *De architectura*, 10.9.

17. Pinto, "Origins and Development." The term "ichnographia" was first used by Vitruvius, *De architectura*, 1.2.2.

18. For the full text of Raphael's letter to Pope Leo X, see V. Golzio, *Raffaello, sei documenti* (Vatican City, 1936). For an English translation, see Carlo Pedretti, appendix to *A Chronology of Leonardo da Vinci's Architectural Studies after 1500* (Geneva: E. Droz, 1962), 162–170.

19. The narrative text is from a contemporary, Pietro Aretino, *Ragionamento della Corti*, Venice, 1538, quoted in Pedretti, *Chronology*, 161–162.

20. Clemente Faccioli, "Giambattista Nolli (1701–1756) e la sua gran Pianta di Roma del 1748," *Studi Romani* 14 (1966): 418; quoted and trans. R. Ingersoll, *Design Book Review* 8, no. 22 (1986).

21. Giambattista Nolli, *Rome 1748*, intro. essay Allan Ceen (Highmount, N.Y.: J. H. Aronson, 1984).

22. *Atlante di Roma*, 2d ed. (Venice: Marsilio, 1991).

CHAPTER 2

1. Clemente Faccioli, "Giambattista Nolli (1701–1756) e la sua gran Pianta di Roma del 1748," *Studi Romani* 14 (1966): 433; quoted and trans. R. Ingersoll, *Design Book Review* 8, no. 22 (1986).

2. Martin Kemp, *Leonardo da Vinci* (Cambridge: Harvard University Press, 1981), 230.

3. Amato P. Frutaz, *Le Piante di Roma,* 3 vols. (Rome, 1962).

4. Steen Eiler Rasmussen, *London: The Unique City* (Cambridge: MIT Press, 1967).

5. Wren, according to his son, Christopher, "immediately after the fire, took an exact survey of the whole area and confines of the burning, having traced with great trouble and hazard the great plain of ashes and ruins" ("Parentalia," 1750, quoted in Raymond Unwin, *Town Planning in Practice* [London: T. F. Unwin, 1909], 77–80).

    The accuracy of Wren's survey has been questioned. He apparently prepared a quick survey of some kind, although there is no record of his field notes. Wren's design for rebuilding London was not produced as an accurate overlay utilizing an ichnographic map of what existed before the fire. See Martin Briggs, *Wren the Incomparable* (London: Allen and Unwin, 1953), 44–56.

6. Rasmussen, *London: The Unique City,* 114.

7. The major European literature available to Wren on the design of cities prior to the mid-seventeenth century included Leone Battista Alberti, *De re aedificatoria,* 1452; Martini Di Giorgio, *Trattato di architettura civile e militare,* ca. 1500; Albrecht Dürer, *Etlicher Unterricht zur Befestigung der Stet, Schloss und Fleckene* (Nuremberg, 1527); Pietro Cataneo, *L'architettura* (Venice, 1567); Andrea Palladio, *Quattro libri dell'architettura* (Venice, 1570); Daniel Speckle, *Architectura von Festungen* (Strassburg, 1589); V. Scarmozzi, *L'idea dell'architettura universale* (Venice, 1615); Jacques Paret de Chambery, *Des fortifications et artifices, architecture et perspective* (Paris, 1601). On the planning of New World settlements, see Philip II of Spain, *Rulas y Cedulas para Gobierno de las Indias,* San Lorenzo, July 3, 1573 (The Law of the Indies); translation and discussion in Axel Mundigo and Dora P. Crouch, "The City Planning

Ordinances of the Law of the Indies Revisited," *Town Planning Review* (Liverpool) 48 (1979): 247–268.

8. During his stay in France, Wren did not visit the model town of Richelieu southwest of Paris, laid out and built 1620–1635, but he would have visited the Place Royal, built in 1604 (now called Place des Vosges) in Paris.

9. Walter George Bell, *The Great Fire of London, 1666* (London, 1920). The Wren, Evelyn, and Hooke plans are discussed in Sydney Perks, "London Town Planning Schemes in 1666," *Journal of the RIBA,* December 20, 1919, 69.

10. Rasmussen, *London: The Unique City,* 115.

11. Baron Georges-Eugène Haussmann, *Memoirs,* vol. 2, cited and trans. Anthony Vidler, "The Scenes of the Streets: Transformation of Ideal and Reality, 1850–1871," in *On Streets,* ed. Stanford Anderson (Cambridge: MIT Press, 1978).

12. Ibid.

13. Cf. Steward Edwards, *The Paris Commune, 1871* (London: Eyre and Spottiswoode, 1971), 8.

14. Robert Hughes, *Barcelona* (New York: Knopf, 1992), 199.

15. According to Alexander Labore, *Voyage picaresques et historique en Espagne* (Madrid, 1812), quoted in ibid., 200.

16. From Allan B. Jacobs, *Great Streets,* chap. 6 (Cambridge: MIT Press, 1993).

17. Anthony Sutcliffe, *The Autumn of Central Paris* (London: Edward Arnold, 1973), 138.

18. Arturo Soria y Puig, "The Project and Its Circumstances," in *Readings on Cerda and the Extension Plans of Barcelona* (Barcelona: Laboratori D'Urbanisme, 1991), 312.

19. Quoted in ibid.

20. Quoted in ibid., 57.

21. Cerda's survey of the social conditions in Barcelona, 1856, in a French translation by Antonio Lope de Aberasturi, *La theorie generale de la urbanisation* (Paris: Seuil, 1979).

22. Ildefonso Cerda, *La theoris general de la urbanization y application de sus principals y doctrines a la reforma y Ensanche de Barcelona* (Madrid, 1867).

23. Hughes, *Barcelona,* 289.

24. Alessandra Di Muntoni, *Barcelona, 1859, Il piano sueza qualita* (Rome: Bulzoni, 1978), figs. 23, 24, 30.

25. Hughes, *Barcelona,* 198.

26. Aldo Rossi, *The Architecture of the City* (Cambridge: MIT Press, 1984).

27. Hughes, *Barcelona,* 201.

28. Unwin, *Town Planning in Practice;* Joseph Stübben, *Principles for Laying Out Cities* (Chicago: International

Engineering Congress, 1893), published in German as "Praktische und ästhetische Grundsätze für die Anlage von Städten," *Zeitschrift des Österreichischen Ingenier und Architekten Verbandes* (Vienna, 1893), 44. See also Joseph Stübben, *Der Städtebau*, 3d ed. (Leipzig: A. Kroner, 1924).

29. Camillo Sitte, *Der Städtebau nach seinen künstlerischen Grundsätzen*, 3d ed. (Vienna: Grasser, 1901).

30. Carl E. Schorske, *Fin-de-Siècle Vienna: Politics and Culture* (New York: Vintage Books, 1981), 25.

31. Ibid.

32. Camillo Sitte, *Der Städtebau nach seinen künstlerischen Grundsätzen,* 5th ed. (Vienna: Grasser, 1922), 92.

33. Ibid., 56.

34. Quoted from a facsimile of the 1929 translation of *Urbanisme*, entitled *The City of Tomorrow and Its Planning*, trans. Frederick Etchells (Cambridge: MIT Press, 1975), 18.

35. H. Allan Brooks, "Le Corbusier's Earliest Ideas on Urban Design," in *In Search of Modern Architecture*, ed. Helen Searing (Cambridge: MIT Press, 1983), 283.

36. Ibid., 282.

37. Maurice Besset, *Who Was Le Corbusier?* (Geneva: Skira, 1968).

38. Erich Mendelsohn and Bernhard Hoetger, "Synthesis— World Architecture," in *Programs and Manifestoes on Twentieth-Century Architecture*, ed. Ulrich Conrads, trans. Michael Bullock (Cambridge: MIT Press, 1970), 106–108.

39. Howard Saalman, *Medieval Cities* (New York: George Braziller, 1968).

40. Congrès Internationaux d'Architecture Moderne, the first CIAM meeting held in June 1928 at Château Sarrar, Switzerland; see the declaration in Conrads, *Programs*, 110.

41. Mendelsohn and Hoetger, "Synthesis—World Architecture," 106.

42. Frank Lloyd Wright, "Young Architecture," in Conrads, *Programs*, 124.

43. Ivor de Wolfe, "The Art of Making Urban Landscapes," *Architectural Review* (January 1944): 3.

44. Ibid., 5.

45. Gordon Cullen, *Townscape* (London: Architectural Press, 1961), 15.

46. Ibid.

47. Kevin Lynch, "Reconsidering the Image of the City," in *Cities of the Mind*, ed. Lloyd Rodwin and Robert Hollister (New York: Plenum Press, 1985), 152.

48. Kenneth Boulding, *The Image* (Ann Arbor: University of Michigan Press, 1956).

49. Lynch, "Reconsidering the Image of the City," 153.

50. Philip Thiel, "Experiment in Space Notation," *Architectural Review* 131 (May 1962): 326–329. Also see Lawrence Halprin, "Motation," *Progressive Architecture* (July 1969): 123–133.

51. Lynch, "Reconsidering the Image of the City," 153.

52. Kevin Lynch, *City Sense and City Design*, ed. Tridib Banerjee and Michael Southworth (Cambridge: MIT Press, 1990), 251.

53. Roger M. Downs and David Stea, *Image and Environment* (Chicago: Aldine, 1973).

54. Stanley Milgrim, "Psychological Maps of Paris," in *Environmental Psychology*, ed. Harold M. Proshansky, William H. Helson, and L. G. Rivlin (New York: Holt, Rinehart and Winston, 1976), 104–125.

55. Ibid.

56. Jan Gehl, *Life between Buildings*, trans. Jo Koch (New York: Van Nostrand Reinhold, 1987).

57. Vineyard Open Land Foundation, *Looking at the Vineyard*, West Tisbury, Mass., January 1973.

58. The drawings also give us a glimpse at a Lynchean Utopia, where development takes place in clusters whose size is defined by topography and vegetation and therefore becomes understandable.

59. Kevin Lynch, *Managing the Sense of a Region* (Cambridge: MIT Press, 1976), 120.

CHAPTER 3

1. George Rowley, *Principles of Chinese Painting* (Princeton, N.J.: Princeton University Press, 1947), 41.

2. Ibid., 61.

3. Christel Habbe, *Die Räumlichkeit der Topographie: Beiträge zum ländlichen Bau-und Siedlungswesen*. Bericht 33, Hannover University, 1991. See also Graf Karlfried von Dürckheim, "Untersuchungen zum gelebten Raum," in *Neue Psychologische Studien*, 6, ed. Felix Krüger (Munich: Beck'sche Verlagsbuchlandlung, 1930).

4. Quotations in this paragraph and the next are from William James, *Psychology: The Briefer Course*, ed. Gordon Allport (New York: Harper and Row, 1961), 147–153.

5. Kevin Lynch, *Managing the Sense of a Region* (Cambridge: MIT Press, 1976), 100; Donald Appleyard, "Understanding Professional Media: Issues and a Research Agenda," in *Human Behavior and Environment*, ed. Irwin Altman and Joachim F. Wohlwill, vol. 2 (New York: Plenum Press, 1977).

6. Peter Kamnitzer, "Computer Aid to Design," *Architectural Design* (September 1969).

7. See Donald Appleyard and Kenneth H. Craik, "The Berkeley Environmental Simulation Project," in *Envi-*

ronmental Impact Assessment, Guidelines, and Commentary, ed. Thomas C. Dickert and R. R. Domany (Berkeley and Los Angeles: University of California Press, 1974), 121–125. See also Donald Appleyard and Kenneth H. Craik, "The Berkeley Environmental Simulation Laboratory and Its Research Programme," *International Review of Applied Psychology* 27 (1978): 53–55.

8. Alvay J. Miller and Jerry Jeffrees were hired to work in computer motion controls for Los Angeles film studios; see Thomas G. Smith, *Industrial Light and Magic* (New York: Ballantine, 1986), 9. Karl Mellander, an optical engineer, supervised Miller and Jeffrees during the Berkeley experiment; see Karl Y. Mellander, "Environmental Problems and How Architectural Engineering Models Solve Them," master's thesis, San Francisco State University, 1978.

9. The Berkeley experiment with model photography was preceded by work at the University of Lund in Sweden under Carl-Axel Acking, G. J. Sorte, and Richard Kueller. See Carl-Axel Acking, "Comparisons between Some Methods of Presentations," in *Evaluation of Planned Environments* (Stockholm: National Swedish Institute for Building Research, Document D7, 1974). See also Carl-Axel Acking and Richard Kueller, "Presentation and Judgement of Planned Environment and the Hypothesis of Arousal," in *Environmental Design Research*, ed. Wolfgang F. E. Preiser, vol. 1 (Stroudsburg, Pa.: Dowden, Hutchinson and Ross, 1973), 72–83.

10. At UC Berkeley, the simulation experiment ended in 1974. John Dykstra, the filmmaker, went on to work with George Lucas on *Star Wars*, a film that brought him an Academy Award for special visual effects. The technicians and computer programmers found employment at Bell Laboratories and at special-effects studios in Hollywood, where they continued work on computerized motion-control systems.

11. Hans Lightman, "The Subjective Camera," originally written for *American Cinematographer* (February 1946); see also *The Movies as Medium*, ed. Lewis Jacobs (New York: Farrar, Straus and Giroux, 1970). Many filmmakers have conceded the rightness of Federico Fellini's answer to his own question: "What's the sense of being 'objective' in films? I don't think it's physically possible." Gideon Bachman interview with Fellini, *Mademoiselle* (November 1964).

12. Lightman, "The Subjective Camera," 61.

13. Alfred Hitchcock experimented with the continuous-shot technique in his film *Rope* (1948). Hitchcock wanted film to seem like a true eyewitness recording, without any condensation of time and change of location. The entire eighty-minute film appears fluid because it was executed in a single uninterrupted traveling camera shot, without a conventional transition like a cut or dissolve. In the film *Rope* the camera points down to a dark surface at the end of a filming session, which turns the entire screen black while the film is projected. Once new film is loaded, the camera pans upward to continue the film, with no apparent interruption of the scene.

14. Smith, *Industrial Light and Magic*, entry for John Dykstra.

15. Kenneth H. Craik, "The Psychology of Large Scale Environments," in *Environmental Psychology: Directions and Perspectives*, ed. N. R. Feimer and E. S. Geller (New York: Praeger, 1983), 67–109.

16. The inclusion of visual concerns in the 1968 Environmental Policy Act had its roots in the 1965 White House Conference on natural beauty. Fifteen panels of experts had been invited to the White House and took as their primary challenge the preservation of landscapes in areas where most people lived and worked—cities, suburbs, and the countryside connecting settlements.

17. Appleyard and Craik, "The Berkeley Environmental Simulation Project."

18. See Stewart Brand, *The Media Lab* (New York: Viking Books, 1987).

19. Donald P. Greenberg, "Computers and Architecture: Advanced Modeling and Rendering Algorithms Allow Designers and Clients to Walk through Buildings before Construction," *Scientific American* (February 1991): 104–109.

20. Stewart Brand, *The Media Lab*, 108.

INTRODUCTION TO PART TWO

1. The West Side Highway simulation project was first described in Peter Bosselmann, "Dynamic Simulation of Urban Environments," in *Environmental Simulation*, ed. Daniel Stokols and Robert W. Marans (New York: Plenum Press, 1993).

2. The force of the preservation movement in Britain, for example, has been documented by Charles Jencks, *The Prince, the Architects, and New Wave Monarchy* (New York: Rizzoli, 1988).

CHAPTER 4

1. Stanley Robarts, "A History of Times Square," in the research report entitled *The Bright Light Zone*, ed. William Kornblum, CUNY, 1978.

2. See Jill Stone, *Times Square: A Pictorial History* (New York: Collier Books, 1982), which includes the author's photographs of Times Square from 1939 on. See also

Lou Stoumen, *Times Square: Forty-five Years of Photography* (New York: Macmillan, 1982).

3. In the mid-1990s, however, the renewed popularity of large-scale musicals has persuaded theater organizations to rehabilitate some of the oldest Times Square theaters.

4. Paul Goldberger, *New York Times*, October 6, 1985.

5. "The Broadway Theater District, A Preservation Development and Management Plan" advocated designating as landmarks the interior and exterior of the remaining thirty-three legitimate Broadway theaters under Chapter 2004 of the city charter. Prepared by Save the Theaters, Inc., New York, December 1983, with Lee Harris Pomeroy, Jack Goldstein, Fred W. Kent, and the Harvard Business School Task Force.

6. *New York Daily News*, headline, page 1, August 28, 1985.

7. The Municipal Arts Society formed an advisory committee for the Times Square simulation project, chaired by Nicholas Quenelle and Hugh Hardy; members were Kent Barwick, Paul Byard, Phillip Howard, and Carol Rifkind. Advisers were Lee Pomeroy and Anthony Hiss.

8. The photographs were taken by Duke Crawford and Doug Webb. The models were built by Gilles Depardon, Michael St. Pierre, Kathryn Ogawa, Timothy Abbel, Mary Judary, Lea Cloud, and Nancie Newman.

9. Paul Goldberger, *New York Times*, October 6, 1985.

10. This figure is based on an 80 percent build-out of twelve development sites around the bow-tie intersection of Seventh Avenue and Broadway, from Forty-second Street north to Fifty-third Street. It did not include the approximately 4 million square feet of development proposed at the time for the Forty-second Street redevelopment project (the City at Forty-second Street), whose 15 million square feet of office space would bring forty to sixty thousand people to the sidewalks of Times Square during commute hours.

11. The 1985 proposal by the simulation team included a mandatory streetwall height of 50 to 70 feet, with a 50-foot setback above the streetwall for the placing of signs. Above that height, building volume would follow a cut-off plane ascending at a ratio of 1:2. If avenue properties were limited to a depth of 200 feet, the resulting floor area ratio would be 1:14. The development potential of the twelve sites in the study totaled 8 million square feet, 30 percent less than the 12 million square feet possible under the 1982 midtown planning controls.

12. A daylight scoring system, intended to preserve adequate light, was developed as part of the 1982 midtown controls. This system, however, should not be applied to an open area like Times Square. Although it defines

tower shapes, it does not limit the volume or height of future buildings.

CHAPTER 5

1. The Mission Bay project, as proposed in 1984, was designed by the architect I. M. Pei and Partners and the landscape architecture and planning firm Wallace, Roberts, and Todd.

2. *San Francisco, 1934–1974: An Animation Film*, Institute of Urban and Regional Development, Environmental Simulation Laboratory, University of California at Berkeley, 1972.

3. Under the auspices of the San Francisco Department of City Planning, the Berkeley laboratory made a short film on the anticipated effect of a San Francisco ballot initiative, Proposition O, voted on in November 1979. The initiative was designed to lower the allowable height of future office buildings to 20 floors in the business district and somewhat lower in other downtown districts. The simulation film showed that buildings designed under the then-current 1974 planning controls would have changed the scale and character of several downtown districts, particularly the retail district near Union Square, the hotel district in the Tenderloin, historic Chinatown, and the area along Market Street.

4. During the 1970s downtown office space in San Francisco had grown by a rate of 1.5 million square feet annually. When word spread that the planning laws were about to change, a rush of building activity took place. The rate in the early 1980s increased to 2.5 million square feet annually. See *Downtown San Francisco Environmental Impact Report, City and County of San Francisco, Growth Management Alternatives for Downtown San Francisco*, Environmental Science Associates, Inc., May 1983.

5. Although the city's legal staff dismissed the idea of tying the allowable height of a building to facade (frontage) length, this concept has merit and could become the legal basis for future planning controls, according to Allan Jacobs, San Francisco director of city planning, 1965–1983.

6. The new path diagrams were modeled after Victor Olgyay, *Design with Climate* (Princeton, N.J.: Princeton University Press, 1963).

7. Peter Bosselmann, "Shadow Boxing: Keeping the Sun on Chinatown Kids," *Landscape Architecture* 73, no. 4 (1983): 74.

8. Peter Bosselmann, Terrance O'Hare, and Juan Flores, *Sun and Light for Public Open Space in Downtown San Francisco*, Institute of Urban and Regional Develop-

ment, University of California at Berkeley, Monograph no. 034, 1983.

9. Eva Liebermann, "User Survey of Downtown San Francisco's Open Spaces," City of San Francisco, Department of City Planning, 1983.

10. L. G. Berglund and Jan A. J. Stolwijk, "The Use of Simulation Models of Human Thermoregulation in Assessing Acceptability of Complex Dynamic Thermal Environments," in *Energy Conservation Strategies in Buildings*, ed. Jan A. J. Stolwijk (New Haven, Conn.: John B. Pierce Foundation, 1978).

11. Edward Arens and Peter Bosselmann, "Wind, Sun, and Temperature," *Building and Environment* 24, no. 4 (1989): 315–320.

12. Peter Bosselmann, Juan Flores, and William Gray, *Sun, Wind, and Comfort*, Institute of Urban and Regional Development, University of California at Berkeley, Monograph no. 035, 1984.

13. Linda Groad, "Measuring the Fit of New to Old Architecture," *Progressive Architecture* 61 (November 1983): 85.

14. Peter Bosselmann and Marsha Gale, "Looking Out for Second Street," *Landscape Architecture* 76, no. 6 (1986): 62–65.

15. Kevin Lynch and Donald Appleyard, *Temporary Paradise: A Look at the Special Landscape of the San Diego Region*, San Diego, 1974, a special newspaper edition by the Marsten Company; reprinted in Kevin Lynch, *City Sense and City Design*, ed. Tridib Banerjee and Michael Southworth (Cambridge: MIT Press, 1990).

16. Ervin H. Zube and J. L. Sell, "Human Dimensions of Environmental Change," *Journal of Planning Literature* 2 (1986): 162–176.

17. Helmut Wohl, "Point of View," *Boston University Journal* (Autumn 1972): 20.

CHAPTER 6

1. Leon Battista Alberti, *Ten Books on Architecture* [1486], trans. Cosimo Bartoli and James Leoni (New York: Dover, 1986), 4.5.79; Andrea Palladio, *The Four Books of Architecture* [1570], trans. Isaac Ware (New York: Dover, 1969), 3.1.60; Tacitus, *Annales*, 15.168.

2. Vitruvius, *Ten Books of Architecture*, trans. Morris Hicky Morgan (New York: Dover, 1960), 4.6., "The Directions of the Streets, with a Remark on the Winds," sec. 8. See also Joseph Rykwert, The Idea *of a Town* (Princeton, N.J.: Princeton University Press, 1976).

3. Philip II of Spain, *Royal Ordinances Concerning the Laying Out of New Cities, Towns, or Villages*, Archivo Nacional, Madrid, Ms. 3017, *Rulas y Cedulas para Gobierno de las Indias*, San Lorenzo, July 3, 1573 (The

Law of the Indies); trans. Zelia Nuttall, *Hispanic American Historical Review* 5, no. 2 (May 1922): 249–254.

4. Thomas Jefferson, letter to C. F. C. DeVolney, Washington, February 1805, in *The Writings of Thomas Jefferson*, ed. A. A. Liscomb and A. L. Bergh (Washington, D.C.: Thomas Jefferson Memorial Association of the United States, 1905), xi, 66–67. Cited in John W. Reps, "Thomas Jefferson's Checkerboard Towns," *Journal of the Society of Architectural Historians* 20, no. 3 (October 1961): 108–114.

5. The medical research findings were summarized and reviewed by the Regional Plan Association in 1929 and presented in Wayne D. Heydecker and Ernest Goodrich, "Sunlight and Daylight for Urban Areas," *Neighborhood and Community Planning* 7 (1929): 142–202.

6. Bruno Taut, *Architekturlehre*, ed. Tilmann Heinish and Gerd Peschken (Hamburg: Sozialistischer Arbeiter Verlag, 1977), 69. Taut is referring to a famous drawing by Le Corbusier from July 1934 inscribed, "This for Algiers and this for Stockholm, for Rio de Janeiro, and for Paris and Antwerp, the green city and its essential pleasure."

7. Peter Bosselmann, Edward Arens, Klaus Dunker, and Robert Wright, S*un, Wind, and Pedestrian Comfort*, City of Toronto, Department of Planning and Development, City Plan 91, Report 25, June 1991. The study discussed here was commissioned by Toronto's Planning and Development Department, Robert E. Millward, commissioner, and was carried out between April 1990 and April 1991 under the supervision of the Architecture and Urban Design Division, City of Toronto, Marc Baraness, director, and Wendy Jacobson, project director. The advisory group included Dr. Christopher Morgan, Gary Wright, and Thomas C. Keefe, staff members of the Planning and Development Department. The following UC Berkeley graduate students helped with field studies, laboratory experiments, and report graphics: James Bergdoll, Marc Fountain, David Ernest, Jane Ostermann, Kevin Gilson, Tim Mitchell, Adil Sharag-Eldin, Zhang Hui, David Lehrer, Alison Kwok, Brian Gotwals, Tom Powers, Colin Drobnis, Elaine Garrett, Kai Gutchow, Masato Matsuchita, Peter Cheng, Tracy Pitt, and Krystof Pavek. Toronto students included Claudio Cellucci, Ken DeWall, Henrik Dunker, Bruno Aletto, Mario Natarelli, and Lisa Laywine.

8. Toronto Transportation Survey, 1986, cited in City Plan 91, June 1991, City of Toronto.

9. This section of Bloor Street has no benches, but in an area with benches or other seating the limit of acceptable wind velocity is 7 mph. Winds stronger than that

would make it impossible, for example, to hold a newspaper. A planner setting a standard to protect those times when people are likely to use the benches would have to decide how often (as a percentage) the standard could be exceeded.

10. For a discussion of wind-speed limits, see Edward Arens, "On Considering Pedestrian Winds during Building Design," in *Wind Tunnel Modeling for Civil Engineering Application: Proceedings of the International Workshop on Wind Tunnel Modeling Criteria and Techniques*, ed. T. Reinhold (Cambridge: Cambridge University Press, 1982), 8–26; Edward Arens, D. Ballanti, D. Bennett, S. Guldman, and B. White, "Developing the San Francisco Wind Ordinance and Its Guidelines for Compliance," *Building and Environment* (London) 24, no. 4 (1989): 297–303; Alan G. Davenport, "An Approach to Human Comfort Criteria for Environmental Wind Conditions," Swedish National Building Award Institute, Stockholm, Sweden, 1976; Julian C. R. Hunt, E. C. Poulton, and J. C. Mumford, "The Effects of Wind on People," *Building and Environment* (London) 11, no. 2 (1976): 15–28; A. D. Penwarden, "Acceptable Wind Speeds in Towns," *Building Science* (London) 8 (1973): 259–267.

11. A. Pharo Gagge, A. P. Fobelets, and L. Berglund, "A Standard Predictive Index of Human Response to the Thermal Environment," *ASHRAE Transactions* 92 (1986): pt. 2; Edward Arens, L. Berglund, and R. Gonzales, "Thermal Comfort under an Extended Range of Environmental Conditions," *ASHRAE Transactions* 92 (1986): pt. 1; and ASHRAE, Standard 55–92, "Thermal Environmental Conditions for Human Occupancy," Atlanta, 1992.

12. See also Ralph Knowles, *Sun, Rhythm, Form* (Cambridge: MIT Press, 1981), 229–297.

13. Because there are very few trees on the streets in Toronto's downtown core, none of the streets modeled for wind tunnel and sunlight studies had trees. Although the effect of trees on comfort could be tested in a wind tunnel, that test would require larger physical models than those used for this study.

INTRODUCTION TO PART THREE

1. Palladio admits as much in the introduction to the *Quattro libri*; see James Ackerman, *Palladio* (Baltimore: Penguin Books, 1966).

2. Johann Wolfgang von Goethe, *Italian Journey, 1786–1788*, trans. W. H. Auden and Elizabeth Mayer (San Francisco: North Point, 1982), entry for September 19, 1786.

3. Ibid., entry for September 21.

4. Ibid., entry for October 26.

5. Ibid.

6. Giovanni Antolini, *Il Tempio di Minerva de Assisi, confronti colle favote, di Andrea Palladio* (Milan, 1883); and Heinz Spielmann, *Andrea Palladio und die Antike*, Kunstwissenschaftliche Studien, 37 (Bamberg: Deutscher Kunstverlag, 1966). Two elevation drawings of the Assisi temple exist. One appeared in *Quattro libri*, plate IV, 26.105. The other, supposedly an earlier drawing—and possibly the original of the one Goethe had with him at Assisi—is at the Royal Institute of British Architects, London. It is drawn in umber ink, with small touches of light sepia wash, at a scale of 5 feet to one Vicentine inch (9.8 mm). See Douglas Lewis, *The Drawings of Andrea Palladio* (Washington, D.C.: Douglas International Exhibitions Foundation, 1981–1982), 52.

7. Heinz Spielmann, ibid., 107; my translation.

8. Charles A. Jencks, "The Rise of Post Modern Architecture," *Architectural Association Quarterly* 7 (October–December 1975): 3–14.

CHAPTER 7

1. Keith Henney, "Cameras," in *Handbook of Photography*, ed. Keith Henney and B. Dudley (New York: Whittlesey House, McGraw-Hill, 1939), entry for "focal length."

2. James J. Gibson, "Pictures as Substitutes for Visual Reality," in *Reasons for Realism: Selected Essays of James J. Gibson*, ed. Edward Reed and Rebecca Jones (Hillsdale, N.J.: Lawrence Erlbaum, 1982).

3. Hans Maertens, *Optisches Mass für den Städtebau* (Cohen, 1890), quoted in George R. Collins and Christine Gasemann Collins, *Camillo Sitte: The Birth of Modern City Planning* (New York: Rizzoli, 1986), 115.

4. *Atlante di Venezia*, trans. Chris Heffer and David Kerr, intro. Donatella Calabi and Edgarda Feletti (Venice: Marsilio, 1989).

5. Ibid., 186. Photomaps show the historic center of Venice and the islands in the lagoon (reduced to 1:1000 from the original 1:500 plates).

6. Donatella Calabi, intro., ibid., 411.

7. Ibid.

8. Edgarda Feletti, ibid., 414.

9. Ibid.

10. The project was undertaken by Thomas Dickert, Peter Bosselmann, Mark Smith, and Brian Smith at the Center for Environmental Design Research, University of California at Berkeley.

11. This cell size was convenient both for recording topographic change and for quantifying the amount and

duration of shading caused by a proposed building. The computer compares the space-time dimension of projected shadows with that of existing shadows and computes the net increase.

12. Martin Kemp, *Science of Art* (New Haven, Conn.: Yale University Press, 1990).

13. Ibid., 315; see also Erich Brucke, *Die Physiologie der Farben* (Leipzig: Kramer, 1866), 204.

14. Kemp, *Science of Art*, 319.

15. Ibid., 316; Kemp refers to Paul Signac on Eugène Delacroix's fresco, painted between 1849 and 1861, in St. Sulpice, a picture considered to be a forerunner of Seurat's brushstroke technique.

16. Ibid., 317.

17. William Henry Fox Talbot, *The Pencil of Nature* (London: Longman, Brown, Green and Longmans, 1844), at plate 10, "The Haystack."

18. Additive optical synthesis was demonstrated by the physicist Sir James Clerk Maxwell at the Royal Institute, London, May 1861. See William Crawford, *A History and Working Guide to Early Photographic Processes* (New York: Morgan and Morgan, 1979), 227.

19. William J. Mitchell, *The Reconfigured Eye* (Cambridge: MIT Press, 1992), 185–189.

20. Thomas A. Funkhouser, Carlo H. Séquin and Seth Teller, "Management of Large Amounts of Data in Interactive Buildings Walkthroughs," SIGGRAPH Special Issue on 1992 Symposium on Interactive 3D Graphics, 11–20.

21. Ibid.

22. Thomas A. Funkhouser and Carlo H. Séquin, "Adaptive Display Algorithm for Interactive Frame Rates During Visualization of Complex Virtual Environments." *Computer Graphics*, 1993, 247–254.

23. John Dykstra, "Miniature and Mechanical Special Effects for *Star Wars*," *American Cinematographer* 58 (1977): 702–705, 732, 742, 750–757.

CHAPTER 8

1. E. H. Gombrich, *Art and Illusion* (London: Phaidon Press, 1962).

2. Amos Rapoport, "Perception of Density," *Environment and Behavior* 7, no. 2 (June 1975). See also William Michelson, *Environmental Choice, Human Behavior, and Residential Satisfaction* (New York: Oxford University Press, 1977).

3. Boris Pushkarow and Jeffrey M. Zupan, *Public Transportation and Land Use Policy* (Bloomington: Indiana University Press, 1977).

4. James Bergdoll and Rick Williams, "Perception of Density," *Berkeley Planning Journal* 5 (1990). The journal is

a student-run publication of the Department of City and Regional Planning, University of California at Berkeley.

5. See Robert Cervero and Peter Bosselmann, *An Evaluation of the Market Potential for Transit-Oriented Development Using Visual Simulation Techniques,* Institute of Urban and Regional Development, University of California at Berkeley, Monograph no. 47, 1994.

CHAPTER 9

1. Community groups opposing downtown development prepared a voters' initiative to limit development in the downtown area. After a narrow defeat in an initial attempt, this initiative, Proposition M, finally passed in November 1987, limiting the increase in downtown floor space to half a million square feet annually, approximately one midsize office building by San Francisco standards.

2. J. Thomas Atkins and William G. Blair, "Visual Impact of Highway Alternatives," *Garten und Landschaft* 8 (1983): 632–635; William Blair, "Visual Impact Assessment in Urban Environments," in *Foundation for Visual Project Analysis*, ed. Richard Smardon, James Palmer, and John Felleman (New York: Wiley and Sons, 1986).

3. Peter Bosselmann, *Five Filmscripts*, Institute of Urban and Regional Development, University of California at Berkeley, Working Paper no. 511, 1990.

4. Michael Oney, "The Skyline That Ate San Francisco," *California Magazine* (May 1983): 72–143.

5. RADIANCE, developed by the Lawrence Berkeley Laboratory, is at the time of this writing the most advanced ray-tracing software for quantitatively modeling light on surfaces under a range of different atmospheric conditions. For qualitative modeling—i.e., the representation of light—RADIANCE perpetuates the problem.

SELECTED BIBLIOGRAPHY

Books and articles are listed alphabetically in five categories:

· Urban Design Representations

· Urban Form and Climate

· Perception, Cognition, and Psychology

· Photography, Visual Arts, and Film

· Computation in Urban Design

URBAN DESIGN REPRESENTATIONS

Ackerman, James. *The Architecture of Michelangelo.* London: A. Zwemmer, 1964.

———. *Palladio.* Baltimore: Penguin Books, 1966.

Alberti, Leon Battista. *On the Art of Building* [1452]. Translated by Joseph Rykwert, Neil Leach, and Robert Tavernor. Cambridge: MIT Press, 1988.

———. *Ten Books on Architecture.* [1486]. Translated by Cosimo Bartoli and James Leoni. New York: Dover, 1986.

Alexander, Christopher, Howard Davis, and Donald Corner. *Production of Houses.* New York: Oxford University Press, 1986.

Alexander, Christopher, Hans-Joachim Neis, and I. Fiskdal King. *Battles.* New York: Oxford University Press, in preparation.

Appleyard, Donald. *Planning the Pluralistic City.* Cambridge: MIT Press, 1976.

———. "Understanding Professional Media: Issues and a Research Agenda." In *Human Behavior and Environment*, edited by Irwin Altman and Joachim F. Wohlwill, vol. 2. New York: Plenum Press, 1977.

Appleyard, Donald, Kevin Lynch, and John R. Myer. *The View from the Road.* Cambridge: MIT Press, 1964.

Ashihara, Yoshimbu. *Aesthetic Townscape.* Cambridge: MIT Press, 1983.

Atlante di Roma: La Forma del centro storico in scala 1:1000 nel fotopiano e nella carta numerica. 2d ed. Venice: Marsilio, 1991.

Atlante di Venezia: La forma della citta in scala 1:1000 nel fotopicano e nella carta numerica. Translated by Chris Heffer and David Kerr; introduction by Donatella Calibi and Edgarda Feletti. Venice: Marsilio, 1989.

Bacon, Edmund. *The Design of Cities.* Cambridge: MIT Press, 1974.

Banham, Reyner. *Theory and Design in the First Machine Age.* New York: Praeger, 1960.

Benevolo, Leonardo. *History of the City.* Translated by Geoffrey Culverwell. Cambridge: MIT Press, 1980.

Blumenfeld, Hans. "The Issue of Scale in Civic Design." In *The Modern Metropolis*, edited by Paul D. Speiregen. Cambridge: MIT Press, 1967.

Bosselmann, Peter. "Experiencing Downtown Streets in San Francisco." In *Public Streets for Public Use*, edited by Anne V. Moudon. New York: Van Nostrand Reinhold, 1987.

———. "Times Square." *Places* 4, no. 1 (1987).

———. "Transformation of a Landscape." *Places* 10, no. 3 (1996).

Bosselmann, Peter, and Marsha Gale. "Looking Out for Second Street." *Landscape Architecture* 76, no. 6 (1986).

Briggs, Martin. *Wren the Incomparable.* London: Allen and Unwin, 1953.

Broadbent, Geoffrey. *Emerging Concepts in Urban Space Design.* London: Van Nostrand, 1990.

Brooks, H. Allan. "Le Corbusier's Earliest Ideas on Urban Design." In *In Search of Modern Architecture: A Tribute to Henry Russell Hitchcock*, edited by Helen Searing. Cambridge: MIT Press, 1983.

Brusquets I Gran, Joan. *Cerda, I el seu Eixample, Laboratori d'Urbanisme Universitat Polytècnica de Catalunya.* Barcelona: Ajuntament de Barcelona, 1990.

Cataneo, Pietro. *L'architettura* [Venice, 1567]. Milan: Edizioni il Polifilio, 1985.

Cerda, Ildefonso. *La theoris general de la urbanization y application de sus principals y doctrines a la reforma y Ensanche de Barcelona.* Madrid, 1867.

Chambery, Jacques Paret de. *Des fortifications et artifices, architecture et perspective.* Paris, 1601.

Collins, George R., and Christine Gasemann Collins. *Camillo Sitte: The Birth of Modern City Planning.* New York: Rizzoli, 1986.

Conrads, Ulrich. *Programs and Manifestoes on Twentieth-Century Architecture.* Translated by Michael Bullock. Cambridge: MIT Press, 1970.

Corbusier, Le. *The City of Tomorrow and Its Planning.* Translated by Frederick Etchells. Cambridge: MIT Press, 1971.

Cullen, Gordon. *Townscape.* London: Architectural Press, 1961.

Delevoy, Robert, et al., eds. *Rational Architecture: The Reconstruction of the European City*. Brussels: Archives d'Architecture Moderne, 1978.

Di Giorgio, Martini. *Trattato di architettura civile e militare*. Ca. 1500.

Dürer, Albrecht. *Etlicher Untericht zur Befestigung der Stet, Schloss und Fleckene* [Nuremberg, 1527]. In facsimile, Unterschneidheim: Uhl, 1969.

Düttmann, Martina, Friedrich Schmuck, and Johannes Uhl. *Color in Townscape*. San Francisco: Freeman, 1981.

Euclid. *The Thirteen Books of Euclid's Elements*. Translated by Thomas L. Hearth. New York: Dover, 1956.

Faccioli, Clemente. "Giambattista Nolli (1701–1756) e la sua gran Pianta di Roma del 1748." *Studi Romani* 14 (1966).

Ferriss, Hugh. "The New Architecture." *New York Times*, March 19, 1922. Reprinted in *Zoning and the Envelope of the Building*, edited by H. W. Corbett. New York: Pencil Points, 1923.

Fischman, Robert. *Urban Utopias in the Twentieth Century*. Cambridge: MIT Press, 1982.

Fox, Hans. *Sequenzplanung in der Stadtgestaltung*. Ph.D. dissertation. Stuttgart University, 1975.

Frutaz, Amato P. *Le Piante di Roma*. 3 vols. Rome, 1962.

Gehl, Jan. *Life between Buildings: Using Public Space*. Translated by Jo Koch. New York: Van Nostrand Reinhold, 1987.

Giedion, Siegfried. *Space, Time, and Architecture*. London: Oxford University Press, 1941.

Goethe, Johann Wolfgang von. *Italian Journey, 1786–1788*. Translated by W. H. Auden and Elizabeth Mayer. San Francisco: North Point Press, 1982.

Hillier, Bill, and Julienne Hanson. *The Social Logic of Space*. New York: Cambridge University Press, 1984.

Huxtable, Ada Louise. *The Tall Building Artistically Reconsidered*. New York: Pantheon Books, 1982.

Jacobs, Allan B. *Great Streets*. Cambridge: MIT Press, 1993.

Jencks, Charles A. *The Language of Post-Modern Architecture*. 5th rev. enl. ed. London: Academy Editions, 1987.

Jordan, David. *Transforming Paris*. New York: The Free Press, 1995.

Kemp, Martin. *Leonardo da Vinci: The Marvelous Works of Nature and Man*. Cambridge: Harvard University Press, 1981.

Kostof, Spiro. *The Architect*. New York: Oxford University Press, 1977.

———. *The City Assembled*. Boston: Bulfinch Press, Thames and Hudson, 1991.

Krier, Leon. "The Reconstruction of the City." In *Rational Architecture: The Reconstruction of the European City*, edited by Robert Delevoy et al. Brussels: Archives d'Architecture Moderne, 1978.

Krier, Robert. *Urban Space*. New York: Rizzoli, 1984.

Lippmann, Walter. *Public Opinion*. New York: Macmillan, 1960.

Loderer, Benedikt. *Stadtwanderers Merkbuch*. Munich: Callwey, 1987.

Loyer, Francois. *Paris, Nineteenth Century: Architecture and Urbanism*. New York: Abbeville Press, 1988.

Lynch, Kevin. *City Sense and City Design*. Edited by Tridib Banerjee and Michael Southworth. Cambridge: MIT Press, 1990.

———. *The Image of the City*. Cambridge: MIT Press, 1960.

———. *Managing the Sense of a Region*. Cambridge: MIT Press, 1976.

———. *Theory of Urban Form*. Cambridge: MIT Press, 1982.

———. *What Time Is This Place?* Cambridge: MIT Press, 1985.

Maertens, Hans. *Der Optische Masstab in den bildenen Künsten*. Berlin: Wasmuth, 1877.

———. *Optisches Mass für den Städtebau*. Cohen, 1890.

More, Sir Thomas. *Utopia*. Translated and edited by Robert Adams. New York: W. W. Norton, 1975.

Moudon, Anne Vernez. *Built for Change*. Cambridge: MIT Press, 1986.

Mumford, Lewis. *The City in History*. New York: Harcourt, Brace, and World, 1961.

———. *Technics and Civilization*. New York: Harcourt, Brace, 1934.

Mundigo, Axel, and Dora P. Crouch. "The City Planning Ordinances of the Law of the Indies Revisited." *Town Planning Review* (Liverpool) 48 (1979): 247–268.

Nolli, Giambattista. *Rome 1748: The Pianta grande di Roma of Giambattista Nolli in Facsimile*. Intro. essay by Allan Ceen. Highmount, N.Y.: J. H. Aronson, 1984.

Norberg Schulz, Christian. *The Concept of Dwelling.* New York: Rizzoli, 1985.

———. *Genius Loci: Towards a Phenomenology of Architecture.* New York: Rizzoli, 1980.

Palladio, Andrea. *Quattro libri dell'architettura.* Venice, 1570. Published in English as *The Four Books of Architecture* [1570]. Translated by Isaac Ware. New York: Dover, 1969.

Pare, Richard. *Photography and Architecture, 1839–1939.* Centre Canadien d'Architecture. Montreal: Callaway Editions, 1992.

Pedretti, Carlo. *A Chronology of Leonardo da Vinci's Architectural Studies after 1500.* Geneva: E. Droz, 1962.

Philip II of Spain. *Rulas y Cedulas para Gobierno de las Indias,* San Lorenzo, July 3, 1573 (The Law of the Indies). Translated by Zelia Nuttall in *Hispanic American Historical Review* 4, no. 4 (May 1921): 743–753; and 5, no. 2 (May 1922): 249–254. Also translated by Axel Mundigo and Dora P. Crouch, "The City Planning Ordinances of the Law of the Indies Revisited," *Town Planning Review* (Liverpool) 48 (1979) 247–268.

Pinto, John. "Origins and Development of the Ichnographic City Plan." *Journal of the Society of Architecture Historians* 35, no. 1 (1976).

Pundt, Hermann. *Schinkel's Berlin: A Study in Environmental Planning.* Cambridge: Harvard University Press, 1972.

Rasmussen, Steen Eiler. *København.* Copenhagen: Gads Forlag, 1969.

———. *London: The Unique City.* Cambridge: MIT Press, 1967.

———. *Towns and Buildings.* Cambridge: MIT Press, 1969.

Reps, J. *The Making of Urban America.* Princeton, N.J.: Princeton University Press, 1965.

———. *Town Planning in Frontier America.* Princeton, N.J.: Princeton University Press, 1969.

Repton, Humphry. *Observations on the Theory and Practice of Landscape Gardening.* London: Taylor, 1803.

Rossi, Aldo. *The Architecture of the City.* Cambridge: MIT Press, 1984.

Rykwert, Joseph. *The Idea of a Town.* Princeton, N.J.: Princeton University Press, 1976.

Saalman, Howard. *Haussmann: Paris Transformed.* New York: George Braziller, 1971.

———. *Medieval Cities.* New York: George Braziller, 1968.

Saarinen, Eliel. *The City.* Cambridge: MIT Press, 1943.

Scarmozzi, V. *L'idea dell'architettura universale.* Venice, 1615.

Scruton, Roger. *The Aesthetics in Architecture.* Princeton, N.J.: Princeton University Press, 1979.

Sitte, Camillo. *Der Städtebau nach seinen künstlerischen Grundsätzen.* 3d ed. Vienna: Grasser, 1901.

Southworth, Michael. *Maps. A Visual Survey and Design Guide.* Boston: Little, Brown, 1982.

Speckle, Daniel. *Architectura von Festungen.* Strassburg, 1589.

Spielmann, Heinz. *Andrea Palladio und die Antike.* Kunstwissenschaftliche Studien, 37. Bamberg: Deutscher Kunstverlag, 1966.

Spirn, Anne Whiston. *The Granite Garden.* New York: Basic Books, 1984.

Stübben, Joseph. *Der Städtebau* [1890]. 3d ed. Leipzig: A. Kroner, 1924.

Taut, Bruno. *Architekturlehre.* Edited by Tilmann Heinish and Gerd Peschken. Hamburg: Sozialistischer Arbeiter Verlag, 1977.

Trieb, Michael. *Stadtgestaltung Theorie und Praxis.* Düsseldorf: Bertelsmann, 1974.

Ungers, Oswald Mathias. *Architecture as a Theme.* New York: Rizzoli, 1982.

Unwin, Raymond. *Town Planning in Practice.* London: T. F. Unwin, 1909.

Varming, Michael. *Motorveje i Landskabet.* Copenhagen: Teknisk Forlag, 1970.

Venturi, Robert, D. Scott Brown, and S. Tzenour. *Learning from Las Vegas.* Cambridge: MIT Press, 1972.

Vidler, Anthony. "The Scenes of the Streets: Transformation of Ideal and Reality, 1850–1871." In *On Streets,* edited by Stanford Anderson. Cambridge: MIT Press, 1978.

———. "The Third Typology." In *Rational Architecture: The Reconstruction of the European City.* Edited by Robert L. Delevoy et al. Brussels: Archives d'Architecture Moderne, 1978.

Vitruvius. *Ten Books of Architecture.* Translated by Morris Hicky Morgan. New York: Dover, 1960.

Whyte, William H. *Rediscovering the Center.* New York: Doubleday, 1989.

Wren, Christopher, Jr. *Parentalia* [1750]. Faonborough, Gregg, International, 1965.

Wurman, Richard Saul. *Cities: Comparisons of Form and Scale*. Philadelphia: Joshua Press, 1974.

URBAN FORM AND CLIMATE

Arens, Edward, and Peter Bosselmann. "Wind, Sun, and Temperature: Predicting the Thermal Comfort of People in Outdoor Spaces." *Building and Environment* 24, no. 4 (1989): 315–320.

Bosselmann, Peter, Edward Arens, Klaus Dunker, and Robert Wright. "Urban Form and Climate." *Journal of the American Planning Association* 20 (1995).

Bosselmann, Peter, Juan Flores, and William Gray. *Sun, Wind, and Comfort*. Institute of Urban and Regional Development, University of California at Berkeley, Monograph no. 035, 1984.

Bosselmann, Peter, Terrance O'Hare, and Juan Flores. *Sun and Light for Public Open Space in Downtown San Francisco*. Institute of Urban and Regional Development, University of California at Berkeley, Monograph no. 034, 1983.

Davenport, Alan G. "An Approach to Human Comfort Criteria for Environmental Wind Conditions." Swedish National Building Award Institute, Stockholm, Sweden, 1976.

Gagge, A. Pharo, A. P. Fobelets, and L. Berglund. "A Standard Predictive Index of Human Response to the Thermal Environment." *ASHRAE Transactions* 92 (1986): pt. 2.

Heydecker, Wayne D., and Ernest Goodrich. "Sunlight and Daylight for Urban Areas." *Neighborhood and Community Planning* 7(1929): 142–202.

Hunt, Julian C. R., E. C. Poulton, and J. C. Mumford. "The Effects of Wind on People." *Building and Environment* (London) 11, no. 2 (1976): 15–28.

Knowles, Ralph. *Sun, Rhythm, Form*. Cambridge: MIT Press, 1981.

Olgyay, Victor. *Design with Climate: Bioclimatic Approach to Architectural Regionalism*. Princeton, N.J.: Princeton University Press, 1963.

Penwarden, A. D. "Acceptable Wind Speeds in Towns." *Building Science* (London) 8 (1973): 259–267.

Rykwert, Joseph. *The Idea of a Town*. Princeton, N.J.: Princeton University Press, 1976.

Vitruvius. *Ten Books of Architecture*. Translated by Morris Hicky Morgan. New York: Dover, 1960.

PERCEPTION, COGNITION, AND PSYCHOLOGY

Acking, Carl-Axel, and Richard Kueller. "Presentation and Judgement of Planned Environments and the Hypothesis of Arousal." In *Environmental Design Research*, edited by Wolfgang F. E. Preiser, 1: 72–83. Stroudsburg, Pa.: Dowden, Hutchinson, and Ross, 1973.

Appleton, Jay. *The Experience of Landscape*. New York: Wiley and Sons, 1975.

Appleyard, Donald, and Kenneth H. Craik. "The Berkeley Environmental Simulation Laboratory and Its Research Programme." *International Review of Applied Psychology* 27 (1978): 53–55.

Bosselmann, Peter. "Dynamic Simulation of Urban Environments." In *Environmental Simulation: Research and Policy Issues*, edited by Daniel Stokols and Robert W. Marans. New York: Plenum Press, 1993.

Bosselmann, Peter, and Kenneth H. Craik. "Perceptual Simulations of Environments." In *Methods in Environmental and Behavior Research*, edited by R. B. Bechtel, R. W. Marcus, and W. Michelson. New York: Van Nostrand Reinhold, 1987.

Boulding, Kenneth. *The Image: Knowledge in Life and Society*. Ann Arbor: University of Michigan Press, 1956.

Broadbent, Geoffrey, R. Bunt, and T. Lloreus, eds. *Meaning and Behavior in the Built Environment*. New York: Wiley and Sons, 1980.

Brucke, Erich. *Die Physiologie der Farben*. Leipzig: Kramer, 1866.

Craik, Kenneth H. "The Comprehension of the Everyday Physical Environment." *Journal of the American Institute of Planners* 34 (1988): 29–37.

———. "Environmental Psychology." In *New Directions in Psychology*, edited by Kenneth H. Craik, B. Kleinmuntz, R. L. Rosnow, B. Rosenthal, T. A. Cheyne, and R. H. Walters, 41: 1–122. New York: Holt, Rinehart and Winston, 1970.

———. "The Psychology of Large Scale Environments." In *Environmental Psychology: Directions and Perspectives*, edited by N. R. Feimer and E. S. Geller. New York: Praeger, 1983.

Craik, Kenneth H., and N. R. Feimer. "Environmental Assessment." In *Handbook of Environmental Psychology*, edited by Daniel Stokols and J. Altmann. New York: Wiley, 1988.

Cunningham, M. C., J. A. Carter, C. P. Reese, and B. C. Webb. "Towards a Perceptual Tool in Urban Design: A Street Simulation Pilot Study." In *Environmental Design: Research*, edited by Wolfgang F. E. Preiser, 1:62–71. Stroudsburg, Pa.: Dowden, Hutchinson, and Ross, 1973.

Downs, Roger M., and David Stea. *Image and Environment: Cognitive Mapping and Spatial Behavior*. Chicago: Aldine, 1973.

Dürckheim, Karlfried Graf von. "Untersuchungen zum gelebten Raum." *Neue Psychologische Studien*, 6, edited by Felix Krüger. Munich: Beck'sche Verlagsbuchhandlung, 1930.

Edgerton, Samuel Y. *The Renaissance Rediscovery of Linear Perspective*. New York: Basic Books, 1975.

Edwards, D. S., C. P. Hahn, and E. A. Fleishmann. "Evaluation of Laboratory Methods for the Study of Driver Behavior. Relationship between Simulator and Street Performance." *Journal of Applied Psychology* 62 (1977): 559–566.

Evans, Gary W., Mary A. Skoerpanick, Tommy Gäring, K. J. Bryant, and B. Bresolin. "The Effects of Pathway Configuration, Landmarks, and Stress on Environmental Cognition." *Journal of Environmental Psychology* 4 (1984): 323–336.

Fuentes, Carlos. "Velasquez, Plato's Cave, and Bette Davis." *New York Times*, March 15, 1987.

Gibson, James J. *The Ecological Approach to Visual Perception*. Boston: Houghton Mifflin, 1979.

———. *Reasons for Realism: Selected Essays of James J. Gibson*. Edited by Edward Reed and Rebecca Jones. Hillsdale, N.J.: Lawrence Erlbaum, 1982.

Gombrich, E. H. *The Sense of Order: A Study in the Psychology of Decorative Art*. Oxford: Phaidon, 1979.

Goodey, Bryan. *Perception of the Environment*. Birmingham: University of Birmingham Press, 1971.

Hagen, Margaret A., ed. *The Perception of Pictures*. New York: Academic Press, 1980.

Helson, William H. "Environmental Perception and Contemporary Perceptual Theory." In *Environment and Cognition*, edited by W. H. Helson. New York: Seminar Press, 1978.

Holahan, Charles A. *Environmental Psychology*. New York: Random House, 1982.

Ittelson, William H. *Environment and Cognition*. New York: Seminar Press, 1973.

James, William. *Psychology: The Briefer Course*. Edited by Gordon Allport. New York: Harper and Row, 1961.

Kubovy, Michael. *The Psychology of Perspective in Renaissance Art*. New York: Cambridge University Press, 1986.

McKechnie, George E. "Simulation Techniques in Environmental Psychology." In *Perspectives on Environment and Behavior Theory, Research and Application*, edited by Daniel Stokols, 169–190. New York: Plenum, 1977.

Markelin, Antero, and Bernd Fahle. *Umweltsimulation*. Stuttgart: Karl Krämer Verlag, 1979.

Metzger, Wolfgang. *Gesetze des Sehens*. Frankfurt: Waldemar Kramer, 1953.

Milgrim, Stanley. "Psychological Maps of Paris." In *Environmental Psychology: People and Their Physical Settings*, edited by Harold M. Proshansky, William H. Helson, and L. G. Rivlin. New York: Holt, Rinehart and Winston, 1976.

Neiser, Ulric. *Cognition and Reality*. San Francisco: W. H. Freeman, 1976.

Sennett, Richard. *The Fall of Public Man*. New York: Vintage Books, 1974.

Sewell, D. W. R. "The Role of Perceptions of Professionals in Environmental Decision Making." In *Environmental Quality*, edited by J. T. Coppock and C. B. Wilson. Edinburgh: Scottish Academic Press, 1974.

White, John. *The Birth and Rebirth of Pictorial Space*. Boston: Boston Book and Art Shop, 1967.

Zube, Ervin H. *Environmental Evaluation, Perception and Public Policy*. Belmont: Wadsworth, 1980.

PHOTOGRAPHY, VISUAL ARTS, AND FILM

Arnheim, Rudolf. *Film*. Berkeley: University of California Press, 1969.

———. *The Power of the Center*. Berkeley: University of California Press, 1988.

———. *Visual Thinking*. Berkeley: University of California Press, 1969.

Dykstra, John. "Miniature and Mechanical Special Effects for *Star Wars*." *American Cinematographer* 58 (1977): 702–705, 732, 742, 750–757.

Gernsheim, Helmut. *The History of Photography*. McGraw-Hill, 1969.

Henney, Keith, and B. Dudley, eds. *Handbook of Photography*. New York: Whittlesey House, McGraw-Hill, 1939.

Hockney, David. "On Photography." Lecture at the Victoria and Albert Museum. New York: André Emmerich Gallery, 1983.

Jacobs, Lewis, ed. *The Movies as Medium*. New York: Farrar, Straus and Giroux, 1970.

Kemp, Martin. *Science of Art*. New Haven, Conn.: Yale University Press, 1990.

Kenworthy, N. P., Jr. "A Remote Camera System for Motion-Picture and Television Production." *Journal of the SMPTE* 821 (1973): 159–169.

Klee, Paul. *The Thinking Eye*. New York: Witternborn, 1961.

Lunsden, E. "Problems of Magnification and Minification: An Explanation of the Distortions of Distance, Slat, Shape and Velocity." In *The Perception of Pictures*, edited by Margaret A. Hagen, vol. 1. New York: Academic Press, 1980.

Pare, Richard. *Photography and Architecture, 1839–1939*. Centre Canadien d'Architecture. Montreal: Callaway Editions, 1982.

Ray, S. *The Lens in Action*. New York: Hastings House, 1976.

Rowley, George. *Principles of Chinese Painting*. Princeton, N.J.: Princeton University Press, 1947.

Smith, Thomas G. *Industrial Light and Magic: The Art of Special Effects*. New York: Ballantine, 1986.

Talbot, William Henry Fox. *The Pencil of Nature*. London: Longman, Brown, Green and Longmans, 1844.

White, John. *The Birth and Rebirth of Pictorial Space*. London: Faber and Faber, 1957.

Ziff, Jerrold. "Background, Introduction of Architecture and Landscape: A Lecture by J. M. William Turner." *Journal of the Warburg and Courtault Institute* 24 (1963): 124–147.

COMPUTATION IN URBAN DESIGN

Brand, Stewart. *The Media Lab: Inventing the Future at MIT*. New York: Viking Books, 1987.

Eastman, Charles M. "Fundamental Problems in the Development of Computer Based Architectural Design Models." In *Computability of Design*, edited by Yehuda E. Kalay. New York: John Wiley, 1987.

Greenberg, Donald P. "Computer Graphics in Architecture." *Scientific American* (May 1974).

———. *The Computer Image*. Reading, Mass.: Addison-Wesley, 1982.

———. "Computers and Architecture: Advanced Modeling and Rendering Algorithms Allow Designers and Clients to Walk through Buildings before Construction." *Scientific American* (February 1991).

Hall, Roy. *Illumination and Color in Computer Generated Imagery*. New York: Springer-Verlag, 1989.

Kalay, Yehuda E. *Modeling Objects and Environments*. New York: John Wiley, 1989.

Kamnitzer, Peter. "Computer Aid to Design." *Architectural Design* (September 1969).

Mitchell, William J. *City of Bits: Space, Place, and the Infobahn*. Cambridge: MIT Press, 1995.

———. *The Electronic Design Studio: Architectural Knowledge and Media in the Computer Era*, edited by Malcolm McCullough, William J. Mitchell, and Patrick Purcell. Cambridge: MIT Press, 1990.

———. *The Logic of Architecture*. Cambridge: MIT Press, 1990.

———. *The Reconfigured Eye: Visual Truth in the Post-Photographic Era*. Cambridge: MIT Press, 1992.

Negroponte, Nicolas. *The Architecture Machine*. Cambridge: MIT Press, 1970.

———. "Computer Graphics and Visualization." In *Computer-Aided Architectural Design*, edited by Alan Pipes. London: Butterworth, 1986.

Sheppard, Stephen R. *Simulation*. New York: Van Nostrand Reinhold, 1989.

Teller, Seth, and Sequin, Carlo. "Visibility Preprocessing for Interactive Walkthroughs." *Computer Graphics* 25, no. 4 (July 1991): 61–69.

Page references in boldface type refer to illustrations.

concept vs. experience, xiii, 18, 28, 35. *See also* maps/plans; perspective

"Construction de Villes, La" (Le Corbusier), 38

contextual movement, 204

Copenhagen, **44**, **45**, 70, 71

Craik, Kenneth: Environmental Simulation Laboratory built by, 92–93, 210n.8

Cullen, Gordon (illustrator), 40–41, 49, 204

daylight. *See* sunlight

decision making, 199–205; accuracy and public nature of representations, 199, 200, 201, 203; objectivity of, 199–201; roles of participants in, 201–2, **202**; in San Francisco Downtown Plan, 199–200 (*see also* San Francisco Downtown project); timing of, 203

Delacroix, Eugène, 178, 214n.15

density, population/residential: of Barcelona, 30; and crowding, 189; and health, 33; of Paris, 30; simulation of, 188–89, **190–91**, 192, **193–95**, 196, **197**; and social problems, 34

Denver, 134

Descripto Urbis Romae (Alberti), 13

design, notation systems for, 42

Deutscher Werkbund (German Association of Craftsmen), 40

disease. *See* health

Disney Company, 107

distance: judgments of, 7, 9, 61, 90 (*see also comparisons under* Venice); measurements of, 13

documentary quality of representation, 99, 203. *See also* objectivity/neutral stance

Downtown Center (Toronto), 142–43

Dreiser, Theodore, 106

Ducos du Hauron, Louis, 178

Duomo (Cathedral of Santa Maria del Fiore, Florence), 3, 4, 18

Dykstra, John, 93, 210n.10

Eliot, T. S., 101

Enlightenment, and abstraction, 22

Ensanche (urban extension plan, Barcelona), **30–31**, 30–34

environment, and visual quality of cities, 92–93, 94, 210n.16

Environmental Policy Act (1969), 92, 94, 210n.16

Environmental Simulation Laboratory (University of California at Berkeley), xiv, 207n.2; built by Appleyard and Craik, 92–93, 210n.8; cost of simulations, 96; model-photography experiment at, **92**, 93–94, **95–97**, 96, 210n.9; objectivity of, 200–201; opened to engineers, designers, and planners, 94; residential-density simulation, 188–89, **190–91**, 192, **193–95**, 196, **197**; role in policy making, 128, 130–32, 199–200; San

Francisco model housed at, 123, 124, **126–27**; San Francisco photo survey by, 176, 213–14nn.10–11; techniques used at, 103; Television City project, 170–72, 171–72; viewing distances studied at, 169 (table). *See also* Mission Bay project; San Francisco Downtown project; Times Square project; Toronto project

Evelyn, John, 25

experience vs. concept. *See* concept vs. experience

Farm Women at Work (Seurat), 178, **179**

Fellini, Federico, 210n.11

1500 Broadway Tower (New York), 107

film: continuous movement in, 93, 210n.13; objective vs. subjective camera recordings, 93, 210n.11

Florence Cathedral (Cathedral of Santa Maria del Fiore), 3, 4, 18

fortified cities, 25, 35

Forum of Trajan (Rome), 11

Freud, Sigmund, 35

future reality, models of, 10. *See also* computer simulations; Environmental Simulation Laboratory

Gehl, Jan, **44**, **45**

General Theory of Urbanization (Cerda), 31, 32

Gilson, Kevin, 168

glass, mirror, 4

Goethe, Johann Wolfgang von, 159–60, 162, 164–65

Goldberger, Paul, 107

Gombrich, Erich, 187

Great Fire (London, 1666), 23

green space, 40

Guggenheim Museum (Wright), 203

Hamstead Garden City (England), 38

Haussmann, Georges Eugène, 25–26

health: and urban planning, 23, 25, 33, 139

Hilberseimer, Ludwig (Bauhaus town planner), 40

Hitchcock, Alfred: *Rope*, 93, 210n.13

Hoetger, Bernhard, 40

Hollar, Wenceslas, 23, **24**

Hooke, Robert, 25

ichnographia, 207n.17. *See also* plan view

Image, The (Boulding), 42

image maps, 42, 45

Image of the City, The (Lynch), 42, **43**, 91

Imola (Italy), map of, **10**, 11, **12**, 13, 21–22, 207n.13

individual style vs. standardization, 40

industrialization, 38, 40

Designers: Steve Renick & John D. Berry
Compositor: John D. Berry Design
Text: Adobe Garamond with Myriad
Display: Adobe Garamond
Printer: Edwards Brothers
Binder: Edwards Brothers